Flawed System/Flawed Self

Flawed System/Flawed Self

Job Searching and Unemployment Experiences

OFER SHARONE

THE UNIVERSITY OF CHICAGO PRESS   CHICAGO AND LONDON

OFER SHARONE is the Mitsubishi Career Development Professor and assistant professor of work and employment research at the MIT Sloan School of Management.

The University of Chicago Press, Chicago 60637
The University of Chicago Press, Ltd., London
© 2014 by The University of Chicago
All rights reserved. Published 2014.
Printed in the United States of America

23 22 21 20 19 18 17 16 15 14   1 2 3 4 5

ISBN-13: 978-0-226-07336-1 (cloth)
ISBN-13: 978-0-226-07353-8 (paper)
ISBN-13: 978-0-226-07367-5 (e-book)

DOI: 10.7208/chicago/9780226073675.001.0001

Library of Congress Cataloging-in-Publication Data

Sharone, Ofer.
    Flawed system/flawed self: job searching and unemployment experiences / Ofer Sharone.
        pages cm
    Includes bibliographical references and index.
    ISBN 978-0-226-07336-1 (cloth: alkaline paper)—ISBN 978-0-226-07353-8 (pbk.: alkaline paper)—ISBN 978-0-226-07367-5 (e-book) 1. Job hunting—Cross-cultural studies. 2. Job hunting—United States—Sociological aspects. 3. Job hunting—Israel—Sociological aspects. 4. Unemployed—United States—Sociological aspects. 5. Unemployed—Israel—Sociological aspects. I. Title.
    HF5382.7.S475 2014
    650.14—dc23   2013011218

♾ This paper meets the requirements of ANSI/NISO Z39.48-1992 (Permanence of Paper).

FOR MY PARENTS, AKIVA Z"L AND AVIVA SHARON
MY SISTER, CARMIT, AND HER FAMILY, YGAL, MICHAEL, AND MICHELLE
MY CHILDREN, AVILEV, ELIYAH, AND TALIA
AND MY WIFE AND BEST FRIEND, ANA

Contents

Acknowledgments

This book would not have been possible without the tremendous guidance and support of my scholarly community. First and foremost, this includes my mentor Michael Burawoy. No less important was the feedback on countless memoranda and draft chapters from my writing group. Several group members provided support over multiple years and significantly contributed to the formation of this book, including Laleh Behbehanian, Marcel Paret, Fareen Parvez, Cinzia Solari, and Kerry Woodward. I received tremendous intellectual and moral support from Kim Voss, Sandra Smith, Gretchen Purser, Jeremy Schulz, Michele Lamont, Steven Vallas, Evelyn Nakano Glenn, John Van Maanen, Paul Osterman, Roberto Fernandez, and Katherine Kellogg. I am deeply grateful to my rabbi, Michael Lerner, for sensitizing me to the pain of self-blame, and most of all to my interviewees, whose willingness to take the time and to openly share difficult experiences made this book possible. I also extend my gratitude to Douglas Mitchell of the University of Chicago Press for his wise advice and enthusiastic support, and to John Elder and Erin DeWitt for extraordinary copyediting.

Finally support for my writing came from family, including my mother-in-law, Michele Murphy, and my dearest colleague, comrade, and best friend: my wife, Ana Villalobos. But perhaps the most significant form of support was ultimately emotional: helping me persevere during the years of writing and editing were my mother, Aviva Sharon; the memory of my late father, Akiva Sharon; my children, Eliyah, Talia, and Avilev; and, most of all, my wife, Ana.

CHAPTER ONE

Introduction

Unemployment Experiences

The widespread layoffs of white-collar workers accompanying the
Great Recession that began in 2008 made dramatically visible a trend
that had been growing since the 1970s: the erosion of white-collar job security. While the bursting of the dot-com bubble at the turn of the mil-
lennium served as a wake-up call to high-tech workers, the Great Recession sounded a loud and unmistakable warning to all white-collar workers
around the world: *No one* is immune to unemployment.

Despite its increasing prevalence, little is known about the day-to-day
experience of white-collar unemployment. Most scholarly studies of unemployment use survey data to trace macro-patterns. These studies are
important for understanding the rates and composition of unemployment,
but they do not reveal the world of job searching and unemployment that
lies behind the statistics. This book delves into that world.

One of the central findings of this book is that the experience of unemployment is largely shaped by the structure of the labor-market institutions
in which job searching takes place. Where others have studied the role
of individual-level factors, such as a job seeker's psychological makeup,
I take a sociological approach. I show that the experience of unemployment varies systematically across societies and, within societies, across
classes. Variations are ultimately rooted in different labor-market institutions that give rise to different job-search "games"—sets of discourses,
practices, and strategies—that job seekers use in trying to find work. Different games generate very different experiences of unemployment.

In the United States, white-collar job seekers are engaged in what I call
the job-search "chemistry game." In this game, hard skills are understood
to be important for getting one's foot in the door but not ultimately deter-

minative. The real key to getting a job is establishing one's fit with a particular employer. More than presenting your skills, landing a job requires effectively presenting *yourself*—the person behind the skills. In this book, I explore the institutional foundations of the chemistry game, how it structures the practices of American white-collar job seekers, and its profound consequences for their distinctive experience of unemployment.

The most striking effect of the chemistry game is to make American job seekers highly vulnerable to self-blame. This turns unemployment into a double crisis: in addition to the financial crisis of wondering how one will keep paying the bills and not lose one's home, there is the personal crisis of wondering, "What's wrong with me?" In turn, self-blame generates equally important secondary effects, including a profound sense of discouragement about the use of further job searching and the widespread understanding of unemployment as an individual and private issue as opposed to one that is public and political. These effects have consequences for society as well as for individuals.

One appreciates the unique character of the chemistry game only through comparison with white-collar job searching in other countries. Among industrialized countries, Israel provides a particularly interesting comparative case because, as will be explained below, it shares important economic and structural characteristics with the United States that would lead one to expect similar unemployment experiences. Yet in Israel a very different set of labor-market institutions generates a very different experience of job search and unemployment—a different game altogether. The Israeli "specs game" does not focus on interpersonal chemistry but on depersonalized and objectified skills and credentials, and a rigid set of characteristics—such as the applicant's age or the existence of an unexplained gap in their résumé—that are taken to be proxies for qualifications.

These distinct games emerge from institutional differences. Although employers in both countries sift potential candidates using varied filters that to some extent consider both objective specs and subjective chemistry, the way in which hiring is mediated by labor-market institutions makes the specs filter more *salient* to Israeli white-collar job seekers and the chemistry filter more *salient* to American white-collar job seekers.[1]

A pair of examples will highlight some of the differences between the chemistry and specs games:

When Beth lost her job as a technical writer in a large high-tech company in San Francisco, she blamed her company's corporate restructuring, which came in the wake of a global economic downturn. At first, her layoff seemed like a blessing in disguise; she had been feeling pretty burned out from her long work hours. She eagerly plunged into her job search, putting a lot of time into crafting her cover letters and résumés and doing a lot of networking. Whenever she applied for a job, she tried to convey not only her professional skills but also her passion for technical writing and her unique fit with that particular company. After a month of intense searching, she was thrilled to be invited to an interview. Yet despite her expressions of enthusiasm for the company and her efforts to present herself as a good fit for its culture, the interview felt awkward. "There was no chemistry," she recalled. She analyzed and reanalyzed how she had "blown it" and what she could have done or said differently. She began to wonder if there was something wrong with her self-presentation or, even worse, something wrong with *her* that interviewers could see even if she could not. After four months of unsuccessful job searching, Beth was virtually paralyzed with self-doubt. She explained that she had stopped searching because the process made her feel that she had a "character defect," that she was "flawed in some way."[2]

Across the ocean, in Tel Aviv, Israel, Eldad was laid off from his marketing position. He, too, understood this to be fallout from the general economic downturn. Working in a region that is home to many of the same multinational corporations found in the San Francisco Bay area, Eldad, like Beth, witnessed many companies responding to the economic downturn with layoffs. Eldad shot off a résumé for every job opening that appeared to demand his skills and was encouraged to get several interviews at staffing agencies that screen applicants on behalf of employers. On his résumé and in his interviews, Eldad tried to convey how well his skills and experience matched the employer's needs, but he could not get past the screening interviews, which focused on whether he met a checklist of very specific requirements. He became increasingly frustrated at the rigid structure of the hiring system, which did not allow him to showcase his underlying strengths. "The system here does not look at you as an individual," he fumed. "You are just a collection of buzzwords." Nevertheless, he continued sending out résumés. While he was no longer as hopeful about his prospects, he figured he had "nothing to lose" if he kept trying.

Caught up in the same global economic downturn, Beth and Eldad both experienced more difficulties in finding work than they had initially expected. Yet the strategies they used to find work, how they understood their difficulties in finding work, and the degree to which they were willing to keep trying were strikingly different. My cross-national investigation reveals that the differences between Beth and Eldad are not reflections of different personalities, genders, or occupations, but of systematic patterns of differences in job searching and unemployment experiences across white-collar job seekers in the United States and Israel.

The comparison raises three questions that go to the core of unemployment and job searching as a social phenomenon:

What are the job-search strategies of white-collar workers and why do they vary cross-nationally? For example, why do American job seekers emphasize their enthusiasm for—and fit with—particular employers while Israeli job seekers emphasize their particular skills? What are the consequences of this difference for the experience of unemployment?

Why—despite searching for work under similar economic conditions— do unsuccessful American job seekers blame themselves while unsuccessful Israeli job seekers blame the system? Job seekers in both countries tend to understand their job loss as a product of structural forces outside their control. Yet when a new job proves hard to find, American job seekers generally shift their focus to individual factors and blame themselves, as exemplified by Beth's feeling of having a "character defect," while Israelis tend to grow angry at the system, as exemplified in Eldad's sense of being reduced to "buzzwords." More broadly, why do unemployed workers in some societies come to see unemployment as a structural and public issue, while those in other societies come to see it as an individual and private matter?

Since the Great Depression, researchers have been puzzled by American white-collar workers' tendency to focus on individual-level factors in understanding their own continued unemployment.[3] This book provides a new perspective on that phenomenon by using a cross-national comparison to a society whose job seekers typically focus on structural explanations of their own unemployment. I theorize a previously unrecognized link between unemployment experiences and the labor-market institutions that structure job-searching practices. Different subjective responses to unemployment arise from playing different job-search games: The chemistry game produces self-blame. The specs game generates system-blame.

What are the effects of these different unemployment experiences? One particularly important effect is the relationship between unemployment experiences and job-search discouragement. At the heart of the unemployment policy debate in the United States is the question of why job seekers lose their momentum and, in some cases, cease searching (the so-called "discouraged workers"). While finding a job usually requires keeping up the intensity of your search, millions of Americans consistently report that they want a job but are not actively looking. As this book will show, such discouragement among American unemployed white-collar workers has much to do with the specific nature of the chemistry game.

Before delving into the specifics of the chemistry game, we will look back at the recent history of white-collar unemployment and job insecurity in the United States. While there is a lively debate on its causes, there is no mistaking the overall decline in white-collar job security.

The Rise of White-Collar Insecurity and Unemployment

Over the past thirty years, white-collar employment relations in the United States have been transformed from secure and stable to contingent and precarious.[4] The post–World War II era was characterized by white-collar job security. While blue-collar workers were typically subject to layoffs during economic downturns, white-collar workers, particularly at large companies, were implicitly promised lifetime employment and were rarely laid off even during hard economic times. For white-collar workers, the firm was often understood as a large family with long-term attachments and a web of mutual obligations, famously captured in William H. Whyte's 1956 book, *The Organization Man*. White-collar workers would enter the firm at the bottom and move up. The worker invested in the firm, and the firm invested in the worker.[5]

In the 1970s and 1980s, however, the implicit bargain of loyalty for security began to collapse. The new heroes of the business world were CEOs like Jack Welch of General Electric, who instituted the practice of annually ranking all of the company's managers along a forced bell-shaped curve and, regardless of economic conditions, purportedly fired the bottom 10 percent. Another CEO who came to symbolize the demise of the postwar era was "Chainsaw" Al Dunlap, who had this to say about corporate loyalty: "If you want a friend, get a dog."

White-collar precariousness is but one manifestation of the transition to a neoliberal political economy, which has also brought a steep decline in the percentage of American workers who are in labor unions, the stagnation or decline of most American workers' wages, and soaring levels of economic inequality unseen since before the New Deal.[6]

The root causes of this neoliberal transformation are the subject of a spirited debate. Some theories emphasize the role of economic forces, technological changes, and globalization, while others focus on the role of institutions and states. Illustrative of this debate are the diverging analyses of two of the most well-known American public intellectuals on economic matters: Robert Reich, professor of public policy and former secretary of labor, and Paul Krugman, *New York Times* columnist and professor of economics. In *Supercapitalism* (2007), Reich argues that the postwar era of job security, wage growth, and strong labor unions was rooted in the particular economic conditions of mass manufacturing. These conditions led American businesses, acting collectively through organizations such as the National Association of Manufacturers, to prioritize predictability and stability. Reich argues that, in this context, gaining a competitive edge required high-volume production, which in turn demanded enormous initial investments. To minimize the risk of such large investments, employers wanted predictability—in the form of barriers to entry for new competitors—which were achieved through government regulations. Employers also needed a cooperative workforce that would not disrupt the flow of production. To minimize worker disruptions, American business agreed to cooperate with unions, which, together with government regulations, contributed to job stability.

Reich claims that this era of stability began to crumble when the economic underpinnings changed. By the 1970s, computers, communication devices, and other technological changes made it feasible to manufacture on a smaller scale and to globalize production around the world. This, in turn, rendered the size of firms and the amount of their initial investments far less significant barriers to entry.[7] The intensified competition arising from these technological changes led firms to focus on cutting labor costs, first and foremost by aggressively busting unions, but also by lobbying the government for deregulation. According to Reich, it is this intensified competition, and the de-unionization and deregulation that came in its wake, that ushered in the present neoliberal era during which white-collar job security collapsed.

Reich's theory is challenged by scholars who claim that it overstates the role of technological and economic forces and that greater emphasis should be placed on institutional changes and the role of the American state. Krugman (2007) traces the same transformation to different causes. In Krugman's story, the relatively strong postwar wage growth, labor unions, and job security reflected the institutional transformation brought on by the New Deal. Correspondingly, the dramatic changes of the past thirty years, in which levels of inequality have returned to pre–New Deal levels, are the result of institutional changes that have unraveled the New Deal. Krugman's analysis focuses on the rise of "movement conservatives," who rose to power with the election of Ronald Reagan in 1980 and rolled back the New Deal through tax cuts for high-earners, cuts in social programs, and a de facto repeal of protective labor laws through lack of enforcement. Krugman's focus on the role of institutions, as opposed to technology and globalization, finds support in studies comparing work conditions in the United States and western Europe. Although western Europe is subject to the same forces of technological change and globalization as the United States, these forces have not led to the same precipitous rise in inequality, collapse of unions, or erosion of job security.[8]

While the Reich-Krugman debate usefully elucidates some of the different approaches to explaining the dramatic changes in the world of work over recent decades, most scholars agree that both economic and institutional factors have played important roles.[9] Regardless of the causes, one dramatic effect of the rise of neoliberal capitalism is the decline in white-collar job security. Since the 1970s, the job-loss rate has increased *more steeply* for college-educated white-collar workers than for blue-collar workers or workers who have not graduated from college. As a result, the class composition of the unemployed has changed. While the vast majority of unemployed workers in the postwar era were those with the least education, in 2008 there were *more* unemployed workers with a college degree than without a high school degree.[10] College-educated workers' vulnerability to job loss has continued to increase, reaching a historic high in 2009.[11]

Not only are American white-collar and college-educated workers increasingly more likely to become unemployed, but, as figure 1 shows, when they lose their jobs, they are more likely than blue-collar or non-college-educated workers to become *long-term* unemployed—defined as remaining unemployed for more than twenty-seven weeks.[12]

In the decade preceding the Great Recession that began in 2008, the share of the unemployed who remained unemployed for over six months had *declined* for workers with only a high school diploma and for blue-collar workers, but had *increased*—to nearly one in three—for white-collar workers and for those with a college degree.[13] In the wake of the Great Recession, among the longest average durations of unemployment were endured by workers in the white-collar information and financial industries.[14] By 2009 nearly half of all long-term unemployed job seekers were white-collar workers.[15]

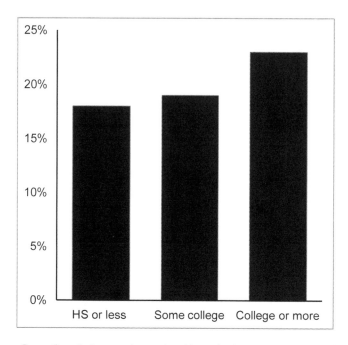

FIGURE I. Proportion of subgroup of unemployed becoming long-term unemployed (Wenger and Stetter 2003).

White-collar workers are thus increasingly susceptible to long-term unemployment with its distinctly damaging effect on financial, psychological, and physical well-being.[16] A comprehensive series of surveys exploring the effects of the Great Recession of 2008–9 makes clear the enormous financial pressures facing long-term unemployed workers, with 55 percent cutting back on doctor visits or medical treatment, 60 percent selling some possessions to make ends meet, and 60 percent borrowing money from family or friends.[17] The emotional fallout from long-term unemployment is likewise devastating, with 85 percent of the long-term unemployed losing sleep as a result of their unemployment, 90 percent experiencing more stress in their relationships with family and friends, and 62 percent simply avoiding some social situations. Perhaps most striking, despite the historically high rates of unemployment in 2011, 74 percent of the long-term unemployed reported feeling embarrassment or shame over being out of work.

Is the American experience of unemployment distinct? To uncover any peculiarities of American white-collar unemployment, it is necessary to compare American job seekers to their counterparts in other countries.

The rise of white-collar insecurity and long-term unemployment is not a uniquely American trend. In other advanced capitalist countries, including most of western Europe, the proportion of the population that is college educated, white collar, and unemployed is even larger than in the United States.[18] However, drawing conclusions from cross-national comparisons can be difficult because economic and institutional differences are hard to untangle. In western Europe, for example, unemployment benefits are much more generous and lengthy than in the United States—sometimes lasting for years as opposed to months—which creates entirely different material conditions for unemployment and job searching.[19]

This book compares the experiences of unemployed white-collar workers in the San Francisco area of the United States and the Tel Aviv area of Israel. Although the political-economic history of Israel is different from that of the United States (as will be described in chapter 4), the comparison is motivated by a striking set of contemporary similarities in the objective conditions of white-collar unemployment. In recent decades, white-collar workers in both countries experienced a profound historical transformation in the nature of the employment relationship, from secure to precarious.[20] As part of a broader set of political-economic changes that diminished the role of the state and of labor unions in both countries' labor markets, institutions that once supported white-collar job security had, by the time of my research, largely given way to neoliberal regimes of flexible employment and job insecurity. Adding to this labor-market insecurity, in recent decades both the American and Israeli governments had cut social welfare protections. At the time of this study, unemployed job seekers in both sites were allotted a maximum of six months of unemployment benefits, a relatively short duration when compared to other advanced economies.[21]

The two areas also share other important similarities. Specifically, the Tel Aviv and the San Francisco Bay areas have the world's highest concentrations of high-tech firms and, on a per capita basis, equal flows of venture capital. This has led Microsoft's former CEO, Bill Gates, to call Israel "part of Silicon Valley."[22] This means that the American and Israeli workers in this study were often seeking jobs with companies operating in the same global economic niche. Given the combination of (a) flexible employment regimes and (b) the dominance of high-tech industries, white-collar workers in both countries experienced similar waves of layoffs following the bursting of the dot-com bubble in the early 2000s. The data for this book were collected during that post-bubble period, when job seekers in both countries struggled in labor-market conditions characterized by an oversupply of white-collar workers.[23]

Given these economic and institutional similarities, one might expect similar white-collar unemployment experiences in the United States and Israel. Yet, as the stories of Beth and Eldad illustrate, the strategies, practices, and subjective experiences of American and Israeli job seekers are very different. Why?

To explore the roots of these different unemployment experiences, I conducted in-depth interviews with 162 American and Israeli job seekers. Each interview lasted approximately two hours. I then followed the interviewees over time with multiple shorter follow-up interviews. While most interviews were with white-collar job seekers in the San Francisco Bay area of the United States and the Tel Aviv area of Israel, to explore cross-class variations within the United States (which are the focus of chapter 6), I also interviewed unemployed blue-collar workers from the San Francisco area. Moreover, to uncover any regional variations within the United States, I interviewed white-collar job seekers from the Boston area. Further details about my research methodologies and sample are discussed in appendix A.

My interview data were greatly enhanced by spending nearly two years as a participant-observer in various support groups for job seekers run by the government or by nonprofit organizations in the San Francisco Bay and Tel Aviv areas. In these groups—which will be more fully described in chapters 2, 4, and 6—I participated in brainstorming sessions about job-searching strategies and listened to counselors and expert guest speakers advise job seekers on strategies. I also observed how job seekers attempted to make sense of their situations, strategize with colleagues, and, perhaps most importantly, express the assumptions behind their strategies. This rendered job-search strategizing—typically an internal and solitary activity—observable and free from any preconceptions that my interview questions might have introduced.[24] Moreover, my mix of interviews and observations allowed me to compare how unemployed job seekers discuss their feelings and understandings when gathered with fellow job seekers and when alone with me in one-on-one interviews.

Almost all of my in-depth interviews were conducted face-to-face. In these open-ended interviews, I asked job seekers about their strategies for trying to find work, their experiences of looking for work, and the obstacles they perceived. Some job seekers were eager tell their stories; others were initially more hesitant. But in almost every case, by the end of the interview, the interviewee had indicated an appreciation of the opportunity to have someone truly interested listen to his or her experiences. Many job seekers confided that they did not want to burden close family members with their own anxieties. Most also felt that friends were not interested in hearing the details of their hardships. Some felt that it was important to maintain a positive front with friends, even if they were experiencing great emotional turmoil inside, because friends were potential sources of job referrals and it was assumed that no one would refer—as one job seeker put it—a "basket case." For all these reasons, the face-to-face interviews offered a rare opportunity for job seekers to openly and fully discuss their experiences.

From a research perspective, the open-ended nature of the interviews allowed me to explore experiences that are typically difficult to access with surveys. While surveys often require that experiences fit one of several predetermined choices, the interviews allowed me to pursue unanticipated issues, such as the degree of personal vulnerability experienced by American white-collar job seekers. Moreover, in the context of the interview, a certain level of trust was established that helped job seekers openly discuss sensitive topics such as their feelings of self-blame.

Job-Search Games and Unemployment Experiences

To understand unemployment experiences—and, particularly, to make sense of the *variations* in these experiences—requires a new theoretical framework. Existing theories tend to focus on universal and generic features of unemployment and thus have difficulties explaining variations. For example, one of the most frequently cited theories about the experience of unemployment focuses on the disorienting effects of losing one's formal work structure.[25] But this loss, however disorienting, cannot explain why Israeli and American job seekers, all of whom experience it, show such systematic variation in their unemployment experiences. Another theory of the unemployment experience focuses on job seekers' diminished sense of self-efficacy from repeatedly encountering labor-market obstacles. But again, because this theory focuses on generic and universal aspects of the unemployment experience—in this case the experience of repeatedly encountering obstacles—it has difficulty accounting for variations in this experience.[26] Following this model, job seekers in any tough labor market, such as the Israeli and American job seekers in my study, can be expected to respond similarly, yet they do not. The universal aspects of the unemployment experience, such as disorientation and repeated frustration, cannot explain why American job seekers tend to blame themselves for not finding work while Israeli job seekers tend to blame the system.

Systematic cross-national variations suggest the need to look beyond universal features of unemployment to specific local conditions. One approach that does consider society-specific factors is found in the literature on unemployment and national cultures. Research on the American white-collar context, for example, claims that the experience of unemployment is rooted in the distinct culture of American individualism.

Katherine Newman's pathbreaking book, *Falling from Grace: Downward Mobility in the Age of Affluence* (1999), provides a vivid account of the devastating self-blame experienced by unemployed American managers and professionals. Newman explains this self-blame by pointing to the culture of individualism. As she puts it: "It is a culture which has the power to reach inside displaced managers and devastate their sense of self-worth" (78). According to Newman, self-blame flows from a cultural belief that labor-market outcomes are a product of one's own actions. Job seekers, Newman claims, "have been steeped in the tenets of the managerial worldview" and its "steadfast belief in the ability of individuals to control the circumstances of their lives" (9).

Newman's (1999) culture-of-individualism theory has a hard time explaining variations and dynamics observed *within* American society. For example—as will be discussed in chapter 6 and as has been documented by others, including Newman herself—American blue-collar workers, who share broad cultural influences with their white-collar counterparts, are nevertheless far less likely to self-blame. Moreover, difficult empirical questions arise even if the culture-of-individualism argument is limited to middle-class managers and professionals—workers who Newman claims are particularly steeped, through the business press, in the American ideology of "meritocratic individualism." As sociologists of culture have generally come to recognize in recent decades, cultures are not coherent and integrated systems but complex and contradictory; instead of providing a particular worldview, they offer a *variety* of "tools" that actors use in different contexts.[27] The American cultural tool kit is not exceptionally coherent, and most recent sociological accounts of American culture point to multiple layers that are often inconsistent and contradictory.[28] Indeed, a multiplicity of narratives can be heard in American white-collar job seek-

ers' accounts of their labor-market difficulties, which focus on both individual and structural factors, including the effects of economic downturns,
layoffs, and outsourcing.[29] This multiplicity of narratives can also be seen
in Newman's (1999) own findings and her descriptions of white-collar job
seekers, whose conflicting subjective responses conjure up the image of
a mental civil war between structural and individual understandings of
unemployment. Ultimately, she argues, individualistic self-criticism "tri-
umphs" over structural explanations.[30] Yet, given the multiplicity of available narratives in the cultural "tool kit,"[31] the question remains: Why does
self-blame "triumph"? Newman's cultural argument does not provide a
theory of the conditions that lead white-collar job seekers to turn to the
individualistic narratives of self-blame.

To explain the "triumph" of self-blame,[32] this book focuses on the relationship between the narratives that job seekers use in discussing their
labor-market difficulties and the institutions that structure the practices
of job searching. My focus on institutional contexts follows Smith's (2011,
125) seminal research, which finds a remarkable pattern in white-collar
job seekers' narratives:

> Managers and professionals viewed only *one* side of the equation—the *cause*
> of their unemployment—as structurally determined, but viewed the *other* side
> of the equation—their search for and inability to find a new job—in purely in-
> dividualistic terms. Despite cognitive recognition of change in economic insti-
> tutions, these individuals internalized responsibility and blamed themselves....

The patterned way in which American white-collar job seekers' understandings of labor-market difficulties shift from structural to individual
suggests that the key factor is not the cultural availability of different
narratives but the institutional forces that shape understandings of outcomes and, specifically in this context, the relationship between the institutions that structure American white-collar job-searching practices and
their individualized understandings of unemployment.[33] In analyzing how
institutional contexts bring to the fore particular cultural understandings and patterned subjective responses, I am also guided by Swidler's
observation that "standard institutional dilemmas produce coherent cultural strands, even when each individual's worldview taken as a whole
may seem incoherent.... [C]onsistent patterns appear in the culture of
many individuals when they all confront similar institutional constraints"
(2001, 134).

The theory developed in this book proposes that to understand why a person sees a particular aspect of his or her unemployment in terms of one available narrative rather than the others, we need to examine that person's day-to-day job-search practices and experiences *and* the institutions that structure them. This approach brings the empirical focus down from universal mechanisms and the abstract generalizations of culture to the *specific* institutions of job searching and hiring. As the following chapters will discuss, these institutions (a) are products of specific political-economic conditions and (b) ultimately structure the daily practices of job searching, which, in turn, generate the varied experiences of unemployment.

Linking Institutions and Subjectivities: Symbolic Violence and Social Games

An institution-focused approach to understanding variations in the experience of unemployment requires two important links. First, one must link labor-market institutions to the daily practices of job searching. Second, one must link these daily practices to subjective responses, such as whether unemployment is understood to be the result of a problematic economic order or the result of a problematic self. Cross-national variation in these subjective responses allows the exploration of the specific institutional conditions under which unemployed job seekers come to see—or not see—the issue of unemployment as private or public and, more broadly, sheds light on how people come to view the role of social structures in shaping their fates.

To explain the relationship between institutions and agents' subjectivities—specifically the institutional conditions that may lead to the subjective responses of self-blame or system-blame—I begin by considering the currently dominant theoretical framework providing a sociological account of self-blame: Pierre Bourdieu's (1998b, 2000, 2001) theory of symbolic violence.

According to Bourdieu, symbolic violence occurs when the "schemes" that agents "implement in order to *perceive and evaluate themselves*" or others "are the product of the incorporation of the (thus naturalized) classifications of which their social being is the product." (Bourdieu 2000, 170, emphasis added).[34] Perceiving and evaluating oneself—and making sense of negative life outcomes like unemployment—through the internalized categories and schemes of dominant social structures results in what Bourdieu calls "self-depreciation."[35] For example, Bourdieu explains that in an educational system that disadvantages working-class children, internalization of dominant schemes "convince[s] the disinherited that they owe their scholastic and social destiny *to their lack of gifts or merits*"[36] (emphasis added). Likewise, in discussing gender inequality, Bourdieu (2001) claims that internalizing "categories constructed from the point of view of the dominant" produces a "kind of systemic *self-depreciation, even self-denigration*" in women (35; emphasis added). He discusses similar internalization processes in interpreting bachelor peasants' "self-mockery" and embarrassment at their failure in the marriage market.[37]

Bourdieu's theory of self-blame rests on a specific mechanism. Agents deeply internalize and embody a set of "schemes of perception, appreciation, and action," which comprise the "habitus."[38] This internalization occurs through lasting exposure to a particular set of social structural conditions.[39] The internalized and embodied habitus, being "inseparable from the structures ... that produce and reproduce" it, perceives such external structures as "natural."[40] Agents take for granted the shape of social structures "because *their mind is constructed according to cognitive structures that are issued out of the very structures of the world*" (emphasis in original).[41]

Since the habitus is the product of the "incorporation of objective structures,"[42] agents acting in the social world, like fish in water, cannot see the role of the structures they inhabit in shaping life outcomes, and thus blame themselves. Bourdieu claims that agents' "*misrecognition* of the social conditions of a harmony" between external structure and the internal habitus makes symbolic violence "a gentle violence, imperceptible and invisible even to its victims."[43] In Bourdieu's conception, self-blame is thus the product of the perfect "adjustment" between the structures of the habitus and the structures of society (1998b, 121–22).

Bourdieu does not assume that the habitus will always be adjusted to a given field. In fact, a mismatch between a habitus formed under one set of conditions and a field characterized by another set of conditions can lead to frictions and resistance.[44] But the theory of symbolic violence and Bourdieu's explanation for self-blame do hinge on a sufficient adjustment between habitus and social structures to produce misrecognition.

While the theory of symbolic violence describes with precision the observed self-blame in the white-collar American context, the mechanisms posited by Bourdieu for the production of symbolic violence cannot account for that self-blame. American job seekers' self-blame is occurring under conditions starkly different from Bourdieu's description of the mechanisms producing symbolic violence, most notably the absence of an adjustment between agents' habitus and external structures. As discussed earlier, in the United States, as in Israel, white-collar employment relations have been deeply and continuously transformed in recent decades from secure to precarious, a transformation that Bourdieu himself observed.[45] Given these rapidly occurring structural changes in the employment relationship, any past experiences and any internalized schemes would clash with the prevailing labor-market conditions. Indeed, this frustration of expectations is heard in Americans' and Israelis' anger over their layoffs and in their initial bewilderment at the rules of the game in the "new economy."[46] Under conditions of correspondence between the internal habitus and external structure, Bourdieu claims that agents have a sufficient "feel for the game" such that no conscious strategizing is necessary, as when an experienced tennis player runs to the net without pausing to think (1990b, 61). However, unlike Bourdieu's tennis player, job seekers strategizing to find work in this new environment are fully self-conscious.[47] Given the rapid transformation of white-collar employment relations and the consequent implausibility of a deeply internalized habitus adjusted to and harmonious with such relations, the mechanisms at the core of the theory of symbolic violence cannot account for self-blame in the American white-collar context.

To explain self-blame—and unemployment experiences more generally—we need a different set of mechanisms that do not presuppose harmonious adjustment between the internal and the external. This book develops such an alternative framework of mechanisms, building on and bringing together Pierre Bourdieu's (2000) and Michael Burawoy's (1979) theories of social games and Arlie Hochschild's (1983) theory of emotional labor.

Both Burawoy (1979) and Bourdieu (2000) use the metaphor of games in theorizing the relationship between agents and structures. Burawoy (1979) developed the theory of "work-games" to explain the subjective consent of factory workers to unequal relations with management. Building on Gramsci's (1971) insight that hegemony under advanced capitalism is facilitated by the expansion of civil society institutions that create spaces of discretion and possibilities for individual gains, Burawoy argues that in the factory, uncertainty over the output of piece-rate manufacturing, combined with the workers' discretion over how to operate their machines, gave rise to games with an individualizing focus on specific production outcomes and away from hierarchical power relations. A subsequent line of studies has developed and applied this framework in a variety of non-factory settings, examining the subjective responses of engineers in a large high-tech company (Sharone 2004), croupiers in casinos (Sallaz 2009), and service workers in luxury hotels (Sherman 2007). All these studies find that certain structural conditions give rise to games that "individualize rewards and relations."[48]

The social games literature sensitizes us to how particular features of institutional contexts may individualize subjective responses by focusing agents' attention on particular strategies and away from broader structural contexts. This individualizing focus is most likely to occur in institutional contexts that (a) generate uncertainty about the likelihood of a desired outcome and (b) grant agents some degree of discretion to take strategic actions that affect that likelihood.[49] As described in appendix B, while Burawoy and Bourdieu disagree on the significance of a habitus, they share an understanding of the role of uncertainty in shaping subjective experiences and particularly its role in absorbing agents in playing a *game*. The key consequence of this absorption is that, as Burawoy (1979, 2012) explains, one cannot focus on playing the game while simultaneously questioning its rules. In the theory of social games, the obscuring of social structures and the forefronting of individual agency does not flow from a deeply internalized habitus adjusted to social structures but rather from the institutional conditions that generate an absorbing game that becomes "an end in itself, overshadowing, *masking* and even inverting the conditions out of which it emerges."[50]

Linking Unemployment Experiences and Labor-Market Institutions: Player Prominence and Emotional Labor

The theory of social games provides a broad framework for analyzing how institutional contexts may individualize subjective experiences and mystify social structures, but requires further development to explain variations; for example, to explain how different job-search games may generate self-blame or system-blame. To this end, I will introduce two previously untheorized dimensions of games.

First, my comparison of unemployed Americans and Israelis will show how social structures vary in the extent to which they render agents' actions *prominent determinants* of uncertain outcomes. While most games involve some exercise of strategic discretion, each game's rules and structures generate distinct understandings among its players of the relationship between the exercise of strategic discretion and the game's outcomes. I call this dimension of games the degree of *player prominence*. Player prominence is *high* to the extent that individual strategies are perceived by the players to be highly determinative of the outcome. Such games have the effect of making the player's role and his or her game-playing capacities *prominent* in relation to the outcome. By contrast, player prominence is *low* to the extent that player's successful execution of strategies is perceived as only marginally important to the outcome.[51]

Chapters 2 and 3 will show how the American white-collar chemistry game, in which job seekers perceive interpersonal fit with prospective employers to be the most important factor in getting hired, is characterized by high player prominence. By contrast, chapters 4 and 5 will show how the Israeli white-collar specs game, in which job seekers perceive a rigid and sometimes arbitrary skills-and-credentials filter to be the most important factor in getting hired, is characterized by low player prominence. Ultimately, low player prominence means that difficulties in finding work are more likely to be attributed to flaws in the system; high player prominence means that difficulties in finding work are more likely to be attributed to flaws in the self.

I introduce a second new dimension to the analysis of games, *emotional labor*, to help explain the white-collar unemployment experience. This concept, coined by Hochschild (1983), captures the dimension of work that requires the production of an emotion, such as sincere concern for a customer. The emotional labor performed by job seekers—as they do their job of seeking work—is to generate the emotions and attitudes demanded by the particular job-search game they are playing.

The chemistry game, which looks beyond a job seeker's skills to intangible inner qualities, requires American white-collar workers to engage in an emotional labor that I call *self-subjectification*—creating a feeling of connection through the projection of the self as a subject with the needed internal attributes to interpersonally fit. The Israeli specs game, by contrast, focuses on fine distinctions in skill levels and credentials and requires Israeli white-collar workers to engage in a very different kind of emotional labor that I call *self-objectification*—projecting the self as an object with the desired specs.

Self-subjectification requires what Hochschild (1983) calls "deep acting." To play the chemistry game effectively, job seekers must actually produce the emotion they need to project. To create interpersonal connection, one must *feel* connected. Producing the feeling of interpersonal connection in turn demands the internalization of, as Bourdieu would put it, the employer's schemes of perception and appreciation. This internalization is not the product of a prolonged and typically unconscious exposure to particular social structures, as in the formation of the habitus, but a purposeful act carried out in response to the demands of the game. In the chemistry game, one works to become the subject that fits the employer's schemes.

Self-objectification, by contrast, requires only "surface acting." To effectively play the specs game, it is sufficient for job seekers to express possession of the requisite attributes and to refrain from exhibiting any subjective feelings that might undermine this outward message. The difference between the deep acting of the chemistry game and the surface acting of the specs game has profound consequences for the experience of job seekers. As this book will show, it is the deep acting required by the chemistry game—the emotional labor of seeking to establish an interpersonal connection—that leaves American white-collar job seekers particularly exposed and vulnerable to ultimately seeing themselves as "flawed" or "defective."

Teasing out the most important elements of the job search that account for unemployment experiences is greatly aided by examining a third job-search game: the "diligence game" played by American blue-collar job seekers. In that context, American labor market institutions apply a diligence filter that focuses on whether the job seeker is reliable, compliant, and a hard worker.

In a surprising finding, of the three groups of job seekers examined in this book—American white-collar workers, Israeli white-collar workers, and American blue-collar workers—the two groups that share neither culture nor class report the most similar unemployment experiences. The American blue-collar unemployment experience bears a striking resemblance to the Israeli white-collar unemployment experience. This similarity makes sense only when one looks beneath the surface and observes the underlying *structural* parallels between the diligence game and the specs game. Both are characterized by low player prominence. While exhibiting a diligent attitude may be assumed to be within the job seeker's strategic control, the dominant American blue-collar labor-market institutions create a highly rigid filtering process (discussed in chapter 6) that typically undermines job seekers' attempts to display their diligence. As in the specs game, the structure of the diligence game makes search strategies seem far less important to the outcome than in the chemistry game. Moreover, both the specs game and the diligence game require surface acting rather than deep acting. It is these structural similarities between the specs and diligence games that explain the initially surprising similarities in the unemployment experiences of American blue-collar and Israeli white-collar job seekers. The diligence game suggests that labor-market institutional structures do more to determine the nature of the unemployment experience than class or culture.

My analyses and comparisons of different job-search games reveal that at the root of varied unemployment experiences lie specific labor-market institutions, often ignored by prior research, that call for specific job-search practices and strategies. The comparison of the job-search games and the unemployment experiences they generate provides a new account of American job seekers' individualized understandings of their labor-market difficulties and, more broadly, an account of how structural conditions shape subjective responses.

The comparison of unemployment experiences sheds light on some of the most important and vexing questions about unemployment. For example, looking closely at the nature of these experiences reveals that job-search discouragement—a phenomenon at the center of the U.S. public policy debates concerning unemployment—is neither a product of insufficient individual resilience nor a universal response to unemployment, but the result of a specific job-search game as structured by specific labor-market institutions. Likewise, whether job seekers blame themselves and interpret their continued unemployment to be a private matter or, conversely, blame the system and understand their unemployment to be a public and political issue is not simply the product of abstract cultural beliefs, but the result of playing a particular kind of job-search game. Beyond unemployment, the analysis of job seekers' experiences in this book will show how seemingly personal thoughts and feelings about ourselves are in fact systematically generated by the social institutions that structure our practices and day-to-day experiences. Recognizing the significance of social institutions in shaping our life experiences and outcomes—and not least in generating the particularly destructive sense of self-blame—is a necessary first step to collectively working to change them.

CHAPTER TWO

The American Chemistry Game

W hen I began interviewing unemployed white-collar workers in the
San Francisco Bay area about their job-search strategies, I noticed
a striking pattern. Whether they were looking for work as engineers, managers, or administrative assistants, they all generally believed that their
skills and credentials were only one factor in getting hired—and by no
means the most important one. Jason, a software engineer, explained: "The
most important thing is 'fit,' not skill. People want to work with people
that they like." Kathleen, looking for work in finance, agreed:

> People hire people that they *like*. Even if you have ideal credentials, even if you
> match one hundred percent of the job description, you may not get the job. If
> you can create *rapport*, you are more likely to get the job than someone who
> has all the credentials.

James, looking for work as a manager, explained that "getting a job is all
about *creating* relationships. This day and age, it's how jobs get found....
If you can establish rapport with someone, they may overlook the fact that
you don't have an exact attribute but that you have other skills. Maybe
you're a cultural fit." Or as Sergio, a system administrator, put it: "Interpersonal connection is probably the main reason why people get hired. [You]
have to establish a rapport.... It's not just about skills or experience."
    The consistency with which these job seekers assured me of the impor-
tance of "rapport" and "fit," no matter what kind of job they happened to
be looking for, led me to wonder: Where is this common understanding
coming from? When I probed job seekers about how they formed their
views about what matters in getting hired, I heard two kinds of answers.
They talked about the advice they had gleaned from books or heard in

workshops or job-seeker support organizations, and they talked about their own experiences at job interviews, where interpersonal fit often seemed to matter more than skills.

Looking more closely at the sources of my interviewees' career advice, I encountered a career-success self-help industry, which has rapidly grown over the past thirty years alongside the rise of insecure white-collar employment relations, discussed in the previous chapter. Through books, videos, workshops, support organizations, and coaching services, this industry offers career advice and job-search training to increasingly anxious workers.[1] By the time I finished my research, I concluded that career self-help is the dominant intermediary institution shaping American white-collar workers' understanding of the labor market and framing what they see as the range of plausible strategies for success in this market. Career self-help is aimed at both employed and unemployed workers, but its effects are much more profound on the latter. As chapter 3 will show, when workers are unemployed, self-help discourses often become their primary framework for understanding the situation they are in and what they should do about it, and self-help practices take on the quality of work itself, structuring job seekers' daily activities.[2]

To delve deeper into the world of job searching, I decided to spend a year as a participant-observer at an organization I will call "AmeriSupport," a career success self-help organization for unemployed white-collar job seekers (which I will describe in greater detail later in this chapter). My year of observations at AmeriSupport and my reading of the best-selling career-success self-help books most often mentioned by my interviewees suggest that the advice discourse on job searching contains two distinct strands:

The *rationalization strand* focuses on the need to define clear career or job-search goals and create a plan of action to achieve them. The core idea is to gain control over one's life through rationally organizing one's time and actions. In the United States, this idea traces back at least as far as Benjamin Franklin and his well-known apothegms regarding time management and self-discipline. Another element of the rationalization strand is the idea that job searching cannot be undertaken in a haphazard manner; rather, it requires one to learn, practice, and improve specific skills. One can, with sufficient diligence, learn these skills. This requires job seekers to approach their job searching as serious work. When the rationalization discourse is embedded in an organization such as Ameri-Support, a further claim is typically made: Performing the work of job searching is greatly facilitated by having a workplace and professional colleagues, as provided by AmeriSupport.

The *chemistry strand* of the self-help discourse focuses on discovering and expressing one's authentic inner self. Ironically, this strand is partly rooted in the American Transcendentalist tradition, made well known by writers such as Henry David Thoreau and Walt Whitman, who urged readers to reject Franklin's disciplined rationalism and to find and celebrate their authentic selves. The self-help fusion of the ideals of self-expression with the instrumental goals of worldly success can already be found in Dale Carnegie's *How to Win Friends and Influence People* (1936). Authentic expression, typically revealed by exuding passion, is not only an end in itself but also a means to achieve your career goals by facilitating interpersonal connection.

The most widely known modern self-help book for job seekers is Richard Bolles's *What Color Is Your Parachute?* (2004). This book makes explicit the connection between exuding an authentic and passionate self and finding a job. It first appeared in the early 1970s, precisely as white-collar job security and work conditions in general began to erode in the United States, and has since sold over nine million copies. It emphasizes that getting a job requires, more than skills and credentials, the ability to convey a self that would be a good interpersonal fit with the prospective employer. Bolles claims that the "job interview is every bit like the 'dating game.' Both of you have to *like each other* before you can even discuss the question of 'going steady,' i.e., a job" (2004, 248; emphasis added). The claim, made consistently and repeatedly by self-help practitioners, is that to get a job, you need to sell not your skills but rather the *person behind the skills*. Job-related skills and experiences are threshold requirements but are rarely sufficient or decisive. What matters most is interpersonal connection, which in turn requires exuding certain intangible inner qualities such as confidence, authenticity, and passion. Getting a job ultimately requires convincing the employer that one possesses the attitudes and dispositions that will make one a good fit. Getting hired requires chemistry.

Job seekers are told that by discovering and expressing their authentic and passionate selves, and by rationally planning and using their time, they can take control of their career fates. The career self-help message aims to inspire job seekers to believe that they can create their own career reality. They *can* make their dreams come true. But—job seekers are warned—it is not necessarily easy. It requires—as the title of Bolles's book suggests—the willingness to take the plunge of jumping with a parachute that reflects one's true colors. Career success ultimately depends on job seekers' successful execution of self-help strategies. As Bolles (2004, 50) puts it: "The *major* difference between successful and unsuccessful job-hunters is not some factor out there such as a tight job-market, but *the way they go about their job-hunt*."

The Chemistry Filter in Hiring

Is there any empirical basis for job-search advice flowing from the self-help industry on the importance of chemistry? As the job seekers I interviewed perceived, chemistry is indeed important at the interview stage with hiring managers, but the level of importance varies by industry and firm. Moreover, specs (skills and experiences) also play an important, if obscured, role in pre-interview filtering.

When conducting job interviews, American managers typically put great weight on interpersonal fit or chemistry. In the United States, after an initial behind-the-scenes filtering of résumés, the most common approach to hiring is a direct interview by the hiring manager,[3] in which interpersonal fit plays an important role. Mills famously described the white-collar "personality market" in which "intimate traits of the employee are drawn into the sphere of exchange." As Mills explains: "Employers again and again demand the selection of men *with personality*," which in most cases is "more important than grades" or other objective indicators of skills (1953, 182, 186).

Recent studies find some support for Mills's observations. A survey of hiring managers found that, in the United States, interviews are *the* most important factor affecting hiring decisions, ranking ahead of "a person's ability to perform the technical requirements of the job."[4] In a qualitative study of hiring in law firms, consulting firms, and investment banks, a majority of hiring managers indicated that interpersonal "fit" is the "the most important criterion a the job interview stage, rating fit over analytical thinking and communication" (Rivera 2012, 1007). Rivera found that while the various firms she studied "could have screened more intensely" using criteria such as "related work experience, writing skills, [or] standardized test performance," they prioritized fit and cultural similarity "because they saw it as a meaningful quality that fostered cohesion, signaled merit, and simply felt good" (1016). Other studies have similarly found that hiring managers' decisions often turn on "chemistry,"[5] on job seekers' self-presentation,[6] or on an ability to "stage characters that generate perceptions of trustworthiness and social similarity."[7] Managers typically discern fit by relying on their "instincts" or their "gut."[8] Kanter (1993) describes the consequences of this hiring process as the "homosocial reproduction of labor," with hiring decisions driven by social similarity or a sense of "easy predictable familiarity."[9]

American companies' reliance on hiring managers' subjective assessment of fit may reflect the sharp decline in the investment made by companies in recent decades in more systematic approaches to hiring. Cappelli explains that while in "the preceding generation, virtually every company of any size conducted sophisticated workforce planning," in recent years companies "appear to have abandoned the systematic approach of managing talent" (2008, 64–65). It is also important to keep in mind that while chemistry may be an important criterion at the interview stage, its relative importance relative to specs—such as credentials and experiences—varies by industry[10] and by firms within the same industry.[11] Moreover, even hiring managers that focus on chemistry factors during interviews nevertheless rely on specs factors to filter the applicant pool at the *pre-interview* stage.[12]

Yet despite these variations, chemistry is the most *salient* element of the hiring process for white-collar American job seekers and colors the entire job-search experience. This salience is a product of the two factors. First, job interviews are typically American job seekers' only direct interactive experience with the hiring process. The filtering of résumés according to specs goes on behind the scenes, while interviews are an intense personal experience that, as we will see in chapter 3, looms large in job seekers' understanding of the success or failure of their job searches. Second, the salience of the chemistry filter is also greatly magnified by the career self-help industry, which consistently presents fit as the key factor in getting hired. The role of the self-help industry in emphasizing the importance of chemistry will be the focus of this chapter.

Self-Help Institutionalized: AmeriSupport

Self-help discourses and practices are institutionalized in self-help organizations. One such organization is AmeriSupport, a state-sponsored support organization for white-collar job seekers in the San Francisco Bay area. It is one of nineteen nearly identical state-sponsored organizations in California, all of which have grown rapidly in the past two decades.[13] My choice to focus on AmeriSupport and other related methodological issues are discussed in appendix A.

AmeriSupport is located in the state of California's Employment Development Department building, on the same floor as a One-Stop Career Center, which is open to all job seekers. The AmeriSupport program, however, is only open to people who self-identify as professionals.[14] Given AmeriSupport's focus on helping professionals, its members—whose past positions range from administrative assistants to corporate executives, and many of whom were engineers and mid-level managers—tend to have higher-than-average past wages and levels of education. Slightly more than half the members are male, the majority are white, and most are in their forties or fifties.[15] The active membership fluctuates between forty and eighty members.

Becoming an AmeriSupport member requires participating in a weeklong series of intensive workshops. The four-hour daily sessions, led by volunteer trainers who are themselves members, cover all facets of job searching. At the end of the week, the graduating cohort of new members forms a "success team," which then begins to meet regularly at the AmeriSupport offices as a group of colleagues supporting one another in their job searches.

I spent one year as a member of AmeriSupport, participating fully in all of its activities. For example, I participated in the weeklong intensive training and became a member of a success team, which called itself the "Quantum Leapers." I also gathered data by conducting repeated indepth interviews with AmeriSupport members and observing all workshops, trainings, and general meetings.

Beyond success team meetings, the main action at AmeriSupport occurs at the weekly general meetings of all active members. These meetings begin with the ritual presentation of "success stories" by any member who found a job in the past week. These are followed by a ninety-minute presentation and discussion led by an "expert" guest speaker, most often a self-help coach or author, who typically elaborated on some aspect of the initial week of job-search training. These speakers, who volunteer to speak at AmeriSupport, often concluded their presentations by pitching their paid services to the members.

Every AmeriSupport member is required to volunteer four hours per week to help with a host of administrative tasks such as maintaining AmeriSupport's website, recruiting new members, coordinating and preparing for the training sessions, inviting weekly guest speakers, and organizing "peer-to-peer" job-search coaching. General meetings are followed by various "departmental meetings" to coordinate this volunteer work. I volunteered to work as a peer-to-peer coach, helping job seekers brainstorm about searching strategies and editing their résumés and cover letters.

During the initial trainings, general meetings, and success team meetings, AmeriSupport puts into action both the rationalization and chemistry strands of the self-help model. First, the work of job searching is rationalized and professionalized in the corporate-like workplace of AmeriSupport's offices, where it is performed with success team colleagues. Second, the substance of the work entails the emotional labor that I will call *self-subjectification*—the uncovering and projecting of one's passions and inner qualities in an effort to produce fit and interpersonal connection with prospective employers.

The Professionalized Work of Job Searching

Self-help's rationalization of the job-search process begins by framing it as a professional activity, like any other. The unemployed members of AmeriSupport are strongly encouraged to view job searching as their new job, which demands expunging any thoughts of this period as involving daytime leisure. This is stated explicitly and repeatedly in AmeriSupport's trainings and general meetings. As one self-help speaker put it: "My best advice is to view your search as a full-time job, not a part-time job, and view [AmeriSupport] as your work site. I've had a few friends who lost jobs and decided to take time off. It has not proven to be a good idea." The speakers are reinforced and bolstered by best-selling self-help authors who convey similar ideas. One of the most influential contemporary authors of this strand of self-help is Franklin Covey, best known for *The Seven Habits of Highly Effective People* (1989). Covey urges job seekers to consciously plan every moment of every day with the aim of fulfilling their "mission" of finding work. Like any other professional work, job searching requires discipline and dedication.

AmeriSupport members police each other on their time management. At one general meeting, Sara, the volunteer president of AmeriSupport, focused on the importance of strictly compartmentalizing leisure:

SARA: I hope people are not forgetting to do things they really enjoy at different hours from their work hours. I like to go dancing. Have other people figured out ways to do things they love without it taking away from job searching?

JENNIFER: I Rollerblade.

SARA: Great. Do you do that on your on weekends?

JENNIFER: Sometimes during the week, for an hour.

ROB: I play softball *in the evenings*. Great for networking.

In this exchange, Jennifer's occasional failure to maintain appropriate boundaries around weekday work hours is only highlighted by Rob's emphasis on his pursuit of play in the evenings, as well as his incorporation of work into play with the reference to networking.

Beyond the construction of temporal structures separating work from leisure, the job search is turned into work at the level of daily practice and experience by its professionalization—the breaking down of job seeking into discrete tasks that can be mastered. The self-help approach to crafting résumés provides one example. Professionalization turns the task of résumé construction into a process of continual editing and revision. As one self-help speaker at AmeriSupport emphasized: "It took me a month to write my résumé, and I do this for a living! People write their résumés too casually. You need to craft it, sculpt it."

The initial weeklong training devotes an entire day to résumés. Members get sample résumés in different formats. They break into small teams to critique each other's initial drafts. The résumé work continues in subsequent success team meetings and in general meetings. Weekly guest speakers often raise various résumé-related topics and provide seemingly endless and often conflicting opinions about the ideal résumé. There are debates about the relative merits of traditional résumés using a reverse chronological format, functional résumés organized around skills and experiences, and various hybrid alternatives. The contradictory self-help advice provides fodder for long strategy discussions at success team meetings.

The rationalization and chemistry strands of self-help come together in the nearly unanimous résumé advice to quantify one's accomplishments and embed them in lively stories. Many job seekers hesitate to quantify achievements without actual data. To help members along, one speaker asked for a volunteer:

SPEAKER: What did you do at your last job?

BARBARA: I improved global processes in customer service.

SPEAKER: Okay. Take a guess about the numbers.

BARBARA: It's hard to make correlations because there are so many factors ...

SPEAKER: A guess?

BARBARA: Okay, fifty percent.

SPEAKER: Your story is "There were lots of customer complaints. I formulated a strategy and implemented a plan, and within six months customer complaints were cut in half."

[Audience claps; Barbara smiles.]

A point often repeated is that mere quantification is not enough. As one speaker explained: "If you just say you saved the company X amount of dollars, employers will know it's bullshit. If you really saved your company a billion dollars, they would not have laid you off!" To make the quantitative claims credible and resonant, and to make the résumé generally compelling, the job seeker must convey more than his or her quantified achievements. Résumés need to communicate something more basic about the job seeker through stories, which are the first step of self-subjectification, the process of constructing and externalizing a particular self.

Job seekers are advised that, to tell compelling stories, they need to avoid jargon and "vacuous phrases like 'dynamic team player,' which come straight out of books and counselors." Instead, résumés should convey stories that are *personalized*. The story must contain the basic elements of "PAR"—problem, action, and result—but more importantly, it needs to convey the qualities of the person who made the action and result possible. To convey the person behind the achievements, résumé stories should cast the job seeker as the hero. As one AmeriSupport self-help speaker put it:

> Write a story about how you increased sales. The real story is *how* you did it.... The résumé is a storytelling tool, a novel that people read. You need four or five of these stories to come alive.

AmeriSupport members are encouraged to "use a sales-and-marketing approach to yourself." The core idea of this approach is that one cannot successfully sell a product simply by listing its functions, but rather by *generating a feeling* about the product. As Dan, the director of AmeriSupport and its only paid staff member (whom I will refer to as "Director Dan"), explained: "A car advertisement usually does not talk about the car's performance but creates an image of its essence as tough or sleek." This analogy is used to bolster the fundamental claim of the self-help discourse that hiring decisions are not ultimately based on an assessment of skills, but rather on the degree of *interpersonal connection.* As Director Dan often repeated: "The personal touch is what gets people hired. People hire people that they like." He added: "I have read hundreds of articles about what employers want, and what comes up consistently is attitude first, reliability second, and skills last. *Skills get you in the door but are not sufficient.*"

One of the most respected speakers, who came to AmeriSupport several times during the year, emphasized the same message and used a similar car metaphor:

> Create chemistry and connection. . . . People make decisions based on emotion. If all decisions were made by brains, we would only buy Toyota Corollas, not Jaguars. Employers are the same thing. You need to create chemistry.

Job seekers are encouraged to create a unique résumé for each job application, highlighting their most relevant attributes to convey fit with that employer. Sally, a job seeker and former quality-control manager at a high-tech firm, expresses this self-help perspective: "It may seem like writing a résumé is about your work history, but it is not that at all. It is a marketing tool and therefore needs to be thought of as such and constructed for particular audiences." As a marketing tool that uses one's work history to produce a connection with different audiences, even minute details of the résumé receive intense focus. In fact, in support-group meetings in which job seekers provide feedback to each other on their résumés, the most commonly discussed issues are aesthetic in nature. For example, if a targeted company or particular job is deemed to require creativity, the résumé should use a more artistic font and imaginative vocabulary. By contrast, applying to a bank requires a more conventional font and wording. The focus on aesthetics is partly attributable to the idea that a résumé should convey much more than the job seeker's skills; it should convey a compelling image. Given the inherently limited expressive powers of a résumé, issues such as font sizes or the ideal amount of white space become the focus for strategizing. Job seekers—especially new AmeriSupport members—spend countless hours perfecting the wording and style of their résumés.

Self-help speakers urge job seekers to try to learn from employer rejections and use new tactics to improve their résumés for the next application. With conflicting views about the proper style, length, font, and format, there is always a new approach to try. The constant working and reworking of the résumé also reflects a larger imperative of the self-help paradigm, which calls for a continuous effort to improve *all* aspects of the work of job searching. This is the seventh habit of Covey's *Seven Habits of Highly Effective People*, called "sharpening of the saw."

Cover letters are as important as résumés. Self-help speakers emphasized that "the real action is in sending a letter that is targeted." As one speaker put it: "Fit [the cover letter] to their *culture*." Since compelling cover letters need to reflect intimate knowledge of the employer, much time must be spent researching targeted companies. For this purpose, speakers suggested that you go to company websites to read press releases and manager bios. It is also advised to do such research by using online social networking sites to identify people you may know at a targeted company and contact them for "informational interviews" (i.e., meetings where the job seekers asks about the nature of the company and the work culture). It is assumed that each company has a unique culture and that getting hired requires displaying your fit with this culture. Like cover letters and résumés, thank-you letters are also seen as important documents for one's presentation of self. In the words of one speaker, they are "your chance to make an impression, to redefine your candidacy, salvage any mistake at the interview."[16]

In addition to résumés, cover letters, and thank-you letters, similar self-help advice is offered for writing of one's social networking profile, which also requires continuous work. At a workshop devoted to using the social networking site LinkedIn, the trainer explained that the profile "is always a work in progress. . . . I change mine all the time." As with other written documents, there is a focus on customization. One expert suggested to "optimize your profile to match the job for which you will be interviewing tomorrow. Customize the first page to the job, using the job announcement." This advice is premised on the assumption that prior to the interview the employer will check the job seeker's social networking profiles. As with résumés and cover letters, there are two goals to the profile. The first is to make sure to include the right keywords so that, as one speaker put it, "people looking for your specialty can find you." Another speaker explained: "Put something that people are searching for. Don't put 'consultant' or 'self-employed.' You need the keyword that the recruiter will be searching for." The keywords should ideally appear "above the fold," which in a digital context translates to the "first screen load of information."

The second goal of the social networking profile is to create connection. Self-help experts emphasize that a social networking profile should be more personal than a résumé or a cover letter. It should be revealing and "alive." Job seekers are advised: "Make it compelling. Don't copy and paste your résumé. This is meant to be a more living document. . . . It has more potential to convey *who you are* than a traditional résumé." One expert explained: "It is more informal. Just like we write e-mails less formally than letters. Profiles are meant to be in that voice."

As with other the construction of other documents, the ultimate focus with social networking profiles is on creating chemistry: "One way to generate chemistry is to tell me about yourself. Tell me your brand, the kind of person you are. It's a way to decide if they like you. Not everyone fits every corporate culture. In your online identity, you want it to come through." Or as another speaker put it: "You want to create chemistry. Include your *personality* so that people will like you." Job seekers are encouraged to put themselves "out there." One speaker advised: "Be out with your outlook on life. It gives you a human face. Be personal as well as professional. Be a human." The approach is summed up as follows:

> Build some chemistry via the [social networking] profile. Don't be dry. Be passionate. Put yourself out there about who you are. Be yourself in your profile. It's differentiating. So many people put stuff that is as dry as toast.

As with the advice for cover letters, it is suggested that job seekers focus on telling stories to convey these personal qualities:

> You can fit six PAR [problem, action, result] stories in your profile. It is much better than telling them your strengths. PAR is proving it and connecting at an emotional level. I believe in stories because stories are fun.

In addition to words, social networking sites provide another salient channel for making connection: one's picture. As a workshop leader said: "When you see a profile, what comes up first? A picture!" Job seekers are encouraged to include a picture because "it makes you more personable, approachable." Speakers explained that pictures add credibility: "A picture makes a difference. People believe content more when there is a picture. It's more credible. Having a photo makes the person more legitimate."[17]

A central purpose of the social networking profile is to facilitate networking, which is the single most important element of the job search, according to both AmeriSupport and the wider self-help literature. Director Dan would often repeat the mantra: "Network, network, network. Eighty percent of new jobs are found through your personal network."[18]

This message is usually accompanied by the reminder that relying on help-wanted ads is almost a waste of time. As one self-help speaker put it, "You need to be out there networking. . . . Sending a résumé over the Internet is not going to do it." Statistics are often marshaled about the low success rates of responding to ads. One speaker asked: "Would you get into a plane with a five percent success rate? That's about the success rates with job boards. So you need to get out there, interacting with folks and telling stories."

Networking requires much more than simply calling up one's acquaintances; that pool of contacts is typically exhausted within the first few weeks of the search. The real work of networking is making *new* connections. As one speaker put it, "You need to keep growing your network and keep it fresh and alive." Various strategies for this are offered. A common suggestion was to attend professional association meetings and conferences. More creatively, Director Dan suggested at a December general meeting that "professional associations are now having holiday events. Crash them! It is a great opportunity because people are in a good mood, drinking alcohol and putting their schmoozer hat on, as opposed to their screener hat." A guest speaker suggested other out-of-the-box approaches:

> Read the wedding announcements in the newspaper which tell you the groom does this, the bride this. Get the names, call and say: "I saw you in the bridal section." If that doesn't work, then start up conversations with strangers at the supermarket. When choosing a line, go behind someone you want to talk to and say: "Hey, I always thought of buying that thing."

Any talk of networking strategies includes at its center a discussion of the importance of using online social networking sites. As the speaker at one workshop said: "It is very powerful to be able to browse the connections of your first-degree contacts." Expert speakers explain the vast pool of potential networking targets made available by social networking sites, as one put it:

> I have 229 first-degree contacts and 50,000 second-degree contacts. That's a powerful resource in a job search. And then I have over 3 million third-degree

contacts. It's mind boggling. Eleven thousand new people are in my network since last week. It is geometric progression.

While most friends and acquaintances will not sit down with a job seeker and describe the career of every person they know, with social networking sites, job seekers now can do just that themselves by browsing through their contacts' contacts. The promise of social networking sites is that one can click and connect, and do it even more effectively than via traditional in-person networking. As a speaker explained, instead of randomly striking up conversations, with social networking sites, you can "find *key* contacts and browse through their contacts. Go in and find the perfect person."

In addition to effectiveness, networking via social networking sites is also presented as *easy*. Most job seekers dislike networking. As will be discussed in the next chapter, despite its perceived effectiveness, job seekers dread networking, fearing they will come across as pushy or as losers. One speaker began addressing the topic of social networking by identifying with these sentiments as a way to encourage the use of the Internet for networking:

> I don't like networking. Anyone else not like networking? [Many hands are raised.] Social networking sites take away the face-to-face encounter with sweaty palms, the nervousness about "How do I talk about myself?" "What do I say?" It is a lot easier to connect. It is a barrier buster.

Once the right connection is identified and the ice is broken, job seekers are then encouraged to meet face-to-face.

The discourse on the importance of using *personal* connections to act as intermediaries between oneself and potential employers—whether such connections are strong, weak, or brand-new—follows the same logic that underlies the construction of résumés and cover letters. In both cases, the strategic emphasis is on finding ways to convey intangible qualities of the self that create chemistry. The often-heard cliché is that networking works because employers assume that "birds of a feather flock together." If someone inside the company refers a candidate (assuming the referrer is considered a "good fit"), the hiring manager will tend to presume that the candidate is also likely to be a good fit. Behind the hiring manager's favorable presumption is the notion that the referrer can intuit or sense a job seeker's all-important internal attributes more directly and efficiently than can be gleaned from a résumé. The focus on the intangible attributes of the self and fit is the reason why even casually formed contacts—whether preexisting "weak" ties in Granovetter's (1974) sense or newly formed ties made at an association meeting—are believed to be effective. Even though the weak or newly met intermediary often knows very little about the job seeker's specific skills, the self-help discourse claims that networking is effective because a "gut-level sense" of the job seeker is perceivable in the first twenty seconds of an interaction and can be easily communicated to the hiring manager.[19]

A frequent guest speaker at AmeriSupport provided step-by-step advice on how job seekers can make an instant connection that can lead to a job referral with someone they just met while in the line for coffee at a professional association meeting:

> Start by saying, "Sure is a big crowd." ... [Then] you say, "I am Mary. I am an accountant. Well, I was until last week when they laid us all off and sent the jobs to India." Notice what I did here. I was very quickly revealing of my need without appearing desperate. That sets the stage for developing the *quick connection*. Then say, "Tell me about you." [She might respond:] "Oh, I am a marketing manager." But she says it in a flat tone. Part of how you *create deep connection instantly* is that you listen not to the words but to what's beneath the words. [Respond] in a tactful way: "Gee, you sound thrilled with that." She gets a little defensive. "Oh, no, it's okay, it's just that with my three kids my plate is pretty full." *Aha*. You found out her *hot button* from her animated voice. This is really important. You make an empathetic statement like: "I can understand. How old are your kids?" ... You share parallel experiences. You show empathy. When you sense she is feeling somewhat connected to you, make *the ask*: "As I mentioned, I am looking for my next accounting job. Might you know somebody I can speak with?" If she knows someone, she is fairly likely to tell you, *even though you just met*.

To make job seekers comfortable with "getting out there" and networking, and to help them create chemistry, AmeriSupport emphasizes the importance of practicing and improving one's "elevator speech." This is the verbal form of the résumé, in which one tries to distill and convey in a catchy way one's skills and, more importantly, one's internal attributes. It is what Vicki Smith (2001) calls the "thirty second me." One speaker explained that "elevator speeches" derive their name from the idea that "if you were in an elevator and Bill Gates walked in, you should be able to tell him who you are and what you're looking for before reaching the twentieth floor." This rehearsed sound bite is also called a "personal commercial" to remind job seekers that, just as in car advertisements, the emphasis should not be on the boring details of the engine specs but on the image. Striking the right tone and using the right body language are essential.

During the initial training week, new members spend considerable time creating these speeches and practicing them on one another. Then, at the climactic moment of the first week, new members are invited by Director Dan to introduce themselves to the other members at the general meeting by giving "their newly minted elevator speeches." As with résumés, the elevator speeches require endless customizing for specific audiences.

The curriculum of the weeklong training encourages job seekers to create an elevator speech using the format of name, description of occupation, description of what one is seeking, and, again, your name.[20] For example, one job seeker's elevator speech was: "I am Doug Shane, and I take technology from concept to product management. If you need someone who actually has a track record of executing on time, I am the person you need to be talking to. I am Doug Shane." The rationalized formula ensures that all the necessary elements are there, but also, by its very nature, tends to undermine the goal of achieving chemistry. Self-help speakers therefore consider it too rigid and advise against it. For example, one speaker who attended the presentation of the "newly minted elevator speeches" later told the group:

> To be honest, when I listened to the people who introduced themselves here, I was unhappy. They were stiff and sterile. *It's all about chemistry and connection.* If you sound like a professional job seeker, it looks like you have been looking for a job too long. Don't do the script with your name stated twice. Stop the scripting. You will look like a loser. Speak your truth informally. Make a connection.

Or as another speaker urged: "Be smooth, but not too smooth." This advice exposes the tension between the twin elements of self-help: the rationalization strand of practice, formulas, and structure, and the chemistry strand of self-subjectification necessary in order to create a connection. In an effort to bridge this gap, the most common word used in elevator speeches is "passion." For example, one job seeker began his elevator speech with: "My name is Ray, and I am a seasoned veteran, *passionate* about having an impact on the business's bottom line." This introductory verbal communication is intended to generate an opportunity for the job seeker to follow up with a longer well-honed story. Just as with résumés, cover letters, and social networking profiles, connection is best achieved through stories.

Stories are most important in the context of the job interview, the job seeker's best opportunity to establish an unmediated connection by conveying the right internal qualities. One speaker stressed the importance of the interview in this way:

> Two percent of the time you have a chance to make a real difference in your life. Ninety-eight percent of time is routine. An interview is one of those two percent moments. What will you do with that two percent moment? Prepare. So when it comes up, you are ready with prime material, stories that make your résumé a whole human being.

The construction of compelling stories is strongly emphasized because, as is often repeated by speakers, they help people "connect with you." The stories should appeal at a gut level. In the words of one speaker, they "cannot be memorized" but should be a "natural reliving of the experience, in all its rich detail, including obstacles, suspense, and, most importantly, how you overcame the obstacles to reach a happy ending with your unique skills, ingenuity, and persistence." The core idea is that employers "respond to stories," not to a recitation of facts. Telling a story that is "full of details, names, and numbers," that "draws a picture," is *the* way to establish rapport—and "*you need the rapport more than anything*." Or as another speaker put it:

> Stories have a way of making people connect with you in a powerful way. . . . It allows someone to buy in and emotionally connect. Little details make it come alive. You need a sense of theater, of dramatic effect. Raise your tone of voice, add spice. You want to absorb.

The crafting, practicing, and delivering of effective stories ultimately demands the emotional labor of tapping into and externalizing elements of one's subjective inner self. To come across as authentic and connecting, this externalization cannot be superficial but should go deep to one's "core." According to the self-help discourse, it is only this authentic discovery and projection of the self that will create the interpersonal connection needed to get hired. The hiring decision is, ultimately, a response not to the well-crafted story but to the nonverbal and intangible qualities it conveys, which create chemistry. One speaker explained that the "purpose of the story is to make you feel good so that you will project good nonverbal stuff, which is the majority of the effect. *Content matters less. Content is important to convince yourself so you project the right stuff.*"

The emotional labor demanded by the work of job searching requires that job seekers not simply fake their connection to the prospective employer but genuinely feel it. In Hochschild's (1983) terms, it requires "deep acting" as opposed to "surface acting." The specific emotional labor demanded of American white-collar job seekers, which I call self-subjectification, requires the internal production of two distinct though related feelings: a generally upbeat attitude and specific and intense passion about the desired work and workplace. I will address these in turn.

The Mandatory Authentic Smile

In the chemistry game, exhibiting a positive attitude is an absolute requirement. Whether crafting cover letters, networking, or interviewing, job seekers must project positiveness and confidence. Self-help speakers stressed that employers are not interested in people who exhibit anger or depression.

The discourse regarding the importance of a positive attitude to career success can be found at least as far back as Carnegie's *How to Win Friends and Influence People* (1936), which emphasizes that successful interpersonal interactions require a "friendly" disposition. At AmeriSupport, one of the most strictly enforced rules is that a job seeker is never to discuss his or her layoff or search process in a negative way. To avoid this, one speaker advised members to never "go into detail about why you are transitioning. Employers don't want any negativity carried in." Or as another speaker put it: "Don't talk about why you are sad because your job search has been difficult. Focus on going forward." With respect to networking, it is claimed that no one will give a referral to a job seeker who is depressed or angry, so job seekers must exhibit to all their social contacts, including their AmeriSupport colleagues, that they are "together" and "positive."

Here again, the construction of stories is recommended. For example, job seekers are encouraged to have a story ready in case they are asked about their "transition" (and *only* if they are asked). Here is one self-help speaker's advice to an AmeriSupport member:

AMERISUPPORT MEMBER: How would you go about finessing being out of work three years?
SPEAKER: What have you done during this period? Coursework? Consulting? Whatever it is, label the period and be ready to talk about it. Ultimately, it boils down to what attitude you project.

The stories should strictly avoid the word "unemployment," typically by using phrases such as "in between gigs" or "in transition." One speaker explicitly exhorted the group: "You are not unemployed; you are free agents." Furthermore, the stories should focus on the positive elements of the current situation, a strategy repeatedly modeled by the self-help speakers themselves. One speaker began her talk this way: "I love being here. I love the excitement about changes." Another insisted that "now is the best time to look at self-actualization" and that "this is your do-over. You can start from scratch and create your life exactly as you want, starting this moment."

In addition to stories, self-help speakers offered a variety of suggestions to generate and project a positive attitude. One common suggestion was to stop listening to the news. Director Dan recommended: "Take a news fast. Read things that are positive." Along the same lines, a speaker rhetorically asked the group:

How can you read the newspaper and stay positive? Be selective. Don't read about *wrongdoing in the world*. It's not the time in your life to focus on that. It's going to rattle your nerves. If your spouse tells you the horrible news in the morning, you can say to her: "This does not support me in my job search."

Another common suggestion is to select social contacts by their effect on one's positiveness. One self-help speaker advised: "Think of all the people you know. Categorize them in terms of who reminds you of your dreams and keeps you positive. Hang out with positive people." The positive-attitude message is even reflected in the posters around AmeriSupport's meeting room. One says "Opportunity," with a picture of a sunrise over water and a small boat sailing to new horizons; another says "Change," with a picture of a scenic winding mountain road.

Members enforce a positive attitude with one another. For example, in

one brainstorming meeting, a relatively new member named Randy spoke
of having been out of the job market for a number of years.

RANDY: I'm old and hope this may open some opportunities with companies using
old systems that young people don't want to touch.
BILL: Don't say "old," say "experienced."
RANDY: Well, I can say it *here*!
LINDA: No. You can't say it here. It's a bad habit.
RANDY: Okay. There is no "old" here . . . [looking irritated and bewildered].

Daniel, the volunteer president of AmeriSupport during the middle
part of my year at AmeriSupport, exemplified the avoidance of negatives
by never discussing his visible disability. Despite having worn a cast on his
right arm for months, Daniel never publicly brought up the obstacle this
posed in his job search. In a private interview with me, he readily volunteered that the injury "changed everything." He explained: "At interviews,
they don't say anything, but you can tell by the way people look, where
the eye is focused, and the interview process doesn't go any further." Yet
when in front of the group, Daniel echoed the spirit of the self-help speakers. He typically told the group how this period "provides a great opportunity to learn about yourself." Only in his final meeting as president did
he indirectly share his situation. When making his usual request to "please
turn off cell phones," he added as an afterthought, "They piss me off because I was rear-ended by a guy talking on one, and it hurt my job and career." In my field notes that morning, I wrote: "The unspeakable cast is finally acknowledged, though in a roundabout way. It is a symbol of all the
other negatives that are not to be talked about."

Passion: Make Your Dreams Come True

Beyond general positiveness, the emotional labor of job searching demands the production of authentic passion for the targeted job. This "deep
acting"[21] is to be achieved, according to self-help speakers, by pursuing
jobs that actually reflect one's true passions. Job seekers are repeatedly
exhorted to "go for your dream job."

The self-help discourse discourages treating work as an instrumental pursuit, instead urging job seekers to look inward, discover their true
passions, and externalize these through the previously discussed job-
searching practices. The decision of what job to pursue should be based

on one's inner desires rather than external labor-market conditions. This claim is ubiquitous in best-selling self-help books. For example, Deepak Chopra (1994) has sold millions of books on the importance of workers discovering their "true self."[22]

The importance of pursuing one's true passion is presented first and foremost in spiritual and philosophical terms. One speaker explained that if you follow your passions, you "can't wait for the alarm on Monday morning because you love every minute of being awake. *Every day wasted not doing what [you] love is a day gone.*" Director Dan made the same point at the end of a meeting: "I want to leave you with a last thought. *What will you do with your one wild and precious life?*"

To follow your passion, you need to find it. AmeriSupport's trainings and workshops, like most self-help books, offer a variety of exercises meant to help job seekers uncover their occupational passions. The initial week of training involves a preliminary exercise of writing down the things that your next job "must have" and "must not have." Speakers at the weekly general meetings encouraged members to go deeper. As one put it: "Listen to the signals internally of what's important to you. What are you passionate about?" There is general agreement that finding your passion requires introspection. As one speaker explained:

> Your life purpose is not on the tip of your tongue. It is down in the darker parts, and you need to find it.... There is buried somewhere deep inside of [you] some part of [you] that already knows what [your] purpose is, but there is just not a good enough line of communication with that part.

To establish this line of communication, job seekers write down the answers to questions such as, "If you had one year with no need for money, what would you do?" In another exercise, members fill in the blanks in phrases such as "I love to ____" and "I get excited by ____." In completing these sentences, members are encouraged to "pick something that is almost too good to be true, something that gives you a jolt." A more unusual exercise asked members to "write down five career options that you have been considering." The self-help speaker explained: "The first answer you wrote is the most conventional and is what you would tell your mom. The second is something you have a strength in and could be good at. The third one is the *real answer.*" After such exercises, there would usually be at least one excited member who said, "I am blown away. This exactly fits me."

As will be seen in the next chapter, the call to follow one's passion often inspires job seekers, at least temporarily, to look for fulfilling jobs. The alluring promise of passion and meaning is bolstered by the more pragmatic claim that pursuing a job that fits one's personal interests will actually *help* one's chances in finding a job. In other words, it is not only the most appealing prospect, but actually the best *strategy*, to look inward rather than outward. As Director Dan often repeated, the best way to find a job is "not to ask what the world needs, but what you have to give to the world."

Passion trumps labor markets or other structural constraints. As one self-help speaker put it: "Your highest probability of getting a job is going for your dream job because [employers] love your passion and enthusiasm." Labor-market conditions, much like skills, are of secondary importance. If you pursue your passion, you will be able to convey the right inner qualities to employers. One self-help speaker summed it up: "When you have passion, everyone wants to hire you."

A contrarian speaker went against the grain of self-help by acknowledging that unemployed job seekers are usually driven by the need for income and not by passion, but even this speaker urged members to engage in surface acting regarding the pursuit of their passions:

> You are really looking for work because you need to pay your bills. But don't tell employers because then they think you will leave. When networking, don't tell people you network with that "I am looking for a job." That sounds like it's about money. Say you are looking for an ideal career fit or opportunity. Say it is your ideal job, your dream job, even if it's just for money. Don't be naive here. People who hear you will think, okay, they will go the extra mile. Work on your vocabulary. "Dream job" is great.

However, this speaker's urging of surface acting and his acknowledgment that many unemployed people want a job primarily to pay the bills was the exception. The far more frequent advice was to truly pursue your dreams. In *What Color Is Your Parachute?*—often referred to as the bible of job seeking—Bolles (2004) explains the motivational benefits of pursuing one's dreams:

> The more you don't cut the dream down, because of what you *think* you know about the *real world*, the more likely you are to find what you are looking for. Hold on to *all of* your dream. Most people don't find their heart's desire because they decide to pursue just half their dream—and consequently they hunt

for it with only *half a heart.* If you decide to pursue your whole dream, your best dream, the one you would die to do, I guarantee you will hunt for it *with all your heart.* It is this *passion* which often is the difference between successful career changers and unsuccessful ones. (186, emphasis in the original)

After being urged by speakers to pursue their dreams, some members were skeptical: "What if your life purpose has no money in it?" The speakers' response was typically to keep asserting that you are wholly in control of your own economic destiny. The following exchange was typical:

AMERISUPPORT MEMBER: How can I overcome the obstacle of not having enough skills for my dream job?

SPEAKER: People always tell me why they can't follow their passion. They come up with list of reasons why it's not possible to do what you love. But this is available in unlimited capacity for everyone here today. . . . Most [of my coaching] clients make more money than ever once they do what they love. Maslow's hierarchy is upside down. Start with self-actualization and other things will fall into place.

ANOTHER AMERISUPPORT MEMBER: But isn't there a gap between theory and reality here?

SPEAKER: We construct our own reality. It's up to us to create our reality. It's a mental construct.

The self-help speakers' insistence on mind over matter—on the power to create one's own reality—is reinforced, legitimated, and echoed by best-selling self-help books. Moreover, speakers can typically counter audience skepticism with the "success stories" of their clients. The most common technique to illustrate the effectiveness of a particular job-search strategy is tell how a client used it and got a job—presumably a dream job. For example, one speaker reported that "last summer I worked with a young woman from Japan who came to California with twenty-seven dollars in her pocket. After going to school and working three jobs, she put a down payment on house that she converted to a hospice. Now she earns thirty thousand dollars a month."

At one general meeting, the guest self-help speaker began by stating: "Your job search has a context." As a sociologist, I pricked up my ears. Did we finally have a speaker who would discuss labor markets and other structural constraints? Instead, he reiterated the claim of individual control, with reinforcement from Director Dan:

SPEAKER: The *context is made up of your beliefs, attitudes, feelings, perspectives.* Some beliefs—like "jobs are scarce," "I have to compromise and reduce my expectations"—are a context. It is not true. It's a perspective, a belief. "I need a job to pay the bills." None of these are true in reality. We relate to them as if they are. *These are contexts, but you can choose to have another one. . . . They are up to you to choose.* Ask yourself: What is my context? My perspective on job search? If the context of your job is "I need to be doing this to survive," your experience will be altered by that, diminished.

DIRECTOR DAN: Yes. It feels like a ball and chain and not a choice.

SPEAKER: You are inventing your perspective. Invent some crazy ones.

AMERISUPPORT MEMBER: I can do anything.

ANOTHER AMERISUPPORT MEMBER: You want it, you go get it.

SPEAKER: How about "jobs are dead"? There is no such thing as a job. "Job" is an anachronism. We are all *free agents.* What if *that* was your perspective? It's *up to you. You get to choose.* How do you choose? Ask what's powerful for you. What will make you *show up* and make you break through the obstacles holding you back?

Audience skepticism is further challenged by speakers suggesting that any perceived obstacles, including skepticism, are within the mind of the job seeker. They often subtly blame job seekers by focusing on the need to remove one's inner obstacles. The following exchange took place at a general meeting:

SPEAKER: What do you need to release in order to embrace your vision? Is it anger? Resentment? Skepticism? Let it go. Get rid of it.

AMERISUPPORT MEMBER: But I do not have experience in the field I want to pursue.

SPEAKER: When you start this process you will get voices of negative self-talk, saying you can't do it. When you give that voice credibility, it can become your reality. Awareness is the first step. Then choose to change the dial. Put on a different station. Turn off the "I am not good enough." Speak affirmations like "I am doing meaningful work and providing financial abundance."

It is sometimes suggested that job seekers unconsciously sabotaged their last job because it was not their dream job. One self-help speaker used herself as an example: "I would get laid off from my administrative jobs. It took me a while to get the message. I kept taking jobs where I was unhappy [and] suffocating until I realized my passion lay in coaching." Another speaker likewise suggested: "The part of you that knows your

purpose ... may have some role in your being here right now. You may
say the company did a layoff, but I am telling you it's *in you* somewhere."
A different type of response focused on the job seeker playing the victim
rather than taking control. One speaker drew from personal experience:

> When I went through a layoff, I went on the Internet to look for work. My
> wife kept asking, "What did you do all day?" I told her, "Get off my back. It's a
> tough economic time and I am a victim here." But later I would feel like a loser,
> and I realized what I was doing was wrong. I was telling myself I am a com-
> modity in a market with an oversupply, but then I realized I *need to take con-
> trol of the situation.*

Taking control often means willing oneself to believe that despite external barriers one will be able to find one's dream job so long as one
follows one's passions. A guest speaker directly addressed the self-blame
that most American job seekers come to feel in order to make his point
that the obstacles are in our minds:

> I am not blowing smoke here. You feel you are an economic orphan. Ninety-
> three percent of people are going to work each morning, so something is wrong
> with me. But there is nothing wrong with you, just how you program yourself
> to think about yourself. Limiting beliefs do a number on you, like I am too old,
> my hair is falling out, I am an immigrant, I am just an engineer. These limiting
> beliefs diminish the power of your message.

The fundamental premise of the self-help discourse is that job seekers are
in control. As Mills (1953, 187) noted half a century ago, in the self-help
discourse "the poor and the unsuccessful simply do not exist except by an
untoward act of their own will." Finding a job, even one's dream job, does
not require the possession of specific skills, the right contacts, an elite education, or experiences outside the job seeker's immediate control. Rather,
it depends on job-searching skills, self-presentation, and beliefs that *are*
within one's control and that can be mastered with the assistance of self-
help practitioners. The common self-help refrain to "take control" urges
job seekers to disregard structural obstacles. One speaker summed it up:
"The main barrier is yourself, not the government, not the market—it's
you." This discourse appeals to job seekers' yearning for control over
their lives and for meaningful and engaged careers. It is seductive and, initially, galvanizing.

The Dominance of Self-Help over Alternative Discourses

The overwhelming majority of guest speakers at AmeriSupport's general meetings are from the self-help industry because self-help speakers readily make themselves available for free, while other kinds of speakers do not. AmeriSupport members in charge of inviting speakers are given a list of past speakers and others who have expressed an interest in speaking there. The list is almost entirely composed of self-help speakers who see this audience as a potential market for their coaching services. Most talks by such guest speakers end with a pitch. For example, one speaker told members that, after the talk, he would post on his website a résumé template that AmeriSupport members could download for free. He then added:

> While at the website, you can also take a look at my book of real stories of people who can inspire you. A book of people who got dream jobs and how to do that. You can all do that. There is nothing special about those people in the book.

Others speakers were even more direct. One concluded her talk with an announcement that she was starting a new self-help support group that would meet over the phone every Wednesday evening, for a fee.

The financial imperative to make a living does not imply that self-help practitioners are not primarily and genuinely motivated by a desire to help job seekers. Many of them, in fact, turned to this line of work after experiencing unemployment themselves, which led them to commit themselves to helping others. But the need to make a living does help explain why self-help practitioners, as opposed to academic sociologists or others, are eager to speak at AmeriSupport and why their discourse is so much of a piece. For example, the emphasis on achieving chemistry with employers, as opposed to skills or credentials, forefronts the critical importance of learning how to best present oneself—exactly the training self-help practitioners are best positioned to provide. Anxious job seekers looking for any way to get an edge are especially vulnerable to this marketing pitch. Likewise, the discourse on following one's passion inspires many people, not only to pursue a fulfilling career path but also—and perhaps mostly—to consume more self-help products and services.[23]

Despite the near ubiquity of the self-help discourse at AmeriSupport, another group of differently motivated speakers occasionally asks to address a general meeting—representatives of temporary-staffing agencies. During my year at AmeriSupport, there were three such speakers.

The staffing agency discourse has some overlap with the self-help discourse, particularly regarding the need for a positive attitude. For example, the speaker from Ace Staffing explained: "Our clients' main concern is attitude. The number-one factor is they want the right attitude." There is also a nod to the importance of interpersonal fit with pronouncements such as: "More clients today are asking about soft skills. Will they fit into my company's culture? Hiring is more like dating." But despite these similarities, there are striking and important dissonances between the two discourses, the most important being an insistence by the staffing agencies that the job seeker have *realistic expectations*. In fact, the positive attitude expected by staffing agencies is explicitly tied to well-adjusted expectations. As one staffing speaker put it, job seekers need to "be flexible, be able to take on a few more things, and be willing to work with an organization." Foremost, the staffing agencies recommend "having realistic expectations and an understanding of what the market is calling for in terms of salaries. We are not going to make the same money as during the [dotcom] bubble." This realism discourse runs contrary to self-help's claims that if you follow your passions and perfect your self-presentation, unlimited career success will follow.

Together with realism comes a different set of job-search strategies. For example, on the issue of cover letters, speakers from staffing agencies urged job seekers to focus on skills, not on the personalized style encouraged by self-help speakers. As one agency speaker put it: "Back away from 'This is who I am' stuff to 'This is my professional demeanor.'" Most direct on this point were the Manpower representatives, who explained that "cover letters get tossed" and are "passé for the most part." This statement, so contrary to the self-help paradigm, compelled Director Dan to chime in with a qualification: "In your business, at least."

Staffing agency speakers explained that their focus in filtering through stacks of applications is *not* personal qualities but a "hot search for the keywords in the résumé." Their suggestion was to include in the résumé—preferably at the very top—whatever words are in the job posting. Whereas self-help speakers suggest a brief summary description of your personal career goals at the top of the résumé, a staffing agency speaker explained that, in his experience, "companies like to see computer skills on top, not your career objective." This focus on skills was further reiterated by a Manpower speaker who explained that, as part of their filtering process, "We conduct behavioral interviews where we will find out what kind of skills you have and we will *test* your software skills." Passion is not only irrelevant but might work against you. A question-and-answer session with a Manpower speaker brought to light a very different perspective on passion:

JOB SEEKER: For administrative medical jobs, what if you come from a business background?

MANPOWER REPRESENTATIVE: It's even preferable. It means you do not have the humanistic thing when it's truly just an administrative job.

From the staffing agency's perspective, having the passion—the "humanistic thing"—only suggests that you might be expecting more from the job than it can offer.

Whereas the chemistry game and the self-help discourses focus on finding one's passion and achieving interpersonal connection with an employer, the staffing agency discourse is instrumental, concerned that job seekers have both the necessary skills and realistic expectations of the work and the pay. In contrast to the chemistry discourse, the staffing agencies' discourse more closely resembles the specs discourse dominant in Israel (discussed in chapter 4) and the diligence discourse in the American blue-collar context (discussed in chapter 6).

Discourses and Structures

The differences between the self-help and the staffing agencies' discourses are not surprising when one considers the different structural locations of their purveyors. As previously discussed, self-help speakers' livelihoods depend on job seekers investing in their services to improve their self-presentations. By contrast, staffing agency professionals depend for their living on efficiently providing employers with appropriate temporary employees. For staffing agencies, therefore, the focus is on easily discernible: credible markers that the applicants have the necessary skills to do the job, along with a cooperative and accepting attitude about the typically rote and poorly paid work.

The coexistence of the discordant discourses on the best strategy for finding a job, stemming from the career-success self-help industry and the staffing agencies, should help dispel any notion that self-help discourses

simply mirror a broader American culture. Rather, the self-help discourses, and the chemistry game they undergird, are a product of the selective mobilization of *particular* cultural schemas. The ideas fused into
the chemistry game are not the only way that Americans can conceptualize the task of getting a job. As the staffing agencies' discourses show,
there are multiple American narratives for what it takes to get hired.

While the self-help industry does not completely monopolize the
job-search discourse, it does enjoy overwhelming dominance. The self-
help perspective was represented by about 90 percent of the speakers at
AmeriSupport. My examination of the speaker lists from other support
organizations around the United States revealed a similar pattern and, in
fact, many of the same self-help speakers. Likewise, self-help books domi-
nate the career sections of American bookstores.

Why does the self-help career advice discourse resonate with American
white-collar job seekers? One reason is that these discourses seem to fit
job seekers' direct experiences. Interviews are typically the only direct
personal experience an American white-collar job seeker has during the
hiring process; filtering the résumés by "specs" happens behind the scenes.
And as discussed earlier in this chapter, hiring managers often do use
chemistry as a filter in job interviews. Given the intense focus on interpersonal connection during job interviews, it is a factor that looms large in
the job seeker's understanding of the hiring decision.

The dominance of the career self-help discourse can also be understood
by considering the historical and political-economic context. It is important to recognize that the self-help industry, often assumed to be a reflection of a timeless American culture, experienced rapid growth only during the past thirty years in the context of white-collar insecurity.[24] While
self-help draws upon discourses that have been part of America's collective cultural "tool kit" (Swidler 1986) for centuries, explaining the timing of this rise requires identifying new circumstances. A likely suspect is
the shift to a neoliberal political economy, described in chapter 1, which
ousted many white-collar workers from their previously secure jobs and
left them in search of new career strategies. McGee (2005) argues that it is
not a coincidence that the rise of self-help was simultaneous with the rise
of white-collar insecurity. The marketing of self-help products and services
capitalizes on workers' growing anxieties and on a general lack of other
sources of information and guidance. Self-help is presented as a compelling solution to—or, as McGee calls it, "a form of insurance" against—
economic uncertainty.

Hochschild (1983) links the rise of self-help to the draining emotional labor demanded by certain jobs, which have deadened workers' sense of an authentic self and led them to turn to self-help in hopes of recovering their inner selves. My findings agree with Hochschild's linking of the rise of self-help to changes in the world of work, but point to a different kind of link between self-help and emotional labor. As this book will show, workers are turning to the self-help industry not to counteract the effects of emotional labor but, on the contrary, to *perfect* ways of engaging in the emotional labor they perceive to be required by the white-collar labor market—producing and projecting the kind of authentic inner self required by the chemistry game.[25]

Self-help discourses also appeal to white-collar job seekers by stimulating their longings for meaningful work. While the staffing agencies are perceived as a route to dreary, low-paying, downwardly mobile jobs, the chemistry game appears to offer a route to a meaningful, passion-filled life. It even has a seemingly subversive or rebellious undertone; job seekers are implicitly told that they should buck the system that is pushing them toward meaningless work and demand more from life than to be cogs in the machine. Although not all self-help speakers talk in this grand way, their underlying message often includes an implicit critique of the banality of middle-class existence. This discourse is seductive and energizing. I myself—a skeptical sociologist all too aware of structural constraints—often felt swept away by the calls to pursue my deepest passions, whatever they might be.

The chemistry game is galvanizing. But as we will see in the next chapter, it also renders American white-collar job seekers vulnerable to a boomerang effect by which the inspirational message of individual control produces a debilitating self-blame.

CHAPTER THREE

The Chemistry Game Experience and Self-Blame

My in-depth interviews with American white-collar job seekers typically started with an easy flow. Job seekers were typically willing—and in some cases eager—to share their career backgrounds and job-search strategies. I sometimes felt I was hearing a version of the elevator speech and that some of my interviewees saw me as yet another networking target.

But as the interview made its way to the job seeker's understanding of the obstacles he or she faced in finding work, the conversation slowed and at times fell silent. At this stage, job seekers frequently shared feelings that they do not usually discuss with others. I heard their fears that they are somehow "defective" or that something is "wrong" with them. For example, Nancy, a thirty-three-year-old woman who had worked in venture capital, described the progression of her feelings:

> At first I felt good when I got all those interviews. But then it got rough when I kept getting rejected over and over. I started to feel there was something wrong with how I interviewed. And then, something wrong with me. I started to have self-doubts. I hit a downward spiral.

Chris, a marketer, said that after four months of unsuccessful searching, "the hardest thing is esteem, confidence. It's killed. I have turned into an introvert. I feel like I've gotten older." Richard, a tax accountant, described his job search as a "terrible emotional experience." A year into his search, he attempted suicide and his wife left him. In describing his emotional turmoil, he said: "I keep asking myself, am I a loser?" Why do so many unemployed American white-collar workers end up feeling like something is wrong with them? In the previous chapter, I primarily drew on my observations at AmeriSupport to describe the chemistry game—the set of interrelated discourses and practices held together by an underlying premise that getting hired depends more on fit than on skills. In this chapter, I will primarily draw on my in-depth interviews to describe what it is like to play the chemistry game and to link the nature of this game to self-blame.

Job seekers engaged in the chemistry game are initially excited about the possibility of taking control of their career fates and finding fulfilling work. At the same time, the early stages of the chemistry game generate a sense of personal vulnerability that, in turn, marks the search experience with intense anxiety. Over time, the chemistry game backfires on those who do not quickly find jobs. The same discourses and practices that produced the initial sense of control now lead job seekers to blame themselves for their difficulties and make it hard to continue searching.

The Initial Boost

Whatever their previous job-search experiences may have been, the intensive first week of training at AmeriSupport typically increases job seekers' confidence and morale, and receives high evaluations for usefulness. This motivational boost partly stems from the comforting idea that job seekers can exercise control in their job search by mastering certain self-presentation techniques. This boost usually lasts two to three months.

Most unemployed job seekers are in that position because they have been laid off, an experience that often undermines a sense of control over one's own life. It is therefore a relief to learn at AmeriSupport (or in almost every book about job searching) that there are concrete and practical steps one can take to become the master of one's own economic fate. Joe, a former manager, described his initial experience with AmeriSupport as a "burst of energy." During his initial weeks, he was engaged in "intensive strategizing with success team colleagues." For Joe and most other members, the perception that the outcome depends on one's own strategic actions has an absorbing and energizing effect.

Job seekers at AmeriSupport are also inspired and engaged by the call to find and follow their passions. For example, Sandy was laid off from a public-health research position. After encountering some initial difficulties in finding work, she joined AmeriSupport. In an interview conducted four weeks after joining, she reported feeling positive and "inspired."

SANDY: The speaker last week led us through the journey of "you've got to figure out what want and go for it."
AUTHOR: What do you think of this message?
SANDY: To a certain extent, you do create your own reality. I agree with the speaker that if, at this point in life, you don't do what's important, how will you feel at the end of your life?

Encouraged to explore new areas of interest, Sandy began considering a career switch to genetic counseling.

Another member, Carole, had worked for a municipal fraud-investigation unit and came to AmeriSupport still upset about being laid off for what she perceived were "political" reasons. "I started out not knowing what I wanted to do," she explained. But after the initial week of training, "I realized what I wanted to do. I realized I loved the arts." Carole decided to pursue jobs in fund-raising that "allows the arts to keep going." For her, as for most of the others, disappointment and anger generated over a job loss was overtaken by the excitement of new potential opportunities. In most cases, while job seekers are unhappy about their layoffs, they also report that their prior job was not wholly fulfilling and that they are relieved to be away from it and hopefully on their way to something more fulfilling. For example, Leslie, who had been a programmer at a large HMO, explained:

I was working in a cubicle, as part of a team, ten hours a day. There was little interaction among team members. The isolation made me crazy. I felt like I was working on Mars. I was very unhappy. . . .

Unlike Sandy and Carole, however, Leslie did not seek an immediate career change. She told me about her nuanced reaction to a self-help speaker at AmeriSupport who had advocated following your passions:

The speaker was looking at it from a spiritual point of view. It was nice, but not real practical. It was a lot of figuring out what you wanted, and then go get it. . . . I have a daughter in college, I need a salary, so I have to be programmer. After that, I will definitely do something other than being a programmer. It's a job, not a career. I don't find it that fulfilling.

Leslie was responding to the self-help message with what she viewed as a pragmatic sequential approach. Her short-term goal was to find a programming job in a friendlier environment that would help pay her daughter's tuition bills. After that, her long-term goal was to switch to a more personally fulfilling career.

Whether seeking a new career or simply a better job in the same career, many job seekers welcomed the opportunity to change workplaces. Most did not mourn the demise of the post–World War II institution of lifelong careers within one firm, and many were not greatly distressed by a layoff per se, which they saw as an expected part of one's work life.[1] For workers who came of age in the neoliberal era, there appears to be little expectation of long-term job security. Ben, an accountant in his early forties, said that after his layoff he sensed "not a single negative connotation" from his friends and family. "It was viewed more as a rite of passage. This happens to everybody. . . . 'Everyone goes through it and you'll get a job' was the attitude." The deep distress that grows over time with difficulties in finding *new* work should not be conflated with the more limited distress following job loss, which is tempered, if not completely overridden, by hopeful excitement over the possibility of a new and better job.

The initial boost of "taking control" and engaging in strategies aimed at finding a better job makes it relatively easy for job seekers to adopt the self-help advice of rationalizing their time use and approaching their search work as they would a real job. Lacking an externally imposed structure, job seekers create a structure. They set micro-goals to be achieved within well-defined work schedules, self-imposing various measures to gauge productivity, such as counting the number of new contacts achieved per week through networking.

The Workday

In the initial two to three months of their search, job seekers typically spend the bulk of their days energetically crafting résumés and cover letters, creating online profiles, rehearsing sound bites, and networking. Sandy would get up each day at around 7:30 a.m. As she described it: "I get right to work checking a series of job-board websites that are bookmarked as favorites. I go through them one by one. If I find something to apply to, I start organizing what to say." Unlike the newspaper classifieds of an earlier era, which appeared only once or twice a week, websites such as Monster.com continuously add new listings, generating the constant sense of new possibilities only a few mouse clicks away. After responding to new ads, Sandy's routine continued: "I also have things to follow up on like sending a thank-you letter or calling to follow up on an application. Then also proactive things like working on my résumé and networking." Sandy was usually done with her work by two in the afternoon.

Jeff, a former marketing executive, was even more rigorous about his schedule. Each Friday he made a weekly plan for how to spend each hour from nine to five during the following week. He showed me his daily grids, which included an hour break for lunch. But he could not always stick to his schedule. He confided: "I am embarrassed to say that I am able to stick to it only fifty to seventy-five percent of the time. I know that it's not enough." Jeff explained that since he was not doing paid work, his family expected him to be more available to help with domestic work such as caring for a sick child. "It's a struggle to protect my space to do job searching."

Other job seekers also had trouble sticking to their schedules and felt guilty about it. Leslie, who had previously discussed her relief at no longer being in a cubicle, confessed: "I could be doing more and should be doing more. I feel guilty about having 'me' time, doing things for me when I should be doing other things, like more job searching."

The guilt about deviations from strict adherence to a work schedule reveals the job seekers' work-like attitude toward their job search. The search, like paid work, is what they *should* be doing; deviations feel like "goofing off." This is also revealed by the clear boundary drawn between work and leisure. Most job seekers bracket off any leisure activities for nights or weekends. Erica reported:

> I spend six to eight hours a day looking for a job. I wake up, look over my phone list, and start making calls. Any leisure is scheduled for non-work time. I leave pleasure reading for evenings. I try not to read for pleasure from eight a.m. to five p.m. The work week is about finding work.... I do try to keep a boundary there.

By creating schedules and routines, white-collar job seekers in the United States (and in Israel, as will be discussed in chapter 5) give job searching the structure of a daytime job and thus proactively counter the temporal disorientation that prior research has shown can accompany the loss of a job.[2]

The Anxious Work of Self-Subjectification

Two types of activity constitute the day-to-day work of American white-collar job searching: constructing documents such as résumés, cover letters, and online profiles, and interacting personally, either by networking to obtain referrals or by interviewing. Both types of activity demand the emotional labor (Hochschild 1983) of self-subjectification—creating a feeling of connection through the projection of the self as a subject with the internal attributes necessary for fitting in with a particular employer. This form of emotional labor requires "deep acting"—actually producing a feeling as opposed to just superficially exhibiting one. In this case, one must produce the feeling of *connection* between oneself and the prospective employer. This emotional labor is most evident during job interviews, which American job seekers often compare to first dates because, in both situations, a successful outcome is understood to hinge on a shared feeling of connectedness and fit.

The work of job searching shares important elements with interactive service work, in which emotional labor has been recognized as central.[3] The emotional labor demanded of job seekers has previously been compared to the emotional labor needed in sales work,[4] requiring the production of a "positive mental attitude" that Leidner (1993) describes in the context of insurance sales. Job seekers and salespersons routinely face a stream of rejections and nonetheless must display a positive attitude to have a chance at succeeding. Yet a focus on the need to maintain a positive attitude misses the core element of the emotional labor required of American white-collar job seekers, which is creating an interpersonal connection or chemistry with prospective employers.

Job seekers perceive that to create the needed feeling of connection, they must look inward and then externalize some part of the self that will create the mutual feeling of fit. In other words, self-subjectification involves the projection of the self as a subject that—when viewed through the employers' schemes of perception[5]—conveys "easy familiarity"[6] and gives rise to a sense of interpersonal chemistry. While this distinct emotional labor is most apparent in job interviews, it suffuses other job-search activities in the chemistry game and creates a distinct vulnerability: the sense of exposure.

At the start of their search, job seekers generally express hopeful excitement, especially with respect to new career directions and opportunities, but when approaching the creation of résumés and cover letters, their excitement is mixed with anxiety. The writing, formatting, editing, and revising of these strategic documents is a never-ending task. Much is perceived to ride on perfecting these documents,[7] which is above all a matter of conveying one's intangible fit with the employer.

At root, job seekers' angst derives from the sense that these documents must reveal something about them, the person *behind* the qualifications. The work of constructing self-revealing documents is fraught with vulnerability. For example, in reflecting on the process of résumé writing, Steven, a forty-three-year-old salesperson, observed:

> Résumés are the hardest things to write because it taps into my identity, my pride, my fears. It's marketing myself; explaining myself to someone else. Putting yourself out to be judged is pretty heavy.

The writing process is time-consuming and exhausting. As Jeff explained, it requires "switching language, transforming the code for different jobs. . . . You try to indicate that you are aware they have a certain culture and that this is your culture."

Erica described her experiences of customizing her résumé for particular ads. She said that her aim was to "convey that I understand their culture, what they do, and that I will fit." This takes at least "four hours [that] are *excruciating, sweating, uncomfortable*." Amy likewise talked about how despite having spent two months looking for work, "résumé writing continues to be hard. I change it for each job, so it takes me forever. I keep revising it." Because the résumé aims to convey information about the person *behind* the experiences and qualifications, the résumé's aesthetic quality is given great weight. Issues such as formats, fonts, margins, and the shapes of bullets become significant areas of strategic focus. A core activity at AmeriSupport and other American job-search support groups is critiquing résumés with a heavy emphasis on aesthetics and style.

Producing a customized résumé is only the beginning of the writing process. Each résumé requires a cover letter, no less an object of anxious wordsmithing than the résumé because it is expected to convey even more openly and at length the job seeker's personality, passion, and fit. Allen, a high-tech manager, described the intense and absorbed anxiety of crafting the cover letter: "I get so caught up in the work that it prevents me from getting a job. It is where all my anxious energy goes. I work it and rework it, fuss with it, change the font." The writing and revision process of each letter often seems endless. Karen talked about working on a cover letter and how "it's kind of taken on a life of its own. I can't believe how much time it takes." Another job seeker reported:

> The cover letter has to sound absolutely right before I send it out. That's the time-sink. If it feels mediocre, I won't send it. I could spend a week or two writing each cover letter. When I apply, I feel like I have a little chance. It is this one little chance, so I have to make it perfect. You have one chance to make a good impression.

The crafting of online social network profiles is another important area of strategic activity. Like the writing of résumés and cover letters, it demands a written presentation of self, but one that must simultaneously appeal to multiple audiences. Job seekers who are contemplating making a career change face particularly difficult choices about what to include in their online profiles. For example, James was an architect who had not had not been able to find work in his field and was considering other positions where his skills might be transferable. "The dilemma," as James said, "is what to put on the website. Should I put my architecture credentials on the website if I am considering getting out of architecture?" The architecture credentials are necessary for any potential architecture position but could undermine James's attempts at making a career change by making him appear overqualified or a bad fit for other types of positions.

Finally, if the job seeker is fortunate enough to get an interview, a thank-you letter must also be drafted. In the chemistry game, résumés, cover letters, social networking profiles, and thank-you letters are small documents with big stakes. Anxiety seems to increase in inverse proportion to the number of words.

Even more important to the job search than the construction of written documents—and, as discussed below, even more anxiety-provoking—is networking. Job seekers playing the chemistry game make strenuous efforts to network and generate a continuous stream of new contacts. For the white-collar American job seeker, a central job-search strategy involves pursuing *new* connections or growing their network by, for example, attending professional association meetings and striking up conversations.[8]

Frank, like the majority of American white-collar jobs seekers whom I interviewed, put networking at the center of his search: "How do I look for work? Networking is the best way. When someone gets the idea to hire someone, they first ask their friends." Or, as Jerome said: "Most of my energy goes to talking with people I know to create contacts that I didn't previously know. That's how your network grows. You talk to someone; they talk to someone." A phrase often repeated by job seekers is that you need "to put yourself out there."

Networking is understood as even more important than résumés or cover letters because it provides an opportunity to directly establish an interpersonal connection. As James put it: "You have a better shot at *making an impression* when you're there in person to make the sale than if you're submitting a résumé." Like most other American job seekers, Jeff placed in-person networking at the center of his strategy: "At Ameri-Support, I learned that you can't be traditional and just look in newspapers; it's about putting yourself out there." Toward this end, he joined the Toastmasters International club, which gave him an opening to go to businesses and distribute information about Toastmasters meetings. Once inside, he explained, "I try to make contacts, build relations with receptionists, and ask for names of executives." He would then cold-call these executives. Other job seekers made collecting network contacts a kind of sport. David, a high-tech manager, said: "The way you will get a job is through people that you know." To get to know people, he used online social networks and attended conferences and events put on by high-tech companies. He pointed to a flash drive that he wore around his neck and proclaimed: "I have five thousand contacts right here!"

Like the construction of documents, the task of networking is never complete, as there are always more potential contacts to pursue. Moreover, networking is hard to compartmentalize. While leisure is not allowed to enter the temporal realm of work, networking tends to spill over into the realm of leisure. Since *anyone* a job seeker meets is a potential contact, and *any* conversation could turn out to be a pre-interview, the job search is always present and the distinctions between friends and colleagues, and between social and professional activities, become blurred. As Vicki Smith (2001) found in her study of white-collar job seekers, this entails a life in which no social interaction is free of professional implications.

The unclear boundary between leisurely social interactions and instrumentally motivated networking leads job seekers, with rare exceptions, to dislike networking. They feel uncomfortable about approaching others, whether friends or strangers, for help. They dread coming across as pushy, annoying, or—worst of all—as losers. Networking triggers some of the same vulnerabilities that writing résumés and cover letters does because it, too, requires externalizing the self for evaluation and judgment. In fact, the vulnerability produced in the course of networking is all the more intense for being face-to-face. One job seeker expressed a typical experience:

> I've learned the importance of networking and I try to network but . . . I'm concerned that I'm perceived as a nuisance. At a party at a friend's house, I met a consultant in the software industry. I explained my situation and asked if I could send a résumé. She said yes, no problem. It seemed that for the rest of the party, I was getting in her way. Every time she was trying to get somewhere, I was there and had to move. It may have been just my perception, that I was conscious of having asked her a favor.

Self-consciousness about networking is endemic. Most American white-collar job seekers believe in the importance of networking, but dread being seen as someone who needs to network. Tina, a paralegal, had been looking for work for nearly a year. She described trying to network but hesitating because, as she explained, "I don't want to be pushy, I don't want to say I don't have a job. . . . It's hard to tell people I'm not working because it sounds like I'm a loser." Beth reported great hesitation about networking because "people will think I am a dork." Ben echoed this sentiment: "I find [networking] difficult to do. There is a hesitation about calling people and *putting myself out there*. It's just difficult." Scott explained that, for him, it is hard to network "without being rude or without being desperate. You feel like the guys who start washing your windows at the intersection on a red light." The personal vulnerability is clear in James's description of networking with strangers:

> It is difficult. It's daunting, scary as hell. Walking into a room full of total strangers and trying to introduce yourself is scary. I have difficulty and end up walking out of some of these open-networking things. . . . Even making phone calls—the phone feels like a thousand pounds. Calling someone out of the blue that you don't know or have just been provided with a warm intro—it's still sometimes tough to take the initiative to reach out. But you have to do it.

But the vulnerability is not limited to interacting with strangers. Rob talked about the vulnerability that comes from reaching out to friends: "Through this you understand who your friends are: Those who try and reach out to you and those who won't return calls." Some former colleagues who Rob thought were his friends were not returning his calls.

Most job seekers cannot fully adhere to the self-help advice of perpetual networking. Sandy, for example, rejected the advice of self-help speakers to network in the supermarket. She explained: "If someone were to tell you their elevator speech when you are at the grocery store, you'd look at them like, 'Are you on the phone talking to someone else?'" Some job seekers cannot bring themselves to network at all. Emily said that while "I like connecting with other people, I don't like insinuating myself or asking for favors from people I don't know." Therefore, she added, "I have not done any networking." Likewise, Joe had a strong network of contacts in the upper-middle-class community where he lived, regularly "chewing the fat with CFOs during their kids' soccer games," but was unable to take advantage of it:

> I can't have the conversation about my situation. I don't want the spotlight as the unemployed guy. I am feeling scared and not wanting to face the rejection and embarrassment that I am not just your son's soccer coach but an unemployed guy looking for work.

Online social networking is immensely appealing to job seekers precisely because it seems to offer the opportunity to connect with others in a less vulnerable way. Online networking means not having to put oneself in potentially awkward and uncomfortable face-to-face interactions. Some job seekers feel like they can be more open and engaging online. For example, Ingrid explained:

> I find it easier. I am very much a digital extrovert. I hate going to live networking events. It's very hard for me to go. . . . To me the online networking has been much more successful just given my personality type and comfort level with a room full of people.

Online social networking is also appealing because it provides an opportunity to carefully manage other's first impression of you. As Matt put it: "If you have a good vocabulary, you can make yourself look like anything or *be anything*. . . . It is a good way to set the stage."

While job seekers find online social networking appealing, most also recognize that ultimately creating connection requires personal interaction. Ellen explained: "Networking over LinkedIn [an online social networking site] is not nearly as good as networking in person. . . . There is nothing like having a face-to-face conversation with someone as opposed trying to network with someone who you might not know by e-mail." Similarly, as Jeff put it: "I personally feel more comfortable in the online stage because I get really nervous in person. But although it's easier, I still think in person is more beneficial." The need to create relationships is the reason most job seekers perceive that using online social networking websites, such as LinkedIn, is useful to identify potential contacts but is not a substitute for face-to-face meetings. James commented:

> LinkedIn can be useful to figure out who the people you know.... But if you allow it to be the sole form of networking, trolling LinkedIn all day has somewhat limited value. It doesn't give you the ability to establish *meaningful relationships*. People won't recommend you to a hiring manager simply because you met on LinkedIn. But if you reach out to them, have coffee with them, establish a good rapport, have similarities—that's when the person says, "You know what? A certain division within our firm has space—let me get you in touch with a hiring manager."

Overcoming the awkwardness that often accompanies face-to-face networking interactions and creating a connection require the emotional labor of self-subjectification. Job seekers need to first suppress their insecurity, which in itself is an extremely difficult emotional task. Abigail explained: "[Networking] is really hard. Talking about the need for work without then saying how you have no money and starting to cry, this has happened to me a couple of times." But beyond suppressing their insecurity, job seekers must also produce its opposite: utter confidence. Likewise, they must suppress any resentment or depression and produce its opposite: constant cheerfulness. Finally, and most importantly, since the ultimate goal of networking is to have another person refer you to a hiring manager, it is critical to produce a *connection* during the networking interaction. Connection requires self-revealing communication that will generate the sense of meaningful shared commonalities. Beyond confidence and cheerfulness, job seekers must achieve interpersonal chemistry.

American job seekers' focus on interpersonal fit reaches its apex in the interview. As Ben explained: "I have learned that there are so many factors that go into this interview process. It's not just what you know and what your experience is, but it's also chemistry with the people.... And this is what sometimes makes or breaks hiring or not hiring that person." Or as Jane described: "What probably they will look for is how you present yourself. How you're dressed. How confident you are. Even the way you sit." The centrality of rapport at interviews was recognized as impor-

tant even by job seekers who did not feel it played to their strengths. Ann
observed:

> There has to be a rapport. Body language is important. Dress is important. . . .
> You can get off on tangents and talk about other things, but you need to have
> a rapport. Perception is reality. And I hate it. I hate that term because it's now
> always true. And I know it, but society is moving so fast that if somebody's very
> good with people, they may not have the same qualifications, but if they can sell
> themselves to the interviewer, they'll get the job.

To achieve chemistry, job seekers engage in various strategies of connection. One of the first steps is research. Increasingly job seekers use online social networking sites to research the existence of any personal links
between them and the interviewer, and then use such links to gather information that may be used to establish a connection. Jacob described his
use of this strategy:

> When interviewing recently I found out the name of the interviewer. After
> looking on LinkedIn, it turned out the interviewer and I had a shared relation-
> ship. I reached out to our mutual friend, who provided me insight about their
> extracurricular activities, their family status. He just had a baby. During the in-
> terview I was able to use this—I picked examples from my experience that
> would generate empathy. At the end of the interview, I mentioned that we had
> a shared friend, to further seal the connectivity with the interviewer.

Sam explained his interactional strategies to achieve connection: "To begin,
I start on a warm and friendly note. I make positive comments about the
office. Maybe ask some sort or personal question, but not too deeply probing. Being friendly and warm is the key. Relationships." Others try to adapt
themselves to the style of the interviewer. Brian said: "You try to assess—
once you get into an interview—the style of the interviewer and you
adapt to it. . . . It's a bit like *going into prom*. You both are dressed up and
trying to present yourself." The dating analogy came up frequently. Joan,
a fifty-year old speech therapist, reported: "I constantly feel like I'm on a
first date."

"First date" interviews are typically the most personally exposing and
emotionally draining moments of the chemistry game. Bill explained that
when he goes to an interview, he feels "everything inside me [is] trem-
bling because I am anxious. This is kind of a humiliating procedure." One

basis for this anxiety is the fear of appearing like a fraud. Ben expressed this fear and tied it to the self-help advice of creating personalized stories:

> In the story thing, there is a premise of not being honest with yourself.... But then these things loom in the background, like shadows hanging over you. Your mind-set becomes one of creating an alternative reality and everyone is saying, "What you want to say is ..." In other words, make something up that has enough of a tie that you can defend it. But creating the alternate reality is stressful because you go into a circumstance where [employers] can expose it.

Erica described a similar sense of exposure in the interview process:

> Interviewing feels like auditioning where you do this dance and there are people behind the screen that you can't see *judging* you. Before my most recent interview, I had an anxiety attack. I didn't know it then but later learned that's what it was.

In sum, playing the chemistry game in its initial phase produces an experience characterized by both excitement and vulnerability. The message of individual control and the galvanizing call to pursue one's passions combine to provide an initial motivational boost that is also, from the outset, mixed with anxiety and vulnerability.

Boomerang

Despite the initial boost, most job seekers do not quickly find new jobs. More than half of my interviewees remained unemployed for more than twelve weeks, and a third remained unemployed more than twenty-seven weeks. Over time, the most salient feature of the job-search experience is the seemingly endless string of rejections. Regardless of the time spent crafting a targeted résumé and cover letter, the most common response received by the job seekers I interviewed was also the most excruciating—no response at all. Job seekers who are just starting to send out applications expect their "phones to ring off the hook," as Jeff put it, but this expectation is almost never met. Bill explained: "I hit the enter key and send a résumé and then it just disappears, like a tree falling in the forest. This is the hardest part."

Job seekers commonly used the metaphor of a black hole to describe their experience of applying for jobs online. As Kevin described it: "When you submit your résumé through Monster, CareerBuilder, and the like, you are throwing your résumé into a black hole." Or as Linda explained: "I have been applying through Monster for quite some time now. It seems like you're applying to a black hole. I know a lot of people say that, but it's true." The common experience of not getting any response at all led one job seeker to report feeling encouraged when receiving a rejection letter: "It actually made me really happy when someone even said, 'Thanks for applying, but we've already hired.' Just knowing that there is at least someone looking at it and that means there could have been a possibility, I guess."

The experience of repeated silent rejections makes it increasingly difficult to muster the practical and emotional energy to keep up the search. With the first or second wave of rejections, the initial burst of energy is sapped. Job seekers get weary revising their résumés. Erica said: "One of the hardest things is modifying my résumé *yet again*. . . . The idea of changing it makes me want to throw up." Job seekers also show signs of being increasingly overwhelmed by the endless advice about how to revise their résumés and particularly by the task of injecting "compelling" personalized stories that create connection. David reported: "I used to like my résumé, but now I hate it because everyone looked at it and said write stories, do this, do that." He showed me five versions of his résumé and continued: "In my field of technical maintenance of machines, you don't have dramas where you save someone's life by fixing a machine, or it's not like you increase sales by fifty percent. It's more like each day you do your work." Another reason job seekers increasingly dislike focusing on their résumés is that their sense of vulnerability increases as the "résumé gap"—the gap between one's most recent employment and the present— grows longer. One job seeker reported being "embarrassed to show my résumé to other people. . . . It doesn't say, 'Last year: read the *New Yorker*,' but it feels like that stuff will peek through."

Even more debilitating than fatigue of revising one's résumé is job seekers' increasing fears, as weeks of silent rejection turn into months, that there must something wrong with them. At this stage the self-help discourses and practices focusing on individual control, having created a boost, boomerang back on job seekers to produce a bust. The premise of individual control generates a focus on perceived individual shortcomings as the source of the rejections. As Gerry, a former manager at an elder-care facility, succinctly said: "I feel like a loser."

The self-blame typically focuses at first on factors that purportedly make one an ineffective job seeker. For example, following the first wave of rejections, many job seekers experience a decline of confidence about their self-presentation. This, in turn, comes to be seen as a major obstacle to finding a job. Rick, a high-tech engineer in his early sixties, had been searching for almost a year. Despite the well-known premium placed on youth in high tech, he did not feel the problem was his age but rather his attitude: "It's not what others think externally—it's *what I think*, and I don't have the *confidence* to pursue work as aggressively as I need to." Emily likewise felt that her problem was "a lack of confidence and insecurity issues." Gerry perceived her major obstacle in the job market to be "low self-esteem." Joe, trying to reenter the workforce after several years of raising his children, reported that his greatest obstacle was not his résumé gap but his increasing inability to keep searching, which he attributed to being "undisciplined." He talked about "not embrac[ing] the opportunity, like in the literature I read. . . . I have not done enough." Leslie reported an apprehension about networking as her biggest obstacle:

> Just getting out there and doing it. I feel confident of my skills and references. I don't feel like age is an issue. I feel I have a lot of experience to offer in areas that are needed. . . . But it's outside of my comfort zone, doing the networking, the informational interviews, *putting myself on the line.*

With the rise of online social networking, another form of self-blame has emerged focusing on one's inability to make full use of this new technology. A common way in which job seekers express this self-blame is to trace their job-search difficulties to the claim that, as Paul put it, "I don't know enough to make the most out of social media." Or as Daniel elaborated: "I've pulled my LinkedIn page together but haven't done much with it yet. I know there's a whole lot more that I could do." Job seekers increasingly sense that their difficulties are the result of not leveraging new technologies to the extent that they should. Erica explained:

> I've definitely torpedoed some of my chances because I don't have a LinkedIn page up and running. I joined LinkedIn and I never did anything with it. I shot myself in the foot on that. And I regret it, you know?[9]

Another form of self-blame appears among the many job seekers who declare that a serious obstacle to finding work is not knowing "what I really want to do." Behind this sentiment is the self-help premise that find-ing a job requires first finding and expressing one's "true" occupational passions. These job seekers believe that others have discovered their pas-sions, leading to career success, and so blame themselves for not being able to do the same. Because so much attention at organizations like AmeriSupport is devoted to figuring out what one "really" wants to do with one's life as a prerequisite for effectively exuding passion and mak-ing connections, members who try to discover their passions and come up with ambiguous results attribute their failure to find work to insufficient self-knowledge.

Chris, an African American marketer, initially suggested that racial dis-crimination might be a barrier: "There is a lot of historical institutional racism, and also in the [marketing] industry.... If you are putting out the commercials to a white audience, why would you think a black guy could know how to deliver the message to a white audience?" However, Chris's view changed over time: "I came to AmeriSupport and saw smart white people unemployed and realized it's not just racism. I have seen all the agencies in San Francisco, they looked at my résumé here and called me, but I did not get anything. Something didn't get passed. *Maybe I am a bad interviewer.*"

These varied explanations for job seekers' labor-market difficulties share a minimization of external obstacles, such as the lack of jobs, that may underlie the loss of confidence or difficulties in maintaining disci-pline. Instead, "inner obstacles," like lack of confidence, are understood as arising from personal shortcomings. The overwhelming sense is of a failure to successfully play the chemistry game. When I asked job seekers about the role of external factors and constraints, they would acknowl-edge obstacles such as a tough labor market, age discrimination, or out-sourcing. But they consistently put their perceived personal shortcomings or so-called inner obstacles at the forefront. In the next section, I will ex-plain how this pattern is generated by the structure of the chemistry game.

The Chemistry Game and Self-Blame

Playing the chemistry game produces self-blame. Job seekers experience waves of rejections while playing a game premised on the idea that finding a job is in their control and depends on their skillful self-presentation. The logic of the game suggests that any difficulties in finding work stem from the actions of the player. This conclusion is unintentionally but repeatedly reinforced at AmeriSupport by self-help speakers' talks about job seekers' control over their career fates. Thus, at any given weekly meeting of AmeriSupport members, a self-help speaker's message of control is simultaneously giving a boost to new members and intensifying the self-blame for veteran members who still have not found work.

Some veteran members become conscious of the implicitly blaming nature of the self-help discourse and drop out of AmeriSupport. Erica, for example, was initially inspired by the self-help discourse to try to start her own consulting business. After five months of failing to get her business off the ground, she dropped out of AmeriSupport. During a subsequent interview, she asked rhetorically:

> Is telling people to just go for what they want a successful strategy? I doubt it. I think it's terrible.... It's easy to talk about. It is emotionally stimulating. But the charge wears out. That's why people drop out of AmeriSupport.

Joe, a former management consultant who also dropped out of Ameri-Support, likewise noted the self-help discourse's boomerang effect:

> The message is that if you execute the process properly, you can do anything you want to do. There is something very empowering in that message. The process can get you to places that you never imagined. You should go for the "right" job, the one that is your highest aspiration. There is a strong judgment that this is the right thing to do and the sincere belief that I can do it if I can follow the processes of getting the information, the right cover letter, hone the elevator speech, that I could get the job effectively.... [But] there is a downside to this: *The high expectations make people feel like there is something wrong with them.* Speakers come in and say that it's easy and a universally applicable process, like anyone can do it, and when you can feel "I can't do it," then what's wrong with me? There is a boomerang effect. You feel you have failed yet again. If it does not work for you, what does it say about you?

Erica and Joe are unusual, however, in their conscious recognition of the boomerang effect. Indeed, the power of the self-help discourse stems from the fact that its claims cannot be easily falsified because they contain partial truths. Job seekers *can* improve their chances by constructing compelling résumés and cover letters. As we saw in chapter 2, hiring managers *do* care about interpersonal fit, and a positive attitude and passion for your desired job may in fact help. The "go for your dream" discourse, which reframes the job search as part of a meaningful life journey with a grand purpose, *does* help some job seekers consider more fulfilling careers. Nevertheless, the reason that this discourse generates a boomerang effect is that it is silent about so many other elements of the job seeker's situation, particularly the structural constraints outside their individual control, starting with the fact that there are many more job seekers than job openings.[10] Ignoring structural constraints leaves job seekers with only one framework within which to understand their difficulties: self-blame.

Self-blame is also the result of intense engagement in the chemistry game's practices that produce the experience that *how* you do your job search critically affects your chances of getting a job. Amy's case provides a good example of the relationship between the practical focus on strategies and the production of self-blame. Amy spent five days putting together a résumé and cover letter for a job she was extremely excited about. Failing to get the job, she reflected on the reasons: "Unfortunately, I think the cover letter was too long and even overwhelming." Amy did not know the *actual* reasons for the employer's decision or even how many other people had applied for the position. Nonetheless, she zeroed in on the one factor that had absorbed the bulk of her time and had generated the most anxiety—her cover letter. Amy's example suggests a tendency on the part of job seekers to attribute causal importance to whatever actions they took just prior to the outcome. Ben provided another example, focusing his job-searching energy on networking. When he still did not find work, he took this to reflect his own failure as a networker: "I had a friend who networked really well and got a job very quickly. This made me feel inadequate. I felt upset with myself that I didn't do it or couldn't network like him." Such second-guessing of oneself is fiercest after interviews. After Thelma applied for a position at an artisanal bakery and got no reply, she reanalyzed the process with a particular focus on whether her attempts at expressing passion had gone too far:

> I wrote on my résumé that food is a spiritual experience for me. I don't know if I wrote the wrong thing. And I may have said the wrong word at the interview. I might have said that food is sensual instead of sensuous. That was really bad.

In my fieldwork, I witnessed the power of this effect most directly while working as a volunteer peer-to-peer coach at AmeriSupport. In this position, I occasionally tried to discuss the larger context of labor markets and structural obstacles with a member who had been turned down by a particular employer, as a reassurance that there was nothing wrong with him or her. But in most cases my attempts were overwhelmed by the job seeker's focus on whatever actions he or she had taken prior to the rejection. Absorption in the chemistry game's practices turns the self-help discourse's partial truths (the measure of influence one does have over one's job search) into the entire story. The focused strategic activity of playing the game foregrounds the bounded universe of the game. It highlights the effects of factors within the player's discretion and obscures factors external to the game. This process, by which absorbed strategic action tends to make more salient certain factors while deemphasizing others, is at the core of the theory of social games as discussed in chapter 1.[11]

The process of playing the chemistry game consigns structural obstacles to the blurry background while the game's discourses and practices place strategic self-presentation at the center. As discussed in chapter 1, social games vary in their *player prominence*, referring to the extent to which individual strategies are perceived as determinative of the outcome. As the preceding section reveals, the chemistry game is characterized by high player prominence because the key determinant of hiring decisions is understood by job seekers to be their successful projection of a self that fits. Since getting hired is perceived to depend on effective self-subjectification, it is the job seekers' strategic moves and emotional labors that become the salient determinants of the outcome. By focusing attention on strategy and execution and away from the larger context of labor markets and structural constraints, the practical lived experience of job searching in the chemistry game reinforces the perception of individual control and thus ultimately leads to self-blame.

Self-Subjectification and Perceiving the Flawed Self

The chemistry game affects not only the tendency to self-blame, but also shapes what job seekers blame themselves *for*. Some scholars link self-blame to the American "culture of meritocracy," which would suggest a focus on objective abilities.[12] However, American self-blame rarely takes the form of job seekers concluding that they are not skilled enough. Instead, the typical progression of self-blame is from focusing on one's inadequacy as a job seeker, as previously described, to focusing on one's inadequacy as a person. In the examples we have already seen, job seekers attributed their failure to find work to spending too long on cover letters, being ineffective networkers, using the wrong word in an interview, lacking confidence, or not knowing what they really wanted to do. Over time, however, this kind of self-blame often gives way to a more fundamental and debilitating doubt of one's self. That is how Patricia felt after four months of unsuccessful job searching: "I've been kicked around enough that it goes to your self-esteem, makes you question your character. You question yourself, your own worth."

In my interviews with job seekers who have been out of work for three months or more, I repeatedly heard phrases like "I feel like a loser" or "something is wrong with me." These self-doubts were rarely publicly shared in group meetings at AmeriSupport but would come out during my in-depth interviews, and most typically at the later stages of the interview (or in subsequent conversations) when interviewees became more open. Self-blame was often described as the most difficult aspect of the unemployment experience. For example, Erica, a manager, explained: "The *hardest* thing is feeling that there is something wrong with me that I am not finding a job."

The increasing blame of one's inner self—as opposed to one's external *self-presentation*—reflects a direct hit to precisely the area of vulnerability created by the emotional labor of self-subjectification. To get a job, one has to put one's self "on the line." The focus on the inner self as the obstacle to finding a job mirrors the focus on the inner self as the central determinant of getting a job in the chemistry game.

The event that most intensely generates this highly personalized self-blame is an unsuccessful interview. Liz's reaction to a recent interview reflects the link between the chemistry game's strategies of personalizing the encounter and establishing rapport and the subsequent sense of rejection:

> I thought I had the best interview. We talked for an hour. I schmoozed them. Then I got a cold, impersonal e-mail. I felt: "How lame." I wrote to ask why, but they didn't respond. I didn't call because it's shameful, like asking a boyfriend, "Why did you break up with me?"

When interviews feel like a date, an employer's rejection is experienced as a breakup.

Interviews disrupt the rhythm of the most disciplined search routine and temporarily become the job seeker's entire focus. In the pre-interview period, there is a surge of hopeful excitement and intense research on the employer. The actual interview is the moment when self-subjectification is at its peak, with the job seeker doing his or her utmost to convey passion for the work and a good fit with the employer. Then, most crucially, comes the waiting period after the interview. Amy explained the pattern: "The rhythm of the search is that you apply—when you get an interview it all shifts to research and specific networking—afterward it's the waiting." After an interview, the only type of entry that Amy can make in her daily journal is: "I didn't hear from Meridian" or "Still waiting to hear from Meridian." Job seekers are often consumed by waiting. Paul said: "After the interview, that week I have an emotional shutdown. I can't do anything until I hear back from this one." Becky likewise reported:

> I had two second interviews last week, so now I'm feeling manic. Can't do any more work, can't continue to look for work. I called one back myself, and they said I didn't make the cut, for whatever reason, but I still have one more. So I am hanging on by a thread.... It's a roller coaster. I may have a message waiting for me when I get home.... I am on a roller coaster now and I can't feel peaceful.

The anxious roller-coaster ride can continue for extended periods when job seekers do not hear back from the employer. Amy *never* heard from Meridian.

Jeff explained that the period of waiting and not hearing is "undermining and devastating." The vulnerability created by self-subjectification both intensifies the post-interview anxiety and severely shakes the job seekers' sense of self in the face of a rejection. It is after unsuccessful interviews that characterological self-blame most often arises.

Nancy, the venture capitalist quoted at the start of this chapter, clearly described the progression of feelings that arise in the wake of unsuccessful interviews. She reported feeling "good when I got all those interviews," but then, when these interviews resulted in rejections, she began to feel that "there was something wrong with how I interviewed," and later, with yet more rejections, that there was "something wrong with *me*."

It is in the context of rejections after interviews that job seekers most often talk of feeling "defective" or "flawed." The increasingly personalized nature of their self-blame reflects the highly personalized nature of the chemistry game.

Since getting a job depends on externalizing one's inner self, the rejection is ultimately experienced as a rejection of oneself. Steven described how, as a result of a series of unsuccessful interviews, "I have had to deal with some self-esteem issues." He paused and then continued: "I think there is something wrong with me."

One consequence of this highly personalized self-blame is a precipitous decline in job-searching activities. Emily said that after the up and down of the interview process and "the undermining and devastating" rejection that follows, she "can't do anything afterward." When the rejection is taken as deeply personal, it is extremely difficult to continue with the search. The relationship between the personalized nature of the rejection and the decrease in job searching can be seen in two separate interviews with Sandy, the public-health researcher who initially reported feeling inspired by the self-help message that you "can create your own reality" and decided to pursue a career in genetic counseling. In her first months of job searching, Sandy stuck to a routine of job searching for six and a half hours a day. However, seven months into her search, she told me that she had ceased to look for work because

> I feel like no one wants me. I am forty-three years old, and I am living off my parents' money. Do you know how that feels? The hardest part is the rejection. Not getting interviews, and then when getting interviews, not getting the job. Rejection.

Joe likewise rhetorically asked: "*Why* am I not doing more? Because of a sense of *failure and rejection*." After an initial burst of activity, he had great difficulty engaging with any aspect of the search, including networking. Chris, the marketer, had been unsuccessful finding work for over four months. He described his difficulty in continuing to network despite feeling like "I need to":

CHRIS: What I found out at AmeriSupport is I need to be aggressive again, but when you are searching for a while and you don't feel like you are getting anywhere ... you get down on yourself. I find myself watching *Regis* and the *Andy Griffith Show*, and then realize I didn't eat.
AUTHOR: But you networked before, so why not now?
CHRIS: There was a time when it was easier.

Maria, a former senior manager, also made the link between the fear of personalized rejections and declining job-search intensity:

MARIA: My success team set up an action plan on a calendar, like Monday: network.... I have made a list of things that need to be done. This week I committed to follow up on six leads. I have set up the structure on paper but have not followed it.... Maybe I should focus more. I would find a job quicker if I was more active and focused on it, tried harder.

AUTHOR: What's kept you from focusing or trying harder?

MARIA: Apprehension. Fear of failure. Fear of rejection.

Becky put it most succinctly. After her two second interviews turned into two rejections, she ceased looking for work. "I feel more like an orphan. No one wants me, and I don't want to impose myself on anyone."

In sum, American job seekers' search intensity drops over time because each further attempt to find work leaves them open to a highly personalized perceived rejection. These already vulnerable job seekers do not want salt poured on their open wounds.

Self-blame and discouragement lead some job seekers to become disillusioned with the self-help model focusing on job-seeker control and the centrality of self-presentation. Erica and Joe, discussed previously, dropped out of AmeriSupport. But other unsuccessful long-term job seekers remain. One might expect their presence to raise doubts about the efficacy of the self-help model. This, however, does not generally happen. The basic premises of the chemistry game, and of the self-help paradigm that structures it, are rarely questioned in public. In the next section, I will discuss how the self-help paradigm is reproduced and how, as a consequence, unemployment continues to be understood as a matter that is private rather than public, and individual rather than structural.

Reproducing the Self-Help Paradigm

The boomerang effect, whereby the presumption of individual control turns to self-blame, depends on job seekers interpreting their labor-market difficulties as personalized rejections rather than as repudiations of the self-help presumption of individual control. It is important, therefore, to examine the practices and discourses that sustain and reproduce the premise of control despite job seekers' experiences that would appear to cast doubt on such premises.

One mechanism of reproduction is the opening ritual of AmeriSupport's general meetings, with Director Dan asking members to share with the rest of the group any "success stories," defined as finding a job or being invited to an interview. Any member with such a story comes up to the front of the room and, following an unwritten rule, begins by thanking his or her colleagues and AmeriSupport and finds some way to explain how AmeriSupport was instrumental in his or her success. In a group of forty to eighty members, it is not surprising that in a given week at least one member will have found a job or been invited to an interview. Thus, week after week, AmeriSupport members hear live testimonials from fellow job seekers who have experienced some job-search success and who interpret that success through the lens of the self-help paradigm. The power of these testimonials derives from the fact that they are delivered by familiar faces who become living proofs of the effectiveness of the self-help practices.

The spotlight on success stories as the opening ritual of general meetings and the de facto taboo on other types of stories create a "casino effect." In casinos, the acoustics are designed in such a way that, in a room full of slot machines, even if only one in a hundred players is winning at any given time, the *amplified sounds* of coins dropping for the one winner create the general impression of constant winning. Winning is loud; losing is inaudible. Success stories amplify singular positive outcomes and drown out contrary experiences. They support the message that the self-help strategies work for those with the fortitude to overcome *internal* obstacles; external obstacles—those immune to self-help methods—simply are not part of the picture.

During the rare weeks when no member had a success story to share, Director Dan filled the gap by drawing on a reserve of e-mailed success stories from former members, some of which he used on two or three occasions. Usually he would read one or two of these backup success stories with all the details and then list even more in rapid-fire succession: "Todd Brown got a job with Big Electric. Ben Roberts got a temp job. Catherine got a job with IT Corp." Beyond the details of any particular story, the overall message was this: Lots of people are getting jobs.

In some cases, the success story described the new job as the member's "dream job." Here is what Betty had to say one week:

> I am very happy right now. A lot because of what I learned here. I am going to be working with people that help disabled children. It is a dream come true. The skills I learned here with the résumé and my cover letter are what got me the first interview, and they even commented on my thank-you note. So *it works*!

In cases where the job finder is not explicit enough in crediting the self-help paradigm, others may step in. For example, here is how Laura reported finding a job: "On the advice of AmeriSupport, I researched the company's mission from their website, and I told them that the work they do is important to the community that I live in." Director Dan seized the opportunity to underline the message: "Yes, it oozes through your pores when you show that this job is about self-actualization. It's not about the money but the mission." Later in that meeting, the guest self-help speaker referred back to Laura's story: "I invite you to be proactive, to go from resigned to inspired. If you are not inspired after hearing Laura's success story today, shake yourself."

Most success stories do *not* contain references to finding work that matches one's passions. Tanya, a woman on my success team, was laid off from a job as a health care administrator. After introspecting about her passions, she developed an elevator speech about transitioning to a career in interior design. However, when the time came to tell her own success story, she reported that she was "thrilled to have found a job as an administrator at a hospital." No one commented on the discrepancy with her previously stated aspirations. What mattered is that another member had been successful in finding work.

Ben, a laid-off accountant, had also been inspired to move from accounting to the sale of medical devices that would help asthmatics like himself. He had taken all the steps—crafting résumés and cover letters and networking diligently—but "never got any responses." Finally, someone in the medical industry told him that without prior sales experience he had no chance. At an interview Ben explained: "They told me, 'It's not about your passion for the product, but what's your record closing deals.' I felt so defeated and so dumb." Ben took an accounting position a month later and announced his "success story" without any reference to his unsuccessful attempt to follow his passion.

Most job seekers at AmeriSupport, like most unemployed American white-collar workers in general, ultimately find a job that comes with a drop in pay and status.[13] Accepting a downwardly mobile job usually occurs as financial and familial pressures mount. After a string of rejections from preferred jobs, the job seekers' spouses—and sometimes their children—tend to urge them to take any job they can get. The self-help model tends to counteract this pressure and urges job seekers to hold out. When AmeriSupport members seek advice on whether to compromise, they are almost always urged to hold out and offered a new strategy to try. Self-help speakers typically encourage job seekers to give themselves "permission" to go for their dream job. Family pressure to take "any job" is countered by success-team colleagues who tend to "take the side" of the job seeker. At a certain point, bills and family pressure usually prevail. Yet even when clearly compromising, job seekers tend to frame their decision as a "step" in the direction of the dream job. For example, Hal, a mechanical engineer who had dreamed of opening his own business, told the group: "I took a job in the plumbing department at Home Depot. The pay is lousy but the commute is good. I will use this as a platform to network as a freelance safety consultant. Network, network, network." To reinforce the framing of this job as a step in the right direction, Director Dan added:

> Speaking of Home Depot, I recall an engineer from AmeriSupport who went to apply there for an entry-level job and their computer kiosk failed. He went up to the manager and said, "I can fix the programming error." He was hired as a programmer. And then another person heard this story here and went to Home Depot. During training he asked: "How does one become a trainer?" And he was hired as a trainer at double the salary.

Director Dan's underlying message was "With pluck and a positive attitude, even a job at Home Depot can be a step toward your dream job."

In rare cases, it was simply not possible to frame a downwardly mobile job as a "good first step" toward the dream job. Jerome, a computer programmer, reported getting a job as a limo driver. He was unapologetic about this downward compromise after months of searching. The audience's discomfort was palpable for a few seconds as members were confronted with the unspoken reality of their own likely downward mobility.

Only once during my year at AmeriSupport did a success story become an occasion to openly share tabooed negative experiences. Paul, an engineer, stood in front of the group to tell his success story:

> I found a job as a technical assistant. I have been out of work for a year and a half. It's been hard. *Suicidal hard.* AmeriSupport was really helpful. Being authentic and being interpersonal was the key.

The room became uneasily silent for a few seconds, and then Director Dan said, "Thank you, Paul." In my field notes, I wrote: "This is a rare moment when the depth of the hardship of this period is openly acknowledged. The words 'suicidal hard' shook this room, and I noticed nods of understanding." This moment was exceptional because it violated the unspoken rule that personal crises do not intrude on the public face of positiveness and success. Even this intrusion came only as a retrospective comment in the context of a success story affirming the self-help model.

While I frequently heard expressions of anger, frustration, and hardship during private interviews, there was usually no sharing of such difficulties among members. Likewise, although members like Joe and Erica were privately critical of elements of the self-help discourse, this critique was not a matter for public discussion.

One reason that AmeriSupport and the self-help paradigm largely avoided open critique is the fact that some members drop out once they become critical of self-help. Their critical voices are therefore simply not around. But even when members who privately critique self-help do not drop out, they almost always keep their critiques to themselves to avoid the charge of *self*-sabotage.[14]

Sandy's case illustrates how the accusation of self-sabotage typically works. Sandy dropped out of AmeriSupport after six months, but feeling increasingly isolated, she decided to give it another try. At her first general meeting upon returning, the speaker—not unlike the speaker who had inspired her a few months earlier to become a genetic counselor—claimed that "you will be amazed that, once you set your mind to it, what things can happen." Sandy stood up and said: "It doesn't work that way. I did everything I could ... and here I am. So it doesn't always work." In response, someone from the audience asked her: "How are you sabotaging yourself?" Sandy sat back down. The discussion turned to how a negative attitude can undermine your chances to find a good job. During a later interview, with visible disgust, Sandy told me: "The only reason I could withstand this blaming audience comment is because I have good friends that love me." Sandy did not speak out again.

Another process by which the self-help paradigm's plausibility is maintained at AmeriSupport—despite visible cases of job seekers who are not able to "take control" of their career fates—is the stigmatization by newer members of more veteran colleagues. Sarah confided in me her view of her longtime colleagues: "AmeriSupport is a do-nothing community. They are not action-oriented professionals. All these baby birds with mouth open."

Because AmeriSupport is partly marketed to new members as an organization for professionals looking to network, new members are sometimes surprised—and disappointed—to find out that their fellow members are in the same boat. As David put it: "AmeriSupport is supposed to be about networking, but no one here has a job. *It's like networking with the dead.*" Todd described his fellow members as stray dogs looking for the bone. There is a sense in the room of people in need of something. A room of unemployed people who are desperate for a job just like you. Ultimately, to what extent will they be your most effective partners? Where is the juice? It's kind of depressing, like a wake kind of feeling. . . . My sense is that these are sad, lost people, like someone on the corner of a street hoping that someone will pick them up for a day's work and take them away.

Ultimately, AmeriSupport members cannot live up to their constructed collective identity as professionalized job seekers going about their work in a positive and passionate manner. The tabooed despairs, fears, and anxieties inevitably rise up through the cracks. When they do, however, they are filtered through the self-help paradigm, which transmutes them into individual failings or pathologies. In place of collective empowerment, we see intensified and collectivized blame.

The Corporate Ethos and Escapes

The previous section discussed mechanisms that help reproduce the self-help paradigm, including job seekers' mutual stigmatization. It might be expected that such stigmatization, as well as other barriers to open communication among AmeriSupport members, would dissipate in the context of smaller groups. In small groups, one might expect open expressions of frustration, a sharing of hardships, and perhaps a recognition of the shared nature of the experience. Yet such sharing does not typically take place, and difficult experiences remain private. One important reason for this is the corporate ethos at AmeriSupport.

The most common type of small groups at AmeriSupport are the success teams formed at the end of a new cohort's weeklong intensive training. Ground rules are usually established to ensure that team members maintain—or at least present—a positive attitude at all times. The following dialogue among a new cohort of job seekers regarding the formation of their new success team is illustrative:

VOLUNTEER TRAINER: Success teams can serve the purposes of honing job-searching skills, networking, accountability, and support. What would you like your success team to do?

BRENDA: I don't have time for a tea party. I want to be in a group that is talking about résumés and interviewing.

MARY: Maybe we can start meetings with a "check-in"?

BRENDA: Can it be ten seconds? Some check-ins turn into therapy sessions, and we don't want to do that.

After this exchange, the group voted on its priorities, the highest being working on résumés and elevator speeches, followed by role-playing mock interviews. The group also agreed that future meetings should last exactly two hours. The bulk of the brainstorming session was spent constructing an agenda for the first meeting, complete with a time limit for each agenda item. When one member suggested adding success stories to the agenda, the group looked for where they could "shave off" five minutes from another agenda item. The imposition of time pressure created the feel of a business meeting.

Both the business-meeting ethos, encouraged by the self-help paradigm's focus on rationalized time use, and the "mandatory smile" discussed in chapter 2 appear to block the forging of deeper connections and the sharing of experiences that might lead to an understanding of the shared nature of seemingly individual predicaments. Without such connections, participation in a success team often becomes a performance. Bill confided to me in an interview that he would start to "shade things" when talking with his success team because "I did not want to disappoint [the other members] by saying I have not done a great thing" in the past week. Similarly, Gerry confided that she "feels like a loser" but explained that "I don't want to talk about *that* with my success team. I am older and they are all IT people, and I don't want to look like a failure."

In one instance a member broke the unspoken rules of maintaining a professional and positive demeanor with her success team. Carole reported:

> I told my success team that I really don't know that any employer would want me. *Everyone was stunned.* I said to them, "You better face this. All of you have this feeling. Feeling I don't have anything to offer." Eventually everyone agreed that they do question, "What do I have to offer? Who would want me? The child in me is feeling that I am just not wanted." And that's the truth.

The "stunned" reaction of Carole's colleagues reveals how the open sharing of fears and insecurities violates the positive-attitude norm and the expected business-meeting ethos.

The business-like ethos of success-team meetings is a manifestation of a broader phenomenon. The entire structure of AmeriSupport is that of a mock corporation. With the exception of one state employee, Director Dan, AmeriSupport consists of unemployed job seekers who organize themselves into a corporate hierarchical structure with various "departments," such as IT, marketing, and member support. These departments come under the "management" of volunteer "vice presidents" who collectively make up an "executive council" that meets weekly—in a conference room behind a glass wall—to make decisions about the "direction" of AmeriSupport. The meetings are run by the AmeriSupport "president." Presidents are council members nominated for this position by the council. When a new president is nominated, the general membership is told—with the perfunctory quality of a corporate shareholder meeting—that a certain person has been nominated to serve as president and "all those in favor please say aye." The vote is always unanimous.

The corporate culture comes with expectations about professional comportment. AmeriSupport members are expected to dress in a "professional manner" and behave as they would in any other workplace. Members all wear badges showing their name, department, and the AmeriSupport logo. For members of the executive council, the badges also include their official title.

The corporate culture is also manifested in the focus on efficiency. During my year at AmeriSupport, for example, the executive council decided to undertake a "re-org." This decision was announced to the membership in a general meeting:

PRESIDENT: We are reorganizing to improve our effectiveness. We currently have eight departments. We are streamlining the organization by creating four divisions instead of eight departments.

AUDIENCE MEMBER: This is a downsizing! Damn. And I don't even get a paycheck [*laughter*].

ANOTHER MEMBER: "Do more with less!" [*more laughter*].

PRESIDENT [*with a serious voice and looking annoyed at the laughter*]: We want to be on a path of continuous improvement and streamlining.

As the back-sass shows, the corporate-like management style provokes some resistance from those who are being "managed."

AmeriSupport's corporate structure and ethos serve two explicit functions and one latent one. The explicit goals are to effectively organize the work necessary to keep the organization functioning and to give volun-

teer members an opportunity for professional development. The latent
function is to provide some job seekers with an escape from the punishing
labor market, a protected space where they can maintain a professional
identity.

The use of AmeriSupport management positions as an alternative identity is more typical of men than women. While there are no clear cross-
gender differences during the initial period of the job search, gendered
patterns do appear in the later stages. Whereas more men than women
seek corporate-sounding positions at AmeriSupport, more women than
men turn to another strategy to deal with their battered identities—
highlighting their non-worker roles, such as being a mother or daughter.[15]

The opportunity for professional development is often touted as an
important dividend of the volunteer work at AmeriSupport. One member reports that he handled the year and a half gap in his employment
history by "putting AmeriSupport as my place of work in computer services" and demonstrating his passion to potential employers by speaking of his "dreams for making AmeriSupport shine." Generally, though,
members who are deeply involved in volunteer positions are not simultaneously very active in the job market. Maria, a former senior manager,
sought to become president of AmeriSupport just as she slowed down in
her job search. In a reflective moment, she told me: "I hope I am not hiding behind being president." Likewise, Chris—the marketer who became
discouraged about his search—took on the task of organizing AmeriSupport's reunion party for former members. He confided in an interview that
his time had been completely taken up by this project:

> It's nice to keep me active, but it's interfering with the purpose of my being
> there by taking up my time. But I like being able to say that I was just working
> on something, and here was my strategy to solve it. People want to hear what
> you can accomplish, and now I have some place to go.

The personal agenda of job seekers in volunteer management positions, whether looking for professional development or escape from the
job search, can get in the way of effectively running the organization. This,
in turn, creates tensions among regular AmeriSupport members and their
volunteer "managers." As seen in the humorous resistance to the re-org,
the projects proposed by vice presidents are sometimes viewed by members as unnecessary work for the members and only designed to improve
the VP's résumé. As one member explained:

> AmeriSupport is a place to do your mock experience. People trumpet that they are the VP of a certain division, and it maintains their sense of stature and leadership. People who want senior positions are crafting senior [volunteer] positions, but it's not about helping people find jobs. The executive council is like a debating society and it's based on hierarchy. It gives [regular members] work and holds them accountable. We act like a company for the purpose of some few individuals. AmeriSupport people are bringing a corporate model of organization, focusing on efficiency, but efficiency doesn't matter here. There is too much exercise of power and hierarchy.

The re-org, for example, consumed months of volunteer work. Linda reflected: "All this was brouhaha that was not about our mission to help people get jobs. It just made the executive council feel important."

The mock corporate style together with the self-help imperative to always maintain a positive and work-like attitude combine to suppress discussion of personal crises. The "backstage" realities of self-blame, discouragement, and fear, which emerged repeatedly during my private in-depth interviews, were not raised on the "main stage" of general meetings.

The financial turmoil that members experience is also kept under a tight lid. Members' situations vary widely; some get by on savings while others rely on financial support from parents or rent out rooms in their houses, and at least two had become homeless. But they all experience utter financial uncertainty and anxiety. And while this came up often in private interviews, it almost never did in general meetings.

An exception, again, made visible the unspoken rule. In one general meeting, the guest speaker—unusual in that he was a financial adviser rather than a self-help coach—began his talk by enumerating the "choices" that "workers in transition" have for health insurance, naming "COBRA, temporary health insurance, and private medical accounts." At that moment, the room simply erupted in a free-for-all discussion. It was the only meeting during my year at AmeriSupport in which the speaker lost control of the audience. The meeting turned into an open exchange of tips and advice on health insurance, with members virtually ignoring the speaker. Audience member comments, recorded in my field notes, include: "One surgery can wipe you out. The last surgery I had cost a hundred and fifty thousand dollars. So it's better to sell your car than be without health insurance." Another member added: "Under state law there is an obligation to treat the medically indigent, but the cost is to have to wait a long time at the emergency room." A third suggested: "Take a class in the community college and sign up for health insurance." The discussion of health insurance led to a broader exchange of ideas on how to cut back spending and save money. Members suggested to each other to convert their mortgages to interest-only loans, to obtain a deferral for the repayment of student loans, or to stop paying for home Internet and use cafés. It was an astonishing moment, which I described in my notes:

> It is an animated explosion of a discussion that is unlike anything I have seen before at AmeriSupport. This meeting is being taken over by members energized by exchanging helpful tips on a topic that is usually taboo. It is completely the opposite of the usual "expert" speaker dynamic where members are passive.

The lid on the personal financial catastrophe of joblessness had blown off for one meeting, but by the next meeting it was back.

*   *   *

The chemistry game takes American white-collar job seekers on a roller-coaster ride—raising them up, only to drop them down again. The self-help discourses and practices structure the game in a way that strongly reinforces the message that winning is within job seekers' control. Job seekers also get an initial boost from the inspirational talks on discovering one's passions and following one's dreams. At the same time, the chemistry game demands the emotional labor of self-subjectification, which, from the outset, makes job seekers feel exposed and vulnerable.

If job seekers do not find a job in the first two or three months, the initial boost disappears and is typically followed by self-blame. The nature of this self-blame, with its focus on internal flaws, mirrors the assumptions of the chemistry game that finding a job is ultimately determined by intangible elements of the *self*. This kind of self-blame is particularly debilitating and leads some job seekers to cease their search.

The typical pattern of the chemistry game, from boost to bust, raises a puzzling question about why AmeriSupport members who are in the bust phase of the game do not share their experiences with newcomers and thus prevent a repetition of this cycle. The second half of this chapter provided several explanations. First, many job seekers in the bust phase continue to believe in the validity of the self-help paradigm and see the problem as purely individual. Second, the minority of job seekers who develop a critique of self-help assumptions either drop out of AmeriSupport or are silenced by a reframing of their critiques as "negative attitude" or "self-sabotage." Third, AmeriSupport members discount the experiences of their veteran colleagues who are experiencing labor-market difficulties by stigmatizing these job seekers as "losers." Fourth, the focus on "success stories" amplifies individual success and powerfully validates the self-help paradigm. Finally, the corporate structure and ethos of AmeriSupport— and of other self-help groups like it—systematically block the forging of deeper ties of solidarity and the open sharing of hardships among members, which leaves the basic premises of self-help uncontested.

When white-collar job seekers first arrive at AmeriSupport, they are looking for a way to make sense of their situations, a map and guide for going forward. They are invited to participate in a seductive game which asks them to suspend their knowledge of external obstacles. But playing this game puts them at a high risk of ultimately feeling defective or flawed. And, as Chinoy (1955) put it half a century ago: "To the extent that workers focus blame for their failure . . . upon themselves . . . American society escapes the consequences of its own contradictions. The social order is thus protected, however, only at the psychological expense of those who have failed."

In the next two chapters, we examine another group of unemployed white-collar job seekers in similar occupations and looking for work under similar economic conditions. Beneath these similarities, however, we discover an entirely different job-searching and unemployment experience. Israeli job seekers play a different game.

CHAPTER FOUR

A Cross-National Comparison

The Israeli Specs Game

Since my research began with a set of initial interviews with American white-collar job seekers, by the time I arrived in Israel, I had begun to take for granted their notion that getting hired, at least for white-collar occupations, was more a matter of fit than skills. I therefore focused my initial interviews in Israel on how job seekers there attempted to convey fit. My questions were met with confused looks.

Israeli job seekers consistently stressed that to get hired, what matters most is to have the right set of "buzzwords" on one's résumé to get past staffing agency screeners and to navigate the seemingly arbitrary pre-employment tests. When I interviewed staffing agency screeners, their descriptions of the process matched those of the job seekers. Yael, a staffing agency screener, was blunt: "I look for buzzwords."

The deeper I probed, the more I realized that the Israeli job-search experience was structured by a different set of labor-market institutions, which are themselves a product of a profound and recent transformation of the Israeli political economy. Like the American labor-market institutions I had already observed, Israeli labor-market institutions undergirded a particular set of job-searching practices, discourses, and strategies—the Israeli specs game.

Ultimately, I concluded that playing the specs game, like playing the chemistry game, generates a distinct unemployment experience and explains why self-blame—one of the most painful dimensions of the unemployment experience among American white-collar workers—is virtually nonexistent in Israel. Unemployment in Israel has its own forms of pain, with job seekers often feeling dehumanized and betrayed. The next two chapters explore the specs game and its consequences. I begin by stepping back to analyze the larger institutional context of white-collar work and job searching in Israel.

The Rise of Neoliberalism and White-Collar Insecurity in Israel

In Israel, as in the United States, the job security once enjoyed by white-collar workers has vanished over the last three decades.[1] In both countries, white-collar workers are increasingly finding themselves involuntarily searching for new jobs in the middle years of their careers.

To explain these changes in Israel, it is necessary to put Israel's neoliberal economy into historical context. From the founding of the state of Israel in 1948 through the early 1970s, the Israeli economy was dominated by the Labor Party, which not only held continuous control of the government, but simultaneously controlled the powerful Histadrut (the general federation of labor unions). The Histadrut encompassed nearly every Israeli trade union and, until the 1970s, represented 80 percent of Israeli workers, making Israel one the most highly unionized countries in the world. This high percentage arose partly due to the Histadrut's control over the provision of welfare benefits, including health care, pensions, day care, recreation centers, housing, workers' education, and soup kitchens. Because these social-welfare benefits, which in most industrialized countries are accorded by virtue of citizenship or residence, were available only to Histadrut members, most Israeli workers sought to become union members.[2] The Labor Party's control of the Histadrut, with its legions of dependent workers, provided it with an unmatchable resource for mobilizing electoral support and maintaining control of the state. In turn, the Labor Party's control of the state guaranteed the Histadrut's continued power and privileges.[3] The Histadrut's power also extended beyond the representation of workers to ownership of some of Israel's largest companies.[4]

Under the control of the Labor Party, the Israeli economy was organized along corporatist lines. Collective agreements on wages, work conditions, and rights of termination were reached in peak agreements among the Histadrut, the state, and employer associations. And, as is the case in western European corporatist economies, these peak agreements were extended by the Ministry of Labor to most other non-organized workers.[5] Because the Labor Party controlled both the state and the Histadrut, two of the three negotiating parties to the peak agreements, and had a powerful role as an employer as well, these agreements essentially involved negotiations *within* the Labor Party. Before the 1970s, Israeli employers saw no opportunity to challenge the Labor Party's supremacy and accepted a de facto exclusion from the wage and work conditions determination process.[6]

The Labor Party's priority in managing the labor market was the maintenance of full employment and job security. From the late 1950s until the mid-1980s, the unemployment rate was usually kept below 3 or 4 percent. This policy priority was tied to a larger Zionist national project wherein full employment was considered necessary to maintain the flow of Jewish immigration.[7] Job security was achieved in several ways, including stringent requirements for severance pay upon termination and the granting of tenure after some period of employment in the large public sector. Collective-bargaining agreements further limited employer flexibility by requiring employers to show "good cause" to terminate employment, thus creating de facto lifetime employment for white-collar workers. The commitment to full employment was also institutionalized in the government-run employment agency, the "Lishka," charged by law with finding jobs for all job seekers.[8]

Both the Labor Party's power and its employment regime began to unravel in the 1970s, due to a mixture of economic, political, and institutional factors. The global economic slowdown of the early 1970s was one important catalyst. Until then, Israel's economy had grown at 10 percent a year, a rate second only to Japan's among members of the Organisation for Economic Co-operation and Development (OECD). But after 1973, Israel's growth rates dropped below that of most other OECD nations. This led to popular discontent with the Labor Party's economic policies. At the same time, a growing number of Sephardic Israelis (Jews of Middle Eastern origins) began perceiving the Labor Party as favoring Ashkenazi Israelis (Jews of European origins), leading to a rise in the electoral fortunes of the Labor Party's historical rival, the anti-statist Likud party. The Likud won a dramatic election victory in 1977, and for the first time in its history, Israel was not governed by the Labor Party.

The Likud's platform embraced the neoliberal view of economists such as Milton Friedman. Yet because Likud had won by mobilizing working-class Sephardic Israelis against the Labor Party and painting the latter as the party of the "elites," it could not immediately implement economic reforms that would transparently benefit the economic elite. Thus, the Likud did not immediately end the state's policy of maintaining full employment,

but instead focused on weakening the Histadrut. It broke the dependence
of workers on the Histadrut through moves—which from a distance may
appear paradoxical for an anti-statist party—such as nationalizing health
care benefits and introducing universal minimum-income guarantees. It
also began to require the privatization of Histadrut-owned companies on
the grounds that it created a conflict of interest for the union and the employer to be ultimately controlled by the same entity.[9] This process, together with large-scale privatization of state-owned enterprises, led to a
dramatic increase in the size and power of the private sector.[10] Divested
of its role as the sole provider of welfare benefits and its status as a large
employer, the Histadrut has seen its membership plunge from 80 percent
of the workforce to 20 percent over the past thirty years.[11] With the collapse of the Histadrut, Israel's corporatist institutions have disintegrated
and wage bargaining has become decentralized.[12]

   These institutional changes have generated levels of inequality in Israel that are now comparable to those in the United States[13] and, of most
immediate relevance, have led to the transformation of the Israeli labor
market. The institutions that supported job security have crumbled, and a
neoliberal "flexible" labor regime has risen in their place. For white-collar
workers in Israel, lifetime employment vanished in the 1990s, replaced by
casualized and flexible employment.[14]

   White-collar casualization was boosted by the rise to dominance of the
high-tech sector, predominantly managed by Israelis who brought, along
with their American MBAs, a "new economy" organizational model that
prioritizes employer flexibility over employee security.[15] This model is institutionalized through the use of temporary and contract workers and
the routine layoffs of permanent workers during market fluctuations.
These practices, which began with the high-tech sector, have spilled over
to change the rules of the game in all other white-collar sectors.[16]

   The high-tech sector's spill-over effect is a product of its tremendous
visibility in Israel, owing to its well-publicized and meteoric growth.[17] The
American-trained managers at the top of Israel's high-tech sector articulate
a discourse—echoed by politicians such as the Likud's MIT-trained Benjamin "Bibi" Netanyahu as well as neoliberal think tanks—which claims
that the high-tech's contingent work regime represents the "American
model." Branding something as "American" was not always a recipe for
success in Israel. In the pre-1970s era, Israel was characterized by a pio-
neering ethos and celebrated collectivist self-sacrifice. Western culture
was seen as decadent, with both television and Coke completely excluded
until 1968. As late as the 1970s, the kibbutz, a communal form of living,

was called "the soul of Israel."[18] However, by the late 1990s the adoption of the American economic model was widely understood as synonymous with progress and efficiency.[19] Its adoption is portrayed as part of the process of Israel joining other advanced economies and adapting to the global economic system. At the core, this discourse links Israel becoming a modern nation with the adoption of the free-market structures of other "truly modern" societies, such as the United States. In this discursive context, all labor-market institutions and regulations generating job security are portrayed as the "old ways," while contingent employment relations are described as symbols of modern "freedom."

Following the typical neoliberal discourse, workers are depicted as benefiting from a flexible labor market, which is "not hampered by unions" and which encourages further investments.[20] The spread of the neoliberal work regime is even discursively linked to Zionist goals. Whereas the Labor Party once claimed that full employment was important for attracting and maintaining Jewish immigrants, the new discourse focuses on the benefits of economic growth. For example, the Shalem Center, a think tank supportive of the neoliberal transformation, argues that economic growth achieved by deregulation and privatization will mean that "immigration to Israel will no longer require a choice between a person's standard of living and his identity as a Zionist and a Jew."[21] Along the same lines, Bibi Netanyahu, in a major speech at the 2003 Herzliya Conference advocating neoliberal economic reforms, claimed, "If we want to encourage Jews to immigrate to Israel, we need a blooming and dynamic economy."

The neoliberal transformation has redefined the role of the state. The Bank of Israel, a leading agent in the reforms, urges "adoption of international standards of management in the private sector" and claims that the role of government is to make Israel "attractive for investors."[22] It is in the name of adopting the "American model," with its purported efficiency, that Israeli workers, including college-educated and skilled workers, have been stripped of job security.[23]

The neoliberal work regime is not only associated with a broad discourse on the nature of efficiency and modernization, but also with a more specific discourse on what it takes to find a job. This discourse claims that getting a job in modern market societies requires successfully competing in a meritocratic labor market by finding a buyer for your skills, education, and experience. The official government pamphlet for unemployed job seekers explains that hiring decisions are based on the job seeker's "relative advantage compared to other candidates" and reminds job seekers:

> Getting or not getting a job is a matter of *supply and demand*. The more people who apply for a given job, the harder it is to get the job, even if you have good credentials. You will often, to our regret, get a negative response despite being definitely appropriate for the offered job. The reason is that there were a number of good candidates and it is only possible to take one and you didn't "win."

This economic supply-and-demand discourse is coupled with the claim that the focus on skills and credentials is both modern and meritocratic as compared to the "old" labor market, which is depicted as dominated by personal connections (*protectzia*) and patronage.

Ironically, while this discourse claims to adopt the "American model," the American white-collar job search is actually dominated by a very different understanding of what it takes to get a job. As discussed in chapters 2 and 3, the chemistry game focuses on the centrality of interpersonal connection and fit. Nevertheless, in Israel the purportedly modern and American approach focuses on the selling of a set of objective skills and credentials, an approach that actively suppresses interpersonal or subjective elements and valorizes market-based instrumentalism, giving rise to what I call the specs game.

While the Israeli discourse is articulated most explicitly in the government literature provided to unemployed job seekers, it is brought to life by the practices of the two dominant labor-market institutions that Israeli job seekers routinely encounter. As described below, the front lines of the Israeli labor market consist of staffing agencies and pre-employment testing institutes, which claim as their *raison d'être* the facilitation of objective meritocracy. Yet, as we shall see, it is the practices of these institutions that sow the seeds of disillusionment and, for job seekers unable to find work within a few months, ultimately generate the experience of betrayal and system-blame.

Israeli Institutions: Screening and Testing

The neoliberal model of flexible employment relations is institutionalized, above all, by staffing agencies, the use of which by Israeli employers has grown *tenfold* since the 1980s.[24] As in the United States, staffing agencies in Israel supply temporary workers to employers. But, unlike the United States, most Israeli staffing agencies also play a critical role in the hiring process of permanent employees by conducting the initial filtering of can-

didates for permanent positions on behalf of employers.[25] Israeli job seekers are well aware of the central role of these agencies, and *every* Israeli
job seeker I interviewed applied to jobs through such staffing agencies. As
Rotem, a computer engineer, explained: "The main way of finding jobs is
staffing agencies"; or, as Nati, a manager, put it: "Eighty percent of work is
gotten through staffing agencies."[26]

From the late 1960s to the mid-1980s, staffing agencies only provided
short-term solutions for employers looking, most typically, to replace a
female worker on maternity leave or a male worker on military reserve
duty. Temp workers were typically paid *more* than permanent workers to
compensate for the lack of job security. This pattern began to change rad-
ically in the late 1980s with the explosive growth and widespread use of
staffing agencies for permanent hires.

The initial impetus for this change can be traced to the Israeli state.
In the late 1980s, in an attempt to stabilize hyper-inflation, the state froze
all new hiring in the public sector. It left a loophole, however, that allowed government agencies to hire personnel through staffing agencies,
which were technically providing "services" and thus did not require formal employment agreements.[27] From the mid-1990s through the present,
economic factors also became important. With global competition putting
more pressure on Israeli companies to reduce costs, the already greatly
weakened labor unions agreed to two-tier collective agreements: one tier
for employees hired through staffing agencies and another for already
unionized workers. From the unions' perspective, this structure appeared
to be the only viable way to protect their current workers' job security
and employment conditions, while for Israeli employers it provided a
way to minimize the scope of union contracts.[28] Finally, as previously discussed, the most recent impetus for the growth of staffing agencies is the
rise of the high-tech sector. Although high-tech companies are relatively
new and therefore do not have unionized workers, they are attracted to
staffing agencies for added "flexibility"—a way around remaining protective legislation for employees such as severance-pay requirements and
the provision of social benefits.[29] The trendsetter continues to be the state
itself, which rarely hires anyone directly. Like high-tech companies, the
state often prefers to let staffing agencies act as the legal employers of
record (even for non-temporary workers) in order to circumvent its own
required protections and benefits.[30] Even public-school teachers are hired
through staffing agencies.

The waves of neoliberal reforms have led to the phenomenon of having three generations of workers doing similar work side by side: "gener-

ation A, who were hired during the corporatist stage; generation B, who were hired after privatization at inferior wages and benefits and no tenure; and generation C, who are hired through [staffing] agencies" and who work under the most contingent terms and with minimal benefits.[31]

The Staffing Agency Filter: Routinization and Rigidity

In comparing the job-search processes of American and Israeli white-collar workers, one of the most salient and important differences is the dominant position of staffing agencies in the Israeli labor market. Because Israeli companies typically outsource their human resources functions to staffing agencies, the human face of the Israeli labor market is not the employer. While the first person an American white-collar job seeker meets is usually a hiring manager who tries to assesses the job seeker's interpersonal fit, an Israeli job seeker typically encounters a young and untrained screener for one of the hundreds of Israeli staffing agencies, who tries to assesses the job seeker with a checklist of skills and credentials.

Staffing agencies laud their expertise at matching job seekers to the needs of employers. Promotional materials are designed to lure employers not only with low costs but also with sophisticated and allegedly well-tested systems for identifying ideal candidates. However, my in-depth interviews with agency screeners indicate that the process of filtering is less a matter of sophisticated systems than of a fast-food-like focus on routinized efficiency.

Screening for a staffing agency is a routinized low-paying job. Yael, a screener at an agency in Tel Aviv, explained that the job of being a screener "is seen as a temp job" with a salary only slightly above the minimum wage, typically taken by young women just out of the army, before they go to university. Screeners are asked to review résumés for qualifications that match an employer-provided checklist of credentials, skills, and experiences and to conduct short and simple screening interviews with candidates who appear to meet the qualifications. The purpose of these interviews is to verify the credibility of the job seekers' claims to meet the checklist criteria and often to find out their salary expectations.

Outsourcing recruiting makes the filtering process highly rigid. The rigidity stems not only from the routinization of the screening work, but also from the structural relationship between the screener and the employer. Unlike American hiring managers who are assessing their "sense of easy familiarity," or chemistry, with potential future colleagues, Israeli screeners typically know nothing more about an employer's culture than what they have read in a company statement. Moreover, given their limited training and experience, they are in no position to be persuaded by a job seeker (or themselves to persuade the hiring manager) that some special skill or quality that the job seeker possesses is actually more important than what is on the employer's checklist.

Yael explained the résumé-screening process:

> I look for buzzwords. I search by keywords. So if the résumé is not clear, there is no chance. I give each résumé fifteen seconds. It must be written in short bullet points. If you write in sentences, it is hard to read. It must be clear what [the job seeker] did.

As will be discussed in chapter 5, this type of screening is particularly tough for job seekers who need to explain their qualifications despite the absence of some "specs," as in the case of job seekers attempting to switch fields who do not meet the direct-experience requirement but who may possess relevant skills developed in a different context.

Adding to this rigidity are the broad proxies used by staffing agencies as indicative of the likelihood of a job seeker being a good worker. For example, job seekers with extended résumé gaps are systematically filtered out. As Galia, a screener for an agency, said, "If someone has been looking for work for more than a year, he is filtered." This is because employers believe that "if he was excellent, he would have found something." Nava, another screener, agreed:

> The gap of time is essential. If they have not worked for a period of time, that is a problem. It's not rational. Employers think: "Why didn't they work? Maybe there is something wrong with them." But it all comes down to the fact that you have so many other applicants. Why deal with someone about whom you have a question mark?

Another issue that raises "question marks" is over-qualification. Erica, a screener, described employers' attitude toward this:

> The over-qualification fear is that they will be bored and leave. Employers fear they will be stuck with someone who is too skilled for the work, so he will deal with politics at work or will sabotage. I don't necessarily think it's a mistake. It is easiest to see in people who used to be managers. They say, "I don't

care. I don't mind [being overqualified], I am going back to the drawing board."
You look at them and think, "Will this person really be able to go back? Will
they, after giving instructions to others, agree to take instructions?" It's a real
obstacle.

Over-qualification is also a problem because it is a sign of "desperation."
As Galia explained:

When I talk to someone on the phone and he sounds desperate, saying, "I will
do anything," even jobs for which he is overqualified, he must have been in a
million interviews. If he was good, he would have gotten a job. People who are
really good have a million offers. Others are not at their peak.

Concerns about over-qualification overlap with concerns raised by another widely used proxy—age. Older workers, like overqualified workers,
are presumed to come with high expectations regarding salary, responsibility, and autonomy. But they also raise other concerns that make age
one of the most difficult obstacles to overcome. Nava, a staffing agency
screener, explained:

Age is a huge issue. I do filter [job seekers] by age because my clients don't
want job seekers over a certain age. In the U.S. it's not the same? Here there
is no shame. The employers who are more sophisticated, say, "I want someone
dynamic with up to ten years' experience," and then you know they want someone younger than thirty-five. But most of them tell you this openly. They say
their workers are young and they want homogeneity among the workers. They
can't imagine how someone in their forties can get along with people in their
twenties and thirties. I totally disagree with this, but I cooperate because if I
send them older workers, they won't take them.... There will be hundreds of
résumés, and age is an easy filter, like education.

Gender is also a critical filter. Unlike résumé gaps, over-qualification,
and age, being female does not automatically exclude job seekers, but it
does result in their selection for low-level jobs and de-selection from
work that has, in the words of Yaffa, another screener, "any potential for
advancement." Yaffa said that employers will not "groom a woman for
a CEO job or any job with a track for advancement." This is because of
concerns that women who receive training will leave upon having children. As Yaffa put it: "From the point of view of the employer, because

they have so many applicants, why should they have to deal with the issue of a woman who might want to go home to be with her kids? It really restricts women. It's true that women don't get equal opportunity." For certain types of jobs, however, the screening by gender can also work against men. Meirav, a screener, elaborated:

> It works the other way too. I get guys who tell me, "I want a secretary job." If they were women, the answer would be yes. But [employers] won't take guys for these kinds of jobs. It's like being overqualified. Even to work as a screener like me, it is all women. Employers think they won't stay. Why would a man work at this level? There is something in the worldview. There are jobs for men and jobs for women. All these sociology BA guys, I won't interview them.... There are no entry-level jobs for them here. They can go to customer service for the cell-phone companies. It's very rigid here. Each person is in his or her box—gender, age, and so forth.

Filtering job seekers by salary expectations is also routine for Israeli staffing agencies. As Noa, a thirty-three-year-old job seeker and graphic designer, put it: "[The agencies'] most important role is to find out how much money you want." For white-collar American professionals, the question of salary typically does not come up at all in the first interview because, in the American context, both job applicants and employers attempt to convey that money is a secondary issue that cannot be discussed without polluting the purity of the expressive and passionate relationship to work. In Israel, however, the question of salary is raised upfront as a threshold matter, which determines whether or not there is any point in talking further about the position. In some cases, interviewees are asked what they expect, while in other cases they are told what the salary is and asked whether it is acceptable. One reason for this aggressive discussion of salaries in the Israeli context is that multiple staffing agencies are competing to fill the same opening based on offering the lowest "price." The agency able to offer up a qualified job seeker with the lowest salary is likely to obtain the placement.[32]

Pre-Employment Tests: Reducing Persons to Specs

In addition to the prominent role of staffing agencies, a second major institutional difference between Israel and the United States is Israel's pre-employment testing industry. While pre-employment tests are unusual for American white-collar job applicants, most large Israeli employers have begun using them in recent years to screen new applicants.[33] In most cases, job seekers who make it through the initial filtering by the staffing agencies are then sent for daylong tests as a second screening mechanism. Of the forty-eight Israeli job seekers whom I interviewed, forty-four reported taking such tests. Of the four who did not take such tests, three had only applied to small companies, and one, an experienced marketing manager, refused on principle to subject herself to the "humiliation of the tests."

Israeli testing institutes use the dominant objective specs discourse to claim that their services enable employers to find the "best" employees, from bank tellers to executives. Their methods are purportedly based on research and are claimed to have proven predictive value for success in different jobs. As one testing company claims: "Using these testing tools substantially improves the quality of the hiring decision and the cost of using these tools is negligible in comparison to the great utility that they bring."[34]

As Yael, the staffing agency screener, explained: "The employers I work with, almost all of them, want [the tests] for secretaries and engineers and everyone in between." She believes that the widespread use of these tests is because they provide cover for hiring managers. If a new hire does not work out, "the manager can say, 'Look, the psychologists did it.'" Another staffing agency manager offered a similar explanation: "There are very few jobs today that don't require [a test]. One reason is to give cover for a manager's bad hiring decisions."[35]

A manager at a high-tech company gave a more substantive defense of the practice:

> The tests look for sharpness and intelligence under the pressure of time. We don't want someone who is slow ... slow thinking is a big problem. Also, we care that the person be social. We emphasize team work. We look to see if they will help. We want someone who works well with others. It's not good if he takes over too much. We also look for how they can deal with routine work, how loyal they are to the organization, how they can deal with frustration.

Whereas the initial filtering by the staffing agencies rigidly focuses on hard skills and credentials, the tests focus on psychological and personality-oriented soft skills. The tests are conducted by private testing institutes.

As with the use of staffing agencies, the Israeli state has led the way in the routine use of pre-employment tests. In fact, unlike private companies, which typically use the test as a secondary filter after the initial staffing agency screening, the state often tests job seekers as the first step in the hiring process.[36]

A typical day of testing lasts between five and nine hours and usually includes several segments. The most straightforward segments examine writing, math, logic, and English-language skills. Depending on the job, there may also be a test of spatial skills using geometric figures. However, the bulk of the test typically focuses on soft skills such as decisiveness, creativity, stick-to-itiveness, leadership qualities, communication skills, and the ability to cooperate. These qualities are evaluated by putting candidates into small groups and observing the "group dynamics." The group of applicants is usually given a collective mission, and a psychologist observes and numerically rates each applicant's performance. For example, Hadas, a job seeker in her early thirties, reported: "The group was told, 'You have five things you need to get done. Prioritize these as a group.'" Another job seeker, Ronen, was part of a group of job seekers being tested who were told: "You are on a ship in the middle of the ocean. In a few seconds, you need to leave the ship for an island. What are the first things that you would take with you?" After hearing the question, the group engages in an open discussion where members try to persuade each other of the cause of action. In some cases, the testing proceeds in the style of American reality television shows with elimination rounds. After each exercise, Hadas explained, the psychologist "passed out notes which told [applicants] whether they should leave or stay. Then the smaller group continued with another role-playing exercise." Hadas believes that these "humiliating elimination rounds" are used because "some employers want to save money and not pay for a full day of testing for all the candidates."

In some cases, applicants for the same position are made to compete directly. Nurit, for example, was in a group-dynamics test with other candidates for the same bank job: "They gave us each a piece of paper and said here is a list of people that you interviewed and you need to decide who to hire. One is sixty years old. One is just back from a yearlong trip. You need to decide as a group. It's like putting lions in a cage and watching them fight."

Soft skills, such as the applicant's trustworthiness, may even be tested during what appears to be the hard-skills part of the test. For example, the English-language section may ask applicants to circle words they know on a vocabulary list. Applicants are naturally tempted to circle more words than they actually know, but later on they are asked to write a story using all the words they had circled. Other components of the test aim to decipher an applicant's personality. In these segments, applicants are shown a picture and asked to write a short story about it. There are also interviews with psychologists who may ask a series of fill-in-the-blank questions such as: "I always dreamed of ____" or "Grunt work is ____." Other segments of the test are more like therapy sessions, with probing questions about the candidate's childhood and relationship with his or her mother. Omer, who is looking for work as a social worker, was questioned by a psychologist for six hours:

> They showed me a picture of a woman crying and asked, "Why is she crying?" They asked me about my relationship with my parents, my wife, and two hours of questions just about me.

Ronen, looking for work as a manager, was asked: "When you see someone suffering, do you run to help them?" Finally, as a part of some tests, job seekers are asked to provide a handwriting sample to be sent to purported experts in graphological analysis of personalities.[37]

After the test is complete, a psychologist summarizes and quantifies the data and writes a report with a "hire or no hire" recommendation to the employer. Thus, while the tests delve into very personal and subjective territories, the end product is a numerical scorecard where various soft skills are objectified; reduced to another list of specs that can be considered by the employer alongside other skills and credentials. By contrast to the irreducible, intersubjective quality of chemistry in the American case, the Israeli job seeker's personality is taken to be something that can be both known and quantified, and therefore can be discussed using the dominant Israeli discourse of objective meritocracy.

Personality tests are used in both Israel and the United States to delve into the job seeker's "inner" self. In the American case, as discussed in chapter 2, the tests are marketed by the self-help industry to job seekers as a tool for self-knowledge and to gain an edge in the chemistry game. In Israel the tests are marketed by a testing industry to employers as a tool with which employers can objectively compare job seekers' soft-skills specs.

For Israeli job seekers, the tests create a second layer of rigid filtering unlike any in the American context. Moreover, they have the unintended consequence of generating further rigidities upstream, in the first layer of already rigid filtering by staffing agencies. Since the tests are expensive and paid for by employers, an employer will not be happy with a staffing agency that consistently recommends applicants to be tested who do not perform well. The screeners, therefore, must focus on the particular skills that are believed to be necessary to do well on the test. As Galia, a screener, explained: "I filter résumés with a thought ahead about who will pass the tests." For example, thinking ahead about tests seems to weed out idiosyncratic personalities who might not do well in the group-dynamics segment of the test. It also exacerbates the practice of filtering by age. Galia said:

> This is not politically correct, but age is definitely an issue. I always try to figure out how old they are. . . . For a regular programmer, above forty is problematic. It's very cruel. I am not for it. But it's a force of reality. In the tests, those who are older have a hard time. It's all about quick thinking, so those above forty fail. The tests push me toward younger people.

If the staffing agencies constitute the front line of the job market, the testing institutes are the secondary reinforcement. The use of these filtering practices creates a very different institutional terrain and job-search experience from that encountered by American job seekers. In the United States, the chemistry filter is the most salient element of the hiring process for American job seekers because interviews with managers are typically their only direct personal contact with the hiring process; and the importance of the chemistry filter is greatly magnified by the self-help industry. By contrast, the staffing agencies and testing institutes constitute the front lines and major points of contact of Israeli job seekers with the labor market. In most cases, job applicants must successfully navigate both of these filters to actually meet a hiring manager for an interview. Thus, for Israeli job seekers, these institutions and their rigid filters are the most salient elements of the hiring process.

IsraSupport and Specs Game Strategies

Job-search strategies proliferate in the spaces where labor-market institutions grant job seekers some degree of discretion and control. In the chemistry game, with its emphasis on interpersonal connection, the space of individual control lies in the job seeker's self-presentation. In the specs game, the rigid filtering mechanisms of the staffing agencies and testing institutes render self-presentation strategies peripheral. Instead, it is the scope and breadth of one's applications that are central.

While the Israeli state provides no support organizations equivalent to AmeriSupport, the nonprofit sector does. Job-search support groups, though not as prevalent in Israel as they are in the United States, provide a revealing site for the explicit articulation of the inner workings of the specs game. It is here that tacit understandings are most openly discussed, and the black box of job-search strategizing is opened to view.

The data presented in this section were primarily gathered though participant-observations at a nonprofit organization aiming to support white-collar job seekers, which I will call "IsraSupport." I became a member of IsraSupport and fully participated in all of its activities for three months. I also conducted in-depth interviews with IsraSupport members.

IsraSupport is located in a well-known bohemian neighborhood of southern Tel Aviv; yoga classes and various self-help workshops are held in the same place as the IsraSupport meetings. This setting conveys the sense that IsraSupport is offering something on the "cutting edge." The group is financed by modest member dues and has roughly equal numbers of men and women. Members are all college-educated and are overwhelmingly Ashkenazi (European-ancestry) Israelis. Most are searching for work in fields such as engineering or management.

As at AmeriSupport, job-searching activities at IsraSupport are characterized as a form of work. IsraSupport counselors repeatedly remind job seekers: "Finding work is work in and of itself. You should look at yourself as a worker. This is your occupation." As in the United States, the work discourse reflects the idea that finding a job requires active engagement in tasks that demand effort and skill. In both sites, job-search support organizations attempt to rationalize the process by breaking it down into discrete tasks and encouraging job seekers to create goals and plans of action to achieve these tasks. Referring to the job search as work also reflects the seriousness with which job seekers in both countries are encouraged to approach it and the underlying fact that, in both cases, the financial and social stakes of finding a job are indeed extremely high.

Although both sites rationalize the search process, the search discourses and strategies are very different. While the American support discourse emphasizes a job seeker's individual control over the outcome, the Israeli support discourse uses probabilistic language, with strategies described as means to increase one's chances. Unlike the American self-help notion that "you create your own reality," the probabilistic discourse emphasizes the highly competitive nature of the job market, while also encouraging job seekers to think strategically about their position in that market. One IsraSupport counselor, for example, gave a group of new job seekers the following sober assessment:

> It is hard to find work. In some fields there is no work at all. In those fields where there is work, there are lots of people jumping on each position. There is intense competition and the chances for any particular position are slight. For every opening, there are hundreds of competitors, and the chances for getting a job interview are very small. But chances do exist, and you can increase your chances by being strategic.

IsraSupport's first strategic postulate is the need to rationally plan the search. Whereas AmeriSupport's rationalist component focuses most on time management, IsraSupport's focuses on methodical action to exhaust all potential opportunities. While a given job seeker's specs—set of skills and experience—is fixed at any given point in time, the demand for it is understood as dynamic. Demand can arise anywhere at any time. Correspondingly, an important strategy is to maximize the number of openings that a job seeker is able to find out about and rapidly respond to. In a game where so many competitors are perceived to have comparable skills and experiences, a speedy response can make all the difference.

The strategic discourse on the importance of locating and responding to all plausible job postings is ubiquitous. The Israeli state's own brochure, given to all job seekers, opens with this bold declaration: "Pay attention! Employment ads are spread out in different parts of the newspaper. You should look at all parts of the newspaper and use several newspapers, including local newspapers!" While the idea of enlarging the pool of potential employers is straightforward, implementing it is not. According to an IsraSupport counselor, next to the obstacle posed by the labor market itself, the next most important obstacle to finding work is not knowing how to find all the ads. He explained:

> It is a sphere where, unlike the job market, job seekers do have some control. It is not easy. You need to devote a lot of work to this. But there is no doubt that, for all job seekers, methodically and systematically finding all available wanted ads is *the most important thing*. (emphasis added)

One private Internet company has capitalized on Israeli job seekers' anxiety over missing relevant job postings by selling an aggregating service called Alljobs, which promises to bring all the job ads together on one website. Alljobs' marketing campaign claims that "there are today in Israel 1,800 different sources where jobs are posted. It is important to know that when you are looking at the 'traditional' sources (other major websites), that these only include half the jobs." Alljobs' motto is: "Check all the options in the market." Because this service is considered essential, a common expense of job searching in Israel is the hefty thirty dollars a month subscription fee, which is paid even by job seekers in financial distress. Yet despite the popularity of Alljobs, most of the Israeli job seekers I interviewed reported that in their view it aggregated only about 80 percent of the jobs. The remaining 20 percent are widely considered *the* most valuable to locate precisely because, falling below Alljobs' radar, they are likely to attract less competition.

Israeli job-searching strategies, which arise in the context of the specs game, are thus very different from American job-searching strategies. Applying to as many jobs as possible, central to Israeli job searching, is peripheral in the chemistry game, where it is derided as ineffective because it does not allow the job seeker to *personalize* his or her appeal. American job seekers do not spend their money on aggregator services such as Alljobs but on private "self-presentation" coaches.

In addition to trying to locate all the jobs posted in their field, Israelis rationalize their job searches by trying to strategically expand the range of targeted jobs. This requires identifying jobs that are in the so-called gray area, where the job seeker has some, but not all, of the required skills and experiences and where there is less competition. At IsraSupport, peers brainstorm about how broadly to apply, taking into account market conditions for a particular set of skills and experiences. The less demand for your skills, the more you need to broaden the scope of your search. The oft-cited Israeli rule of thumb is that if you cannot send out several résumés per day, you need to broaden the categories of jobs you are applying for. But this broadening is constrained by the rigid filters of the specs game. As an IsraSupport counselor explained: "You need to be a professional, someone who has experience and knowledge in the field. So if you don't have experience, it's almost impossible to break in. You can't start with no experience."

For many Israeli job seekers, identifying *which kinds* of jobs to pursue outside their immediate field becomes an important area of strategizing.

One of the core activities of IsraSupport is having members take turns making extended oral presentations to their peers about the jobs they are targeting. The presentation and the discussion that follows is called a SWOT analysis, an English acronym that stands for strengths (internal), weaknesses (internal), opportunities (external), and threats (external). It is an analytical exercise imported from the business world to the context of job searching. Unlike the American self-help model, which encourages job seekers to look inward to their passions and to remain doggedly positive, the Israeli practice of SWOT asks job seekers to reflect on both their weaknesses and their strengths and—in even greater contrast to the self-help approach—to give equal weight to structural obstacles. One of Isra-Support's trainers explained that SWOT is "a technique" where we "map ourselves, look at the internal and external, the positive and negative … create a new perspective, and learn to accept weaknesses." SWOT provides a systematic way to examine external barriers, such as a flooded market, and to consider alternatives directions. IsraSupport counselor Lev explained the hoped-for outcome of the analysis: "With the strengths, we can deal with the weaknesses. With the opportunities, we can deal with the threats." Eytan, another IsraSupport counselor, said that the "ultimate goal [of SWOT] is to walk out of the session with a concrete plan, which requires self-knowledge."

Amos, a forty-two-year-old former hotel manager, was looking for work in the hotel industry but was also developing a backup plan to start his own business. He gave a presentation to his IsraSupport colleagues about his plan to provide relationship workshops to couples and drew a two-by-two table on the board to organize his thoughts on each element of SWOT. The other members offered feedback about the strengths and weaknesses of his plan. In fact, IsraSupport members are *required* to give feedback, both positive and negative; they are encouraged to start with a positive comment but are expected to continue with constructive critical feedback. Typical feedback therefore begins with a ritual phrase, such as "very interesting," followed by difficult questions about the plan's market viability. Amos was bombarded with tough questions such as "What's new here in what you are providing?" and "What other workshops exist and how do you distinguish yourself from others?" The group consensus was that Amos's ideas lacked focus and did not adequately deal with the threat of the market being flooded with similar offerings. After brainstorming on this issue, Amos decided to tailor his workshop to couples over the age of forty-five who want to "spice up" their relationship. This outcome was typical in that most SWOTs ultimately focus on how job seekers can better distinguish themselves from their competition.[38] Such analysis is at odds with the dominant American self-help emphasis on one's inner passions and deemphasizing of the external market.

The chemistry and specs games differ not only in their strategic foci but also in their ways of helping job seekers stick to the search. While AmeriSupport's focus is on inspiring job seekers with a sense of control over their search and with admonitions to follow their passions, IsraSupport emphasizes the importance of overcoming any tendency toward procrastination and making a firm commitment to action. The belief in the benefits of continuously remaining in action is one of the core animating principles of IsraSupport. Lev, a facilitator, repeatedly told the group that "the way to deal with fear is action." Nadav, another facilitator, laid out IsraSupport's philosophy in a kind of pep talk at the start of a meeting on how to keep oneself going in the search:

> It stems from organizing yourself and giving your all to the search. The real problem is staying optimistic and the key is the doing, the action. People start to lose all hope, start thinking of leaving the country. But you need to wage a war. You need to be like a wheel that is in motion and keeps going from inertia. Don't stop the wheel. You are not discouraged. A discouraged person does not fight. You are fighting. It is hard, but hard does not mean discouraged. Just keep going. Nothing matters as long as you are going.

The key to keeping oneself in motion is methodical action or, as Nadav calls it, "systematicity." In a private interview, he elaborated:

> It is hard to find work. But when you believe in the system, if it is a good system, you will win the game. The system is the essence. People are looking for something to hang on to, and the system is something that gives people something to do. Just having a system, any system, is what helps.

Whereas at AmeriSupport members are expected to be excited about their job search because it is rooted in a passionate commitment, in the Israeli case looking for work is assumed to be dreadful and therefore to require discipline. Action is not meant to be inspired by internal drive but by disciplined practices. For example, at the end of each IsraSupport meeting, facilitators tape up sheets of paper on which each member writes his or her goals for the following week. Each member then describes what actions he or she took on last week's goals and talks about the new goals. Eytan, one of the facilitators, explained that these should be "tangible goals that can be measured. Ideally, things that we can put a deadline on. Schedule when you'll do it. Commit. Overcome the hesitation and write down goals." Lev, another facilitator, elaborated: "Think of when to do the goals. Life can get in the way of goals. We want to create responsibility."

At one meeting, Geula, a job seeker, was the first to go. Her goal the previous week had been to "create a business plan":

GEULA: I didn't create a business plan. I am not ready for it.

LEV (FACILITATOR): Just do it. Take eight hours and do it. The doing is what matters.

IRIT (MEMBER): You will not have to start from nothing when you go do it next time.

EYTAN (FACILITATOR): With a car, the biggest output of energy is to start it. Then it flows.

GEULA: Okay. I will do it for next week.

Alex was next. He wrote on his poster that he would contact a manager at an industrial firm "as soon as I get the contact information." Lev challenged him:

> This kind of goal puts the responsibility on someone else. What will you do to get the contact information? Not wait. *Goals can't be dependent on others' actions.* When you have a difficulty facing you, you have to do something. No one can walk for you. Take action and take it seriously. It's your only life.

Each person's plan was analyzed with similar rigor. If a task was to be done, it should be scheduled for a particular day. If it had not been done by the following week, the job seeker would be asked, in front of everyone, "How do you explain not doing it?"[39]

In addition to rational planning and discipline, another focus of IsraSupport is practicing one's oral presentation for job interviews. Self-presentation is not central to Israeli job searching, but it is addressed as a secondary concern. The state unemployment agency brochure provides rudimentary advice such as not to "cut off the interviewer in the middle of a sentence" (which apparently is all too common in Israel) and to "put your cell phone in your bag, not on the interviewer's desk." Practicing oral presentations is the only overlap between the kinds of support offered at IsraSupport and at AmeriSupport. At IsraSupport, however, the focus is on practicing *concise* and *clear* oral sound bites. Each member articulates a summary of his her skills and experience within a two-minute time limit strictly enforced with an oversize hourglass in the middle of the room. The feedback tends to address the need to be concise. Eytan, the facilitator, emphasized: "Stick to the clock. Imagine you are standing in front of someone and have couple of minutes to communicate." Lev likewise explained: "In life you have time limits. People give only a certain amount of attention." Unlike the American focus on projecting enthusiasm and making a "connection," the goal here is to precisely convey one's professional capacities. After the presentations, members are asked to write down what they remember from each other's pitches. If people do not remember much about your pitch, then it was not clear.

The focus on clarity and conciseness is rooted in Israeli labor-market institutions and their filtering practices and in the corresponding set of discourses about what it takes to establish fit between the candidate and the job. Unlike the chemistry game, in which fit is either purely interpersonal or between the candidate and the distinct corporate culture that every company is assumed to have, establishing fit in the specs game is a matter of one's ability to perform the required role. Israeli companies are not deemed to have unique cultures, but are viewed more generically as organizations that do a specific type of work. In preparing for interviews, Israeli job seekers at IsraSupport encouraged each other to learn about the typical expectations and demands of the given kind of job, but not of the particular company's culture. As an IsraSupport counselor explained:

> Think of the ideal candidate profile and think of how to match it with your experience. Then try to get the interviewer to tell you what they are looking for. This requires doing research about the company and the industry. The secret is that for each job there is a profile. You need to figure out the puzzle of the perfect profile.

Whereas fit in the chemistry game hinges on a perceived connection, fit in the specs game hinges on perceived capacities.

Pulling Strings: The Old Paradigm Lingers

Israel's specs discourse, with its focus on modernity and meritocracy, is often articulated and clarified through a comparison to a caricature of the purportedly old paradigm of using contacts to "pull strings." The use of contacts is typically depicted as a throwback to a corrupt pre-meritocratic era. *Protectzia*, the Hebrew word for using connections, comes from the Russian word meaning protection—that is, protection from the rigid hiring system, and implies getting something because of who you know and not because of your merit. It is diametrically opposed to the dominant discourse in which success depends solely on objective factors—and emphatically *not* on personal, non-professional, factors.

Despite the stigma associated with *protectzia*, personal connections continue to play an important role. Colleagues at IsraSupport remind each other that, in addition to engaging in their standard job-searching activities, they should, in the words of one job seeker, "remember to also use the 'grandma' method, the old way of using contacts and *protectzia*." This is viewed by many job seekers as a necessary evil. It is widely assumed that having the right personal connection inside a company can pierce any barrier to employment, including the rigid obstacles posed by staffing agencies and testing institutes. In fact, most job seekers I interviewed believe that getting a rare "good" job, one with good benefits and some security, typically requires personal contacts. The *protectzia* discourse thus survives as a secondary way to talk about and understand finding work, much as in chapter 2 we saw that American job seeking has a secondary non-dominant discourse emanating from temp agencies.

On the surface, the Israeli *protectzia* discourse seems to resemble the American emphasis on networking. Yet the gulf between the chemistry and specs games becomes clear when we examine the Israeli understanding of how and why personal contacts are effective. In Israel the use of personal contacts is understood as a *corruption* of the merit-based employment system through favoritism, an open violation of the exchange of objective skills for money. For example, Gil told me that a city government job for which he had applied had been given to the mayor's son, who had no relevant background. Finishing the story, he exclaimed, "That's Israel." This common refrain is used to emphasize the supposedly banana-republic character of Israel, often with the addition that such practices would "never fly in orderly countries" such as the United States. Israelis typically imagine that the specs game is in fact the *American model*, which represents progress and modernity.

This understanding of using personal connections as a corruption of the hiring process stands in sharp contrast to the understanding of networking in the chemistry game, which is not seen as corrupt at all, but rather as an *efficient* way to convey one's fit. Because, as the American saying goes, "birds of a feather flock together," using personal intermediaries is understood in the United States as a legitimate way to communicate one's possession of the desired intangible qualities that indicate good fit. In the chemistry game, networking is simply a more direct way of communicating the intangibles that American job seekers already attempt to communicate in their résumés and cover letters.

As discussed in chapter 2, an important element of job searching in the United States is the attempt to create *new* contacts, which one can do with the right elevator speech at networking events or through effective use of Internet social networking sites. When I asked Israeli job seekers about the American strategy of developing new contacts at professional conferences and elsewhere, I was met with bewildered looks. Audrey, a young lawyer, asked: "Why would they refer me if they don't really know me? I would not refer someone that I don't know." For contacts to help you, another job seeker explained, "requires some kind of mutual obligation, something from the past."

Within the specs game, the use of personal contacts to obtain a referral can only be seen as a personal favor because the intermediary is asking the employer to make an exception to the usual hiring process. For the intermediary to take such action would necessitate using some of his or her political capital at the workplace, and therefore any such action is presumed to require a past history of mutual and reciprocal help. By contrast, in the chemistry game, the person acting as the intermediary can assume the role of a matchmaker who is helping to bring together two suitable parties for their mutual benefit. Since networking is treated in the chemistry game as a legitimate and efficient practice, which potentially benefits all parties, there is far less cost to acting as an intermediary, while the potential benefit is a returned favor in the future.

The above differences between the specs and chemistry games mean that networking—the core American white-collar job-search strategy of trying to meet expand their network to obtain a referral—is ineffective in Israel. One clearly observable manifestation of this difference is that "networking events," which are ubiquitous in the United States, do not exist in Israel. With the exception of job seekers who had spent some time in the United States, Israeli job seekers had difficulties understanding what I was actually talking about when I asked about such events. Jamie, who had looked for work in both the United States and Israel, explained: "In the U.S., networking is a lot more professional and orderly; you go to networking events. In Israel, there's no formal networking. In Israel it's seen as a friend thing, and there are no networking events or structures of any sort." Liat, an Israeli looking for work in Boston as a radio producer, likewise noted that "in Israel I never heard of an event where people go and introduce themselves. . . . In Israel networking happens if my friend hears of a job opening and they pass along my résumé. There is no physical meeting. There are no gatherings."

Another indication of the difference in networking practices is that by contrast to the rapid rise in the use of online social networking among job seekers in the United States to reconnect with old contacts and connect with their contacts' contacts, Israeli job seekers generally do not use online social networks as part of their job search.[40] Job seekers who are familiar with how social networking sites like LinkedIn are used in the United States and Israel were best positioned to explain the difference. As Masha, an Israeli looking for work in Boston, put it: "Israelis use LinkedIn, but not like they do in the United States. They might use it for more social purposes, like to talk to friends. I think it's more for communication."

Nirit, an Israeli job seeker, explained that for job searching in Israel: "Internet social networks are not highly useful. Networking is done in other ways." The "other ways" predominantly refers to asking for help from your family and close friends. As Ronny said: "I can tell you, I'm getting a lot of e-mails for networking, and it's not because I'm on LinkedIn, but because I served in a certain unit in the army." Friends from the "army days," referring to the period of mandatory military service that most Israelis go through in their late teens and early twenties, are the most often mentioned group of relevant connections. Using your army connections, or other close personal ties, is sometimes referred to as taking "vitamin P" with the *P* standing for *protectzia*. As Michal put it, "You take vitamin P when you look for work where your cousin works or in the business your old army commander now runs." But without strong preexisting ties, contacts will not help. As Eldad told me: "Personal connections are important, and if they are your friends, they will hire you regardless of skills. But if they don't know you, forget it."

The obstacles to expanding one's network for job-searching purposes could also be seen at IsraSupport. During the period of my participant-observations at IsraSupport, Eytan and Lev, facilitators at IsraSupport who had been reading about job searching in the United States, decided to encourage members to provide a list of their personal contacts for other members to use. But this idea generated resistance. At one meeting, Eytan handed out sheets for members to fill out with their list of contacts, including their workplace and the nature of the connection. He explained: "We are creating a list of contacts from members in a database. We see this as an important tool. There may be people here under our noses with contacts that can be really useful." Yet most members were reluctant to share contacts this way. Ruti claimed that she had "nothing to add to the list," which sparked the following dialogue:

LEV (FACILITATOR): Where does your husband work?
RUTI: No. What does my husband have to do with this? He can't talk to anyone. Do you know what he went through to get his work? Seven levels of hell!

Under the facilitators' pressure, a few contacts were reluctantly provided, and Eytan asked the group to use them. The following week, he asked: "Has anyone used the list since last week?" No one had. The attempt to spread connections in this way had failed. IsraSupport members remained firm in their assumption that for an insider to "pull strings" on behalf of a job seeker, to expend capital within his or her organization, there had to be a preexisting long-term relationship of reciprocal exchanges.

Institutions, Neoliberalism, and Culture

This chapter described the emergence of Israel's dominant labor-market institutions, which underlie the specs game, as part of a broader shift to a neoliberal political economy. Such a shift is generally marked by a decline in the power of labor unions, a rise in the power of private firms, and a retreat of the state. Specifically, in the case of labor markets, a move toward a more neoliberal political economy typically goes hand in hand with increased employer power and flexibility to dictate the terms and duration of employment. This broad shift is evident both in the United States, as described in chapter 1, and in Israel, as described in this chapter. However, a comparison of the two reveals that the shift in the political-economic balance of power does not necessarily go hand in hand with any particular set of labor-market institutions. As this chapter shows, the neoliberal-era institutions that developed in Israel for the white-collar labor market are markedly different from those described in chapter 2 for the American case. Israel's labor-market institutions—specifically the powerful staffing agencies and pre-employment testing institutes—are no more inevitable outcomes of the shift to a neoliberal political economy than the American self-help industry or American hiring practices. In each site, labor-market institutions and practices are a product of the interaction between the shift to neoliberalism, on the one hand, and the historical configuration of institutions that preceded this shift, on the other. The historical legacies of the preceding relations between workers, employers, and the state delimit the kinds of problems that newly empowered actors attempt to solve through institutional reforms or the construction of new labor-market institutions.

Just as specific labor-market institutions are not merely the inevitable products of neoliberalism, neither are they merely reflections of wider cultures. As discussed in chapter 2 with respect to the American self-help model, Israeli labor-market institutions draw on a subset of the available cultural schemas or "tools."[41] As described in this chapter, the forces propelling the rise of institutions like staffing agencies are political-economic in nature and not cultural. Israeli labor-market institutions do draw on specific subset of Israeli discourses of modernization, meritocracy, and the efficiency of market economies, which are essential for their legitimacy. Yet these institutions are in striking tension with hallmark elements of Israel's culture—its interpersonal casualness and directness. Israelis generally take great pride in this interaction style, which purportedly establishes an authentic and immediate connection without the barriers of politeness. *New York Times* columnist David Brooks (2009) describes it a "reticence-free" culture.[42] American interpersonal dealings are typically perceived by Israelis as distant, overly polite, and exasperatingly stiff. However, as the discussions of the workings of staffing agencies and testing institutes in this chapter show, Israeli labor-market institutions are highly formal and impersonal. It is hard, in fact, to imagine anything more at odds with the blunt and casual Israeli style of interaction than the rigid screening interviews performed by staffing agencies. Thus, any argument that seeks to reduce the origins of labor-market institutions to culture would encounter the paradox that Israel's culture of informal interpersonal bluntness and free-flowing expression is coupled with rigid labor-market institutions that depersonalize the job-search process,[43] while the individualistic American culture, with its comparatively distant interpersonal relations, is coupled with labor-market institutions that emphasize interpersonal chemistry.

While this chapter explored the institutions, discourses, and strategies that make up the specs game, the next chapter will delve into the day-to-day practices and experiences of Israeli job seekers. It will illustrate how the playing of the specs game gives rise to a distinct unemployment experience and to a subjective understanding among Israeli job seekers of their difficulties in finding work that turns American self-blame on its head: instead of self-blame, we will find system-blame.

CHAPTER FIVE

The Specs Game Experience and System-Blame

While unemployed American white-collar job seekers end up feeling internally flawed, their Israeli counterparts end up feeling objectified, dehumanized, and betrayed by a flawed system. In-depth interviews with Israeli job seekers—whether engineers, managers, or administrative assistants—revealed a consistent and intense set of emotional responses to being unemployed: feelings of arbitrary exclusion, invisibility, anger, and not knowing what to do. Eldad captured the essence of what many other Israeli job seekers conveyed:

> The system here does not look at you as an individual. You are just a collection of buzzwords. They don't care who the person is, only that you know X, Y, and Z. They don't look you in the eye to see who you are.

Different unemployment experiences are the consequences of different job-search games. While Israeli and American job seekers may appear to be engaged in similar job-search practices, such as creating and sending résumés in response to job postings and interviewing with prospective employers, the apparent similarities vanish upon closer inspection. Job-search practices that are generally assumed to be universal, such as writing résumés and interviewing, take on different meanings and forms within the context of different games.

This chapter will explore the practices and experiences of job searching in the context of the specs game. My analysis of the specs game will highlight important—though previously overlooked—ways in which the practices and experiences of job searching can vary. For example, job-searching experiences can vary systemically in the extent to which job seekers perceive that their actions affect the ultimate outcome; that is, job-search games can have different levels of player prominence. While the chemistry game is characterized by high player prominence, with job seekers' perceiving their actions to be highly determinative of the search outcome, the specs game is characterized by low player prominence. For Israeli job seekers, finding a job seems largely determined by external factors and not by their own strategic actions. Moreover, different job-searching games may require different forms of emotional labor. Whereas the chemistry game demands self-subjectification—the projection of a passionate and connecting self—the specs game requires self-objectification, the projection of a professionalized self who can suppress and compartmentalize his or her private self. Ultimately, it is the combination of these characteristics of the specs game that lie behind the Israeli unemployment experience.

Determined Browsing and Self-Objectification

Most Israeli job seekers, like their American counterparts, begin optimistically. In both countries, job seekers typically report that their most recent jobs were in some respects unfulfilling and that the job search presents an opportunity to find a better job. Nevertheless, the specs game gets off to a slower start, with a lower level of absorption and a greater sense of tedium. While the initial stages of the chemistry game, as described in chapter 3, involve an engaging, and at times even inspiring, process of internal discovery and projection of one's passions, the specs game begins with an external focus on the competitive nature of the labor market and the constraints it imposes on the job seeker.

While hopeful that there will be a happy ending, Israeli job seekers talk of gearing themselves up for a long and tough process. They know they are playing a game that may require many rounds to win, a view reflected in the probabilistic discourse discussed in chapter 4. Gil, a high-tech engineer, said that when he was first laid off, "I told myself it will take at least three months. So three months I am not going to count as anything because there are so few jobs."

The day-to-day experiences of the search are generated by putting into practice the specs game strategies. Chapter 4 described the strategic importance of methodically locating all possible job postings. This strategy translates to a very particular search process, with significant attention and energy devoted to developing systems for finding postings dispersed in dozens or, for some occupations, hundreds of websites. By contrast to American job seekers who typically approach browsing job boards in an ad hoc manner, often referring to their "favorite websites" without clear rationales for their choice of one job board over another, Israeli job seekers give attention not only to finding all relevant job boards, but also to the far more complicated task of determining the optimal search method for each. This requires identifying the keywords that pull up the most relevant postings. Different sites require different combinations of keywords depending on their method of classification. Israeli job seekers often experiment with different keyword combinations, using various ways to classify their prior work experiences, and attempt to set up a master list of relevant sites and site-specific search methods. The most disciplined job seekers have a scheduled routine for going through the master list in a manner that takes into account the frequency with which the sites update their postings. For example, Oron's work week was spent methodically going through 160 job boards and individual company websites that he had bookmarked. He explained: "I prioritize [the order], and once or twice a week I start at the top." Another Israeli job seeker started his search process by obtaining a database of all 3,500 high-tech companies in Israel; over the next several weeks, he systematically faxed his résumé to each one.

The rote nature of this kind of search work requires Israeli job seekers, even more than their American counterparts, to impose strict work schedules on themselves. For example, Noa, a thirty-three-year-old graphic designer, reported that she did not allow herself to have any "fun" on the computer, whether surfing the Internet or going into any chat rooms, before first completing her six-hour scheduled routine of searching through all relevant job boards. Shoshana, formerly an administrative assistant to a CEO, was likewise strict about spending her daytime hours on nothing but the job search. She had self-imposed rigid rules about what she was allowed to do during the day, explaining: "I am not allowed to have fun or even do non-work things because everyone else is working. I do everything, like grocery shopping, after five p.m. During the workday, even if I am just sitting immobilized, I will not go out for a walk, which I normally love to do."

Some job seekers attempt to spice up their dull search routines. Gabi, a forty-nine-year-old former manager, focused on finding "hidden job postings," which transformed his rote search into a bit of a treasure hunt. He spent much of his time "going into company websites to try to guess which companies will be hiring *before* they advertise," working from clues such as postings about a planned expansion or the landing of a new contract. If it appeared that a company was about to hire, he would apply before the position was advertised. Once it had been advertised, he explained, "yours is one among a huge pile of résumés and it is hard to differentiate yourself." But while such treasure hunts have their moments of excitement, Israeli job searching is for the most part highly routinized and requires methodical work.

The construction of résumés, a universal and seemingly unremarkable practice, reveals some of the essential differences between the specs and the chemistry games. In the specs game, the construction of a résumé is perceived as a straightforward task. Israeli résumés come in only one format—a reverse-chronological listing of past jobs and functions and of educational credentials. There are no American-style summaries at the top of the résumé and no functional or hybrid résumé formats to choose from. The aesthetics of the résumé, typically of great concern to American job seekers, are a non-issue in Israel. Don, an Israeli who is now looking for work in the United States, expressed surprise upon realizing that in the United States "there is a different mentality in how you approach the search. To look for work [in the United States] requires *working* on the résumé, making sure it will *look* a certain way."

Whereas the significance of résumé construction in the chemistry game is evident from the multiple shelves of books devoted to this topic in any large American bookstore, even the largest bookstore in Tel Aviv does not sell a single book on how to write a résumé. While at least a third of the meetings at AmeriSupport are devoted to the crafting of résumés, job seekers at IsraSupport typically never critique each other's résumés. In the specs game, refinements of style are not perceived as plausible strategic moves that might increase one's chances of getting a job.

The straightforward Israeli résumé can only be understood by situating it within the larger specs game. Israeli labor-market institutions, particularly the staffing agencies focused on objective assessment, are largely blind to aesthetic maneuvers. As Guy, a forty-eight-year-old manager, put it: "It's not like the tablets from Mount Sinai. *It's the product specs.* How the résumé is written does not matter. What matters are the skills. Either you have them or you don't."

Israeli job seekers' résumé-construction practices are explicitly linked to the practices of staffing agencies. Résumés must focus on buzzwords or quick descriptions of skills and experiences that will leap out at the staffing agency screener. As Channan, an engineer, explained, since the screeners at staffing agencies do not know the details of the job or even the specific occupation for which they are screening, "you have to be able to look good on paper, fit the keywords that the employer provided to the [staffing agency], have the external markers." Moreover, unlike the American case where a central focus of résumé construction involves establishing one's fit with the employer, Israeli résumés must focus on generic keywords. This difference is also directly tied to the staffing agencies and the fact that their screeners are external to the hiring company. Guy explained that beyond the checklist of skills and credentials, "screeners usually know nothing about the employer and the possible fit between you and the employer. . . . You cannot attempt to match yourself to the employer."

The Israeli résumé is both straightforward and a straitjacket. Its simple construction emancipates Israeli job seekers from the aesthetic anxieties of the American chemistry game but also constricts their strategic flexibility. They must adhere to the straightforward listing of work history. The feedback or strategic advice on résumés most commonly offered at Isra-Support, whether by counselors or peers, is to make the résumé more professional by depersonalizing it. For example, Israeli résumés should not allude to hobbies or non-work activities. Depersonalization is also achieved by the convention of using the passive voice, which puts the focus on the action and not the person. As one IsraSupport member explained to another, "The subject is the doing and not you." Or as another member explained, "Don't use the first person. Don't say 'directed' but 'responsible for directing.'" This advice is diametrically opposed to that given in the United States, where the cardinal rule of résumé writing is to use active verbs that focus on the job seeker as the acting subject. The rigid format and style requires self-objectification—the submersion of the personal and subjective and the projection of the professional and objective.

The same pattern applies to the construction of cover letters. While cover letters are of central strategic importance in the American chemistry game, where job seekers attempt to project their passion for the work and their fit with the employer, such letters are no more than a formality in the Israeli specs game. One IsraSupport counselor explained: "A cover letter should mention the job you are applying for, [but] the letter has almost no weight." It is generally presumed that employers and their agents are not going to bother with the letter and will go straight to the "facts" in the résumé. One Israeli job seeker familiar with American-style cover letters, put it succinctly: "There are no cover letters in Israel." In unusual cases where an Israeli job seeker does write a substantive cover letter, it focuses on explaining the relevance of his or her skills and experiences. Unlike the chemistry game, where each employer is deemed to have a unique culture and job seekers typically spend long hours researching so as to articulate their fit with this culture, in the specs game, employers are not deemed to have individual cultures, only generic needs for certain skills.

As with résumés, Israeli job seekers link the irrelevance of cover letters to the rigid screenings of staffing agencies. As Oren, a thirty-five-year-old engineer, said: "Agencies don't care about letters. They don't even read them. They just want the buzzwords." When I asked Israeli job seekers about the possibility of sending American-style cover letters, they typically felt that even if such a letter would actually be read by the employer, it would seem like an inappropriate insertion of the personal into the professional, and might even be perceived as an attempt to use personal manipulation. For example, when I asked Noa about the American practice of expressing subjective passion for a particular job, she replied: "In Israel, they won't believe you. It will seem like bullshit." Mirit likewise opined: "It would feel strange to put such things [in a cover letter]. It is not professional. It's not because you really want the job that they will hire you."

Israeli job seekers' perspective on cover letters is a product of the specs game. The rigid screening by staffing agencies on the basis of skills, or purported proxies thereof, creates no strategic space for the cover letter. My interviews with agency screeners confirmed the job seekers' view of the unimportance of cover letters. As Galia, a screener, explained:

> The cover letter is not something I read. I will peek at it only if I have a question. To start telling something about yourself, like "I really want to invest myself," is pathetic. We only take people who had good grades at a good university and worked at a good place. The cover letter is where they try to convince you to overlook that. It is a waste of time.

A similar logic applies to thank-you notes. This draining and consuming task for American job seekers has no equivalent in Israel. When I asked about the possibility of sending thank-you notes, my question was met with bewildered looks and a counter-question: "Why would I *thank* them?"

Strategies that flourish in one game are unintelligible in another. The skeletal and impersonal Israeli résumé, the two-sentence cover letter, and the absence of thank-you notes all flow from the logic of the specs game. Similarly, as previously explained in chapter 4, the central job-search strategy in the chemistry game—expanding one's network to obtain referrals— is a non-starter in the specs game context.

Job interviews starkly illustrate the differences between the games. In contrast to American job seekers, who frequently compare interviews to a first date, Israeli job seekers see each interview as an oral test. As we saw in chapter 4, interview preparation in Israel is focused on analyzing the imagined profile of the ideal employee for a given position and attempting to enact this ideal. The specs game renders unimportant the emotional labor of producing passion and connection, which is *the* central element of a job interview in the chemistry game. In fact, as with cover letters, American strategies to make a personal connection might backfire in Israel. Israeli job seekers believe that expressing passion for the job during an interview will be perceived as an attempt to manipulate the interviewer. Yaffa, a thirty-two-year-old technical writer, was advised by her brother, now living in the United States, to say at interviews that this is "the job I most want in my whole life." But in Israel, she explained, to say that "kind of stuff would be a turn-off because no one will believe you." Insertion of the personal—whether in a résumé, cover letter, or interview— undermines the professionalized self that employers (and their front-line screeners and testers) are looking for.

Israeli self-objectification requires projecting a strictly professionalized self while *suppressing* the personal and idiosyncratic. At job interviews, where the American job seeker playing the chemistry game attempts to be connecting, enthusiastic, informal, and chatty, a job seeker playing the specs game tries to appear knowledgeable, respectful, and pleasant.

*   *   *

Self-objectification, the emotional labor associated with the specs game, demands that job seekers project a disciplined and professional worker who is able to submerge his or her private self and fully focus on the needs of the organization. Unlike the emotional labor of self-subjectification in the chemistry game, which requires the deep acting of actually producing the emotion of connection, self-objectification only requires the surface acting of suppressing emotions and displaying the expected role (Hochschild 1983). Self-objectification demands that Israeli job seekers show an ability to subdue and suppress whatever subjective self lies beneath the surface and externally maintain a professional demeanor.

Whereas self-subjectification requires externalizing the self, self-objectification requires hiding the self.

The Specs Game Experience

The distinct experience of job searching in the specs game is rooted in its low player prominence. Israeli job seekers experience a limited and diminishing sense of individual control over the outcome and a growing sense that getting a job largely depends on a host of external factors. Unlike the chemistry game, which emphasizes the critical importance of self-presentation techniques that are understood to be *learnable and perfectible* (and therefore within the job seeker's short-term control), the specs game focuses on one's set of objective skills and credentials, or the proxies thereof, which cannot easily be changed by any immediate action. In chapter 4, for example, we saw how Israeli job seekers perform a SWOT (strengths, weaknesses, opportunities, threats) analysis of their personal strengths and weaknesses in relation to particular types of jobs and to the opportunities and threats in the environment. None of the four elements of a SWOT analysis are subject to short-term manipulation by the job seeker. Rather, they are the given context of the search and delimit the space of strategic maneuverability. As previously shown, the structure of the specs game renders *irrelevant* the most common strategies of the chemistry game, such as crafting a customized cover letter or developing an elevator pitch to expand one's network.

Given the limits of strategic action, upon encountering difficulties in finding work, most Israeli job seekers describe a growing feeling of *choser onim*, a Hebrew phrase that literally means not knowing how to respond to the situation or being at a loss. This is coupled with a feeling that the labor-market institutions they encounter dehumanize them and render them invisible. As quoted at the start of this chapter, Eldad's experience with the Israeli labor market captures this sense of invisibility: "The system here does not look at you as an individual. . . . They don't look you in the eye to see who you are."

Like Eldad, most Israeli job seekers who have difficulty finding work feel they are up against a powerful system that simply does not *see* them and blindly weeds them out according to rigid criteria. The helpless feeling of *choser onim* is generated by the repeated experience of one's determined efforts being thwarted by unyielding filters. Rinat, looking for work as a marketer, described her up-and-down experience:

To see a new job posting is very exciting. To see that you meet the qualifications, it's a rush. When I get interviews, it's the biggest high. The worst moments
come when you wake up and you get dressed nicely, you plan what you will
say at the interview, and you begin to hope, and then you have an experience
where the staffing agency screener is an idiot and she will decide your fate, and
you see others going through the same humiliation. To see *who* is deciding your
future is terrible. At those moments you say, "I will never go to another interview," and you think, "I want to leave the country."

The screeners often bear the brunt of job seekers' frustration because
they are the human face of the "system." The screeners' minimal training and routinized approach to weeding out job seekers not only adds
insult to the injury of rejection, but also strongly reinforces the job seekers' sense that there is nothing they can do. Given the mechanical nature
of screening by checklists, there is no chance of convincing the screener
to take a closer look. It would be, as one job seeker told me, like trying to
request a special order from a cashier at McDonald's. Uri explained: "All
the [staffing agencies] care about is buzzwords that they can check yes or
no. If I could talk to a manager, I could explain and convince, but here I
get filtered out. They want to get me as a *commodity*, like when they buy
a computer with specifications."

The essence of the experience that generates *choser onim* is the fact
that there is no one on the other side to whom you can explain or whom
you can try to convince. This leads job seekers to the conclusion that their
actions have little effect on the outcome. As Hadas explained, she felt
choser onim because "it is not up to you. . . . *Your fate is not in your hands.*"
The specs game simultaneously constricts the job seeker's strategic maneuverability and generates an experience of dehumanization. Whereas
Uri felt like a commodity, Eran felt more like a piece of meat:

> The staffing agencies are a meat market. It's disgusting because, usually in these
> agencies, you get a young twenty-five-year-old screener, not a professional, and
> you need to explain your field to her. They know nothing. It creates the biggest
> humiliation. Staffing agencies are a meat market.

Contributing to the meat-market atmosphere are aggressive questions by
screeners about salary expectations. Whereas in the chemistry game salary is either not brought up at all in the first interview or only toward the
end, in the specs game it is often raised right off the bat and, as Hadas ob-

served, "the answer to this question can rule you out." Ruti, a bookkeeper, discussed her "degrading" experience at an agency: "I was one of twenty girls being interviewed, each for five minutes. It was like a conveyor belt. The only important thing was the salary. How low is she willing to go?"

From the job seeker's perspective, Israeli employers are like someone buying a used car. Of course, s/he wants a car that works, but s/he does not want to overpay, so s/he hires a mechanic (the staffing agencies and testing centers) to examine the car and aggressively bargain for the best deal. This is in diametric opposition to the American employer who is more like a prospective lover looking for passion and connection, seeking to find *the one* with whom he or she will experience ineffable chemistry.

The rigidities of the specs game are particularly glaring to job seekers attempting to change fields. Liora, for example, had worked as a high-level hospital administrator but was now looking for administrative jobs in non-hospital settings because demand for hospital workers had decreased. Despite having the relevant skills, she was repeatedly screened out because the buzzword description of her hospital experience did not fit the generic checklists used at staffing agencies. She explained: "Screeners don't think what I did [at the hospital] is relevant." Rigid filtering likewise poses serious obstacles for job seekers who have relevant skills but lack the desired degree. Daphna, for example, was applying for bookkeeping jobs and had worked for fourteen years as a bookkeeper, but her degree was in geography rather than economics. She explained that, because of having the wrong degree, "I get weeded out automatically at the staffing agencies."

Age discrimination is a significant cause of the sense of *choser onim* for job seekers over forty. As we saw in chapter 4, age discrimination is pervasive and openly acknowledged by screeners. Einat, a thirty-six-year-old job seeker, described this happening even at the state's unemployment office, which occasionally provides job referrals to unemployment insurance recipients:

> The clerk began to tell me that a bank is looking for such-and-such a worker and then interrupted herself saying, "Oh, how old are you? Oh, thirty-six. It is not a fit. They are looking for people thirty-five or younger." The state itself is violating the law!

It is difficult to avoid being screened by age. Even though employers are legally forbidden to ask for this information, it is not only expected but *recommended* that a job seeker list his or her age, marital status, and number of children at the top of his or her résumé; the state's own brochures for job seekers includes that suggestion. At IsraSupport, counselors explained: "It may seem like a good idea not to mention it if you are too old or too young, but hiding this information will become obvious and may ultimately hurt you." Total disclosure is the recommended approach because anything else runs the risk of making you seem "evasive." Thus, even job seekers who know they are likely to be filtered out due to their age feel they are better off including it on their résumé. As Menashe, a forty-six-year-old job seeker, explained, to do otherwise would make it "appear like you are hiding something." Likewise Alex, a fifty-five-year-old job seeker, said: "If you don't put your age on the résumé, it lacks transparency."

While most job seekers assumed that screeners will be even quicker to discard résumés for lack of transparency than for age, some older workers took a different view. Forty-nine-year-old Gabi explained his strategy:

> I don't show my age in my résumé to try to look young. The agencies know the trick and they say that if you don't put your age, the résumé goes straight to the garbage. But I know that if I put my age, it will 100 percent for sure go to the garbage. Without it, maybe it is only 90 percent?

Yet even if Gabi's strategy works, it would seem only to postpone the inevitable. Fifty-year-old Limor discussed her experience of going to interviews at staffing agencies that did not know her age in advance:

> There are always seven or eight others waiting [to be interviewed] there, and I am always the oldest. They ask me, "How old are you?" When I say, "Fifty," they respond, "Okay, we will let you know." I know they won't. They almost never bother to call.... When you are my age and looking for work, they assume something is not right about you, that your brain is screwed up.

Fifty-three-year-old Moti, a high-tech worker, reported how screeners were excited when they saw his work experience, "but when I tell them my age, there is silence, and then they say this work is for younger people." He compared the revealing of his age to "pouring cold water on their enthusiasm. I can see that the whole process gets grounded when they find out my age. There is no chance."[1]

While arbitrary filtering occurs in every hiring system, and surely takes place behind the scenes in the American chemistry game when the applicant pool is whittled down to a few finalists, the institutional features of the specs game render this filtering process more transparent and salient. The experience of routinized screening interviews at staffing agencies provides Israeli job seekers with a direct experience of the rigid filters being used to exclude them from the labor market.

The experience that most intensely generates the feeling of *choser onim*—even more than being filtered by buzzwords and proxies—is the experience of the pre-employment tests. In the American chemistry game, job interviews are typically the most personally exposing and emotionally draining events of the job search; in the Israeli specs game, it is the pre-employment tests that are the most frustrating part of the job search. As one job seeker described it, these are the *"Via Dolorosa* of job seekers." The tests, which are described in chapter 4, epitomize the larger structure of objectification and dehumanization.

Hadas reported that the tests create a feeling that "you are invisible." Or, as Noa put it, "Employers *miss me* through these tests." Oren elaborated:

> No matter what I do . . . no one is really checking *me* out for real. When I go to these tests, I am boiling with anger. The tests are humiliating. These are idiotic situations that are determining your fate. I don't understand. What do they want from me? You feel like you are up against a wall that you can't get over. I just want to work and these feel like obstacles that I can't overcome. . . . It creates a feeling of *choser onim*. You feel like, "What can I do?"

Job seekers are most frustrated by the vagueness of the group-dynamic exercises and personality tests, which reinforce the sense of having no control. As one job seeker explained, "There is no way to prepare yourself for these kinds of tests. Should you be aggressive? Cooperative? You don't know what the company wants." Einav echoed this feeling: "The tests create a sense of no control. How can I know what kind of tree they want me to draw? *Choser onim*." Several Israeli job seekers reported feeling "tortured" by the vagueness of these test questions.

The conventional wisdom among Israeli job seekers is that the soft-skills part of the pre-employment test, which is the bulk of it, is by design impossible to prepare for. Most job seekers can recount many examples of "impossible" questions they have encountered. One recalled being asked, "Do you agree with the following: 'It is hard for me to work with people who do not stick to a schedule.'" He explained that it was impossible to know whether that employer was looking for discipline in sticking to a schedule or flexibility in working with others. Another job seeker recounted being asked this question: "Do you agree or disagree: 'I am ready to take big risks in order to succeed at work.'" The job seeker could not decide whether agreeing with the statement would reflect admirable dedication or a dangerous propensity for risk taking.

Job seekers' understanding that it is impossible to prepare for the tests is reinforced by the testing institutes themselves. For example, the largest testing institute informs job seekers that "you do not need to learn any material for the tests" because "there are no right or wrong answers, but a variety of responses that reflect the habits, preferences, and personality of the testee in relation to different situations."[2] Job seekers' inability to prepare for such tests is, in fact, how the testing institutes try to reassure their actual clients (the employers) that the tests cannot be gamed and therefore the results are valid.

There are books and classes that claim to help candidates prepare for the tests, not unlike American SAT-preparation companies. But all the job seekers I interviewed expressed resentment over their exorbitant fees—in the hundreds of dollars. Eli angrily pointed out that these preparation companies are "exploiting the people who can least afford it."[3] But beyond the price, Israeli job seekers are also deeply skeptical that preparation would actually help. Of the job seekers I interviewed, only Mirit, who was looking for work in a bank, consulted a book on how to take the tests. She told me that the book taught her that the "best way to draw a tree" is with "lots of roots and branches." But at her actual test, she was not asked to draw a tree but rather to talk about her social life in high school.[4]

The vagueness of the test questions and the perceived impossibility of preparing for them generate an intense experience of objectification and lack of control. At the test, as at the screening interviews, job seekers directly experience the objectifying and, at least from their perspective, arbitrary mechanisms that transmute their selves into a set of quantities on a scorecard, which in turn determines their career fates.[5] A screener at a staffing agency who has seen many job seekers go through the testing process put it thus:

> The tests cut the person up. They analyze the person in a very cruel way. It's all in numbers. These tests are cruel in how they turn a person into a set of numbers and say things like "not sharp." My husband thought of trying to work at

another company and I was afraid of him taking these tests, that it would cut him up to pieces. I didn't want to see it.

For Israeli job seekers, the only way around the rigid agency screenings by buzzwords and pre-employment tests is to go outside the specs game and attempt to use their contacts, *protectzia*. But even this alternative route is marked by rigidity and a sense of lack of control. As we saw in chapter 4, the strategy of establishing new contacts for the purpose of obtaining a referral is not plausible in Israel, where referrals are only made on the basis of long-standing relationships of mutual reciprocity. Thus, for the purposes of job searching, one's social ties are a given and are typically limited to one's close friends, mostly importantly from the army, and one's parents' close friends.[6] Even Uri, one of the most energetic Israeli job seekers I met, described his personal network as a *fait accompli*:

I don't have good friends or family that can help. Some people don't have appropriate connections. What can you do? People around me are blue collar and don't know high-level people. That's the situation.

There is no verb "to network" in Hebrew; one's network is one's network.

System-Blame and Betrayal

Whereas American white-collar job seekers who encounter difficulties finding work in the context of the chemistry game typically come to think that there is something wrong with them, Israeli job seekers playing the specs game typically come to think that there is something wrong with the system.[7] We have just seen how frustrated and angry Israeli job seekers become with the seemingly arbitrary filtering practices of the staffing agencies and testing institutes. There is also much anger directed at the employers. One example of the cross-national differences in the subjective reaction of job seekers to employers can be seen in their response to having to wait to hear about a job. In both the Israeli and American hiring processes, the employers manifestly have greater power, in part because they control the pace and timing of the process. For example, employers in both sites set the time of the interview, and job seekers, knowing they will be judged on their timeliness, strive to arrive early. Yet stories abound in both sites of how employers hold up the scheduled interviews for any number of "more important" contingencies. The power disparity is even more apparent in the (often long) wait for a response after the interview. Here we have the job seekers, figuratively and perhaps literally, "waiting by the phone," while the employers seem to feel no obligation to respond promptly or even at all. American job seekers typically respond to these events by discussing their sense of rejection, analyzing and reanalyzing the details of the interview to understand where *they themselves* went wrong. In contrast, one of the most common topics of discussion among Israeli job seekers is their indignation at having to wait to be interviewed and their even greater indignation at the arrogance of agencies or employers who do not respond afterward. This waiting comes to symbolize their experience of powerlessness and repeated humiliation.

Israeli job seekers also attribute some of their difficulties to the tough labor-market conditions for someone with their level of skills and experience. For example, a marketing manager explained his difficulty: "I think I am one of many people looking in the field and, because of this, the employers can be much more picky about the level of experience they demand." Whether stated in more sophisticated economic terms by a lawyer who observed that "in the end, it is a matter of supply and demand," or in a more straightforward way by a clerical worker who thought that "the biggest problem is that other people are applying for the same jobs," the role of market conditions is perceived as important in determining one's own chances.[8]

However, when digging deeper into Israeli job seekers' subjective response, it becomes clear that, for most, blame also lies with the state. The state is seen as standing behind both the dominant labor-market institutions (the "system") and the current market conditions. Moti was explicit: "Bibi [Netanyahu, then the minister of finance] is responsible for the fact that I am unemployed.... *Bibi* and those who elected him decided my sentence. He has put a death sentence on people like me." Some job seekers blame the state for its actions and policies while others blame it for inaction. Gabi exemplified the former: "The minister of the finance and the bureaucrat economists in the Ministry of Finance are responsible for [the layoffs]. They make policies that are disconnected from reality by using economic models that are about the U.S. stock market [with no] connection to Israel." Menashe focused on the state's inactions: "While I understand some of the [neoliberal] changes because there does need to be some more efficiency, I don't see a policy that will absorb the workers that are let go. I don't see an attempt to create new jobs."

Job seekers frequently go beyond merely blaming the state and express feelings of *betrayal*. After discussing how the state is actively or passively to blame, job seekers often bring up their own personal sacrifices to the state—for example, their military service or that of their children—to explain their expectations of reciprocity. Menashe, for example, after claiming that the state should do more to create jobs, continued:

> I always did reserve duty [an annual month of military service required of men under age forty], but I don't feel like that interests anyone. . . . I did serve the country. While doing reserve duty, they cut you off from your life and you have to go serve in the "the territories" [the West Bank and Gaza]. I left my family for the state. They should give more help because of that. There is something not so fair here.

Moti, whom we heard above claiming that the finance minister had sentenced him to "death," also brought up his army experience: "I feel betrayal. I served in the army, in a combat unit. I served in the reserves. My brother died in the army. But the state only takes and does not give. There is no help, no support. Betrayal." Hadas linked her sense of betrayal to a desire to emigrate:

> I feel a desire to leave this country. After I gave it two years for the army, the state is not helping me. I served in Lebanon during rocket attacks. Now the state says, "Who are you? What do you want? I am not responsible for you." The state of Israel, because it requires so much of its citizens, because you have to serve in the military, has to supply jobs. I have a lot of anger about the state and a feeling of alienation.

While past military service is one important reason for heightened expectations of the state, Hadas and others made clear that their expectations also arise from the promise of Zionist collectivism. As Hadas put it: "We live in a bubble of Zionism. There is an ideology of togetherness, which is everywhere, and then one day you find yourself in the job market and no one is helping you. You invest yourself in this vision, in this society, and all you get is a slap in the face." Aurora likewise tied her sense of betrayal to the promises of Zionism:

> Betrayal comes from the fact that the state keeps pounding patriotism into your head. Give to the country. If you want us to be patriotic, give *us* something,

too. . . . The education here is that individual fate is tied to the fate of the state, your fate is the state's fate. If that's true, then the state should worry about us in the way that we are asked to worry about the state. The state always talks about "we," but when I need them, where are they?

When I began my research in Israel, I expected Zionist ideology to have the opposite effect. I speculated that a sense of collective mission and identity among Jewish Israelis might mitigate the individual pain of unemployment. I reasoned that job seekers' investment of their identities in such a collective project, which is not tied to their individual career success, would lessen the personal blow of unemployment. Yet, to my surprise, the collective identity only seemed to heighten unemployed workers' sense of being invisible. Part of my research took place at the height of the national drama of Israel's withdrawal from the Gaza Strip, which involved the forcible removal of Jewish settlers. For weeks Israeli radio and television dealt with nothing else. But rather than being swept up by these events, many unemployed job seekers adamantly rejected any collective identification, explaining that they had enough crisis and drama in their personal lives to also ride the emotional roller coaster of the national saga. If anything, the attention paid to that saga seemed to reinforce their sense that no one cared about *them*.

Corporatist Legacies and the Lishka

Job seekers' focus on the state as ultimately responsible for their difficulty in finding jobs is in part a holdover from Israel's earlier corporatist political economy, as discussed in chapter 4. The Israeli employment agency, the Lishka, is the historical embodiment of the state's institutional commitment to provide jobs or retraining. Prior to the neoliberal era, which began in the 1970s, an Israeli job seeker could go to the Lishka and expect to receive referrals for a new job in his or her field or support for retraining.[9] Today, the Lishka's main function is to disburse unemployment benefits to those who qualify and to persuade or pressure job seekers to accept lower-level jobs. The Lishka's history turns the experience of going to collect unemployment benefits into a loaded affair; its historical role as a source of support clashes visibly with its current role of coercively pressuring job seekers to accept downwardly mobile jobs.

The state employees working in the Lishka are fully aware of job seekers' expectations and resentments and try to counter these by "educating" job seekers about the new reality. In contrast to the American self-help discourse, which raises expectations by encouraging job seekers to go for their dreams, the Lishka sees its goal as lowering job seekers' expectations. In fact, its discourse resembles that of the American temp agencies, which also emphasize the importance of realistic expectations. The Lishka assumes that job seekers remain unemployed because they are turning down jobs that involve a step down in pay or status.[10]

The attempt to educate workers out of their inflexibility is observable in workshops provided to job seekers who receive retraining through the Lishka. At the end of each retraining program, job seekers are given a one-day workshop on "how to search for a job." The Lishka outsources this workshop to a private company called Improve, and, as Miriam, the instructor, explained to me, the primary goal is to "address the gap between workers' expectations and existing jobs." The thrust of the workshop's message was that in the *modern* economy there is no job security, and that workers need to learn to take *initiative and responsibility*. The workshop emphasized that workers need to move "forward" with the times. Miriam told the class:

> The work world has been transformed. There is a gap between expectations and what there is in the market. The jobs that people had at Bezek [a large state-owned company] didn't prepare them for the kind of jobs that exist today. There is no more tenure. Employers are looking for people with initiative, people who are responsible. The era of tenure is over. It doesn't exist anymore.

To help solve the perceived problem of worker inflexibility, the Lishka also uses coercive tactics to pressure job seekers to be more open to downwardly mobile options. When job seekers come to sign up for unemployment benefits, the Lishka sporadically provides them with job leads that they *must* pursue. To continue receiving unemployment benefits, job seekers must, at a minimum, apply for these jobs and make a good-faith effort to be hired.[11] For example, Nurit, an office manager, was given a lead for a job cleaning houses. After she refused this work, she stopped receiving unemployment compensation for three months. Likewise, Yariv, a former finance manager who wanted to find "more meaningful work in a nonprofit company," was deemed a "refuser" and had his unemployment benefits cut off because he did not follow up on a job lead with the police department. He began going to interviews with all referred employers simply to keep receiving his unemployment benefits.

The Lishka is also experienced as coercive in its strict enforcement of the rule that job seekers must physically sign in every week on an assigned day to continue receiving benefits. For example, Leon's unemployment benefits were suspended when he signed in one day late. He explained: "I didn't go sign because my daughter was born at the time I was supposed to be there. I showed them the medical records, but that was not an excuse for them." Most Israeli job seekers are full of horror stories about the cold treatment they have received at the Lishka. As Ruti put it, "The Lishka people treat you like shit. The attitude of the government offices is crushing. When I walk out of there, I feel as if I had been run over by a car."

When I accompanied Gil, a high-tech engineer, to the Lishka, he was greeted by a clerk who chewed her gum while she spoke and conveyed through her words and body language that she was doing Gil a favor by letting him sign in. As we walked away, Gil told me this clerk was "relatively okay compared to others."

To gain further insight into the Lishka, I asked to speak to a manager. I was told to knock on a small office door; a voice inside said, "Yes, open." Chaim barely looked up from his papers as I opened the door. "What do you want?" he asked. I told him I was doing research and asked if I could have a list of other offices similar to this one. Chaim responded in an impatient tone, "Where are you from again?" When he discovered that I am from California, everything changed. He smiled and told me his sister lived in Los Angeles and immediately invited me to dinner at his house. Suddenly, we were like long-lost relatives. He explained that he initially thought I was an unemployed job seeker. "Some people want to take advantage of unemployment benefits and not to work," he explained, "or they work under the table and don't report it." He could not estimate how common this problem is, but he assured me that "it is not small." This kind of abuse was his major concern. It was challenging, he went on, because "they don't say they don't want a job, because I can cut their benefits. Instead, when they get a referral, they show up late or come dressed in shorts." Chaim also complained that there are too many "health regulations" that restrict referrals, like the fact that he cannot refer someone with a bad back to a physically demanding job. This, he explained, "makes it very hard."

Chaim's attitude appeared to emanate from the very top of the Lishka and the Israeli state. As I approached the national headquarters of the Ministry of Labor in Jerusalem, which runs the Lishka and is housed in a large building across the street from the Israeli Parliament, I walked by a tent city of protesters demonstrating against cuts in welfare and the state's implementation of an Israeli version of a welfare-to-work program. As I came closer, I encountered a different group of protesters, people in wheelchairs protesting cuts in disability benefits, chanting in unison into microphones. Edna, the Lishka spokesperson who had agreed to be interviewed, met me in the lobby of the building and reassured me that it had been "much worse before, when the protesters took over the lobby of the building for months."

Edna claimed that the protesters and the unemployed in general were wrong to blame the Labor Ministry, explaining: "We here are not responsible for creating jobs." The Lishka's main difficulty, she went on, was dealing with unemployed job seekers' "attitude that the government should 'give me.'" Like Chaim, she explained that the people who come to the Lishka are those "who do not compromise on the job. They have a condition we call 'entitlism.' But in the modern economy, it is about individual responsibility." The Lishka's discourse mirrored that emanating from the very top of the government. Most notorious was Bibi Netanyahu, the finance minister at the time of my research, who often proclaimed in the media that "there are jobs" and admonished the unemployed to "just get out there and work."[12]

The state's coercive, suspicious, and patronizing attitude toward job seekers acts to reinforce the sense of anger and betrayal on the part of job seekers.

Anxiety, Search Intensity, and Downward Mobility

The experience of a lack of control, what I call playing a game with low player prominence, generates a distinct form of anxiety. Eran, who had just found a job at the time of the interview, looked back on his two-year unemployment spell and explained how he had needed to pretend that he had some control in order to keep going:

> The situation is not in your control. . . . Nothing is in your control. But you need to act *as if.* The situation is so hard. You are fighting hundreds of people, all of them good. You go through tens of interviews. The fact that there are tons of people out there, that is not in my control. But if I won't struggle, there is no chance. I was fearful. I didn't sleep at night. I was terribly afraid because I am just one person in a mass. My hands shook with fear. To this day I am in fear and I will never get rid of it because I know it's not in my control. . . . Even if you are the best in the world, there is also a *huge amount of luck.*

Menashe similarly explained that "unemployment has changed my sense that I can control everything," and, for this reason, he said, "I cannot relax. The feeling is terrible. The anxiety of uncertainty never leaves me. Uncertainty is what kills a person."

The sense of losing control and the system-blame associated with the specs game are different from the unemployment experiences associated with the chemistry game discussed in chapter 3, and these differences have important consequences. One such consequence is the effect of the unemployment experience on job-search intensity. Over time Israeli job seekers see no way to break through what they perceive to be a rigid and arbitrary system. The increasing sense that one's fate is not in one's hands and that one's strategic actions are useless lead to greater uncertainty about how to proceed and less motivation to try. As Anat explained:

> I don't know what to do anymore. I sometimes feel like I will never find work, and I am sick of it. I sit at home each morning and think, "What am I going to do today?"

Several job seekers specifically linked the seeming futility of their attempts to penetrate the rigid screens of the staffing agencies to their decreasing search intensity. As Niv explained: "The staffing agencies reduce motivation. . . . The humiliation of the meat market is one the biggest things that leads people to give up."

This kind of discouragement, however, is different from that which American job seekers feel due to self-blame; for them, continued searching is like putting salt on the open wound of one's own inadequacy. Inaction due to not knowing "what to do" is precisely what IsraSupport attempts to counter, as described in chapter 4, by insisting on sustained and methodical action. IsraSupport's support strategy discussed in the prior chapter, which focuses on fighting fatalism and disciplining oneself to just keep going with the search, can be thus understood as a well-suited response to the specific subjective difficulties that arise in the course of playing the Israeli job-search game.

As described in chapter 3, the American job seekers in my sample energetically searched for work in the early part of their unemployment, but over time the intensity of their search, as reflected in the number of hours devoted to looking for work each week, dropped. By contrast, Israeli job seekers' initial levels of job searching were below those of their American counterparts, *but* their levels of intensity remained comparatively more steady over time.[13] Given these different trajectories, after four months of searching Israeli job seekers, despite somewhat decreasing their search intensity over time, were typically spending *more* time searching and were less likely to become "discouraged" and cease searching, when compared to their American counterparts.

The specs game's low player prominence means that successive failed attempts at finding work reinforce the perceived rigidity and arbitrariness of the "system" but leave one's sense of self untouched. Israeli job seekers typically feel like they have "nothing to lose" in continuing their job search. Eldad, an Israeli job seeker who expressed feeling indignant about being reduced to "buzzwords," nonetheless continued job searching. He explained: "An important part of all this is just luck. I continue sending out my résumé because *I have nothing to lose.*" Unlike most American white-collar job seekers, Eldad's self-worth was not "on the line" with each application.

While continuing to look for work, over time Israeli job seekers increasingly confront a tough question: Should they continue searching for jobs matching their skills and experience, or should they compromise downward, as the Lishka (the unemployment agency) urges? Israeli job seekers, like their American counterparts, typically do not consider downward mobility in the first months of unemployment. But over time they are often forced to reassess. In my sample, an economist who had worked for the state took a job, after a year of searching, as a part-time security guard at an elementary school. A fifty-six-year-old former high-tech manager took a job driving a shuttle van. A librarian was pushed by financial stress to look for a job as a secretary. When she found that the market for secretaries was "flooded," she began seeking work as a supermarket cashier but had thus far not succeeded in obtaining even this kind of low-wage work.

Financial stress as well as mounting pressure from family members pushes job seekers in Israel, as in the United States, toward downward mobility. Nurit explained the pressure she felt from the incessant questions of her family and friends:

> The hardest thing is the questions of people. "Have you found a job? Why not? My daughter found a job in a week!" I want a good job that I can stick with in the long run, but people don't understand that.

The social pressure to compromise can be intense. Yehuda described how his friends and family found it difficult to believe that "someone who is so skilled can't find work," which led to the question, "Are you too picky?"

He said that the questions "come from a place of worry," but "this attitude makes it really hard. I don't go to family functions so that people will not ask me what's going on with me." Yet, just when the job seeker would prefer some distance from his or her family, the family tends to become more involved. Anat related: "It's hard because they [her parents] call me more. They want to know what's going on. I've turned into their little girl again." Family members often begin to suggest that the job seeker take *any* job he or she can find. Rinat, a thirty-two-year-old former human resources department manager, had been unemployed for five months. She lived with her brother, who had begun to say that he did not understand why she did not just take any job and had expressed his disappointment with her. When she was offered a minimum-wage job, she did not want to take it because, as she put it, "It was humiliating to work at these terms. I know what I am worth." She called friends to "ask for legitimacy not to take this job." Some of them, however, advised her "take it until you get something else." She said that this was "not what I wanted to hear," but she took the minimum-wage job.

Friends and family often interpret reluctance to take downwardly mobile jobs as reflecting excessive pride. One job seeker I interviewed, although he himself had just accepted a good job after struggling for months not to compromise down, opined that "those who are unemployed are a little spoiled. There is always something.... You need not feel that work is degrading."

Even at IsraSupport, the general advice is to compromise. Nadav, a counselor, put it this way:

> Should you compromise for lower wages? Yes. Job searching wears you down to the bones. You need to support your family. Take what there is because a low salary is more than no salary. To get a job is like parting the Red Sea, but it's much, much harder to interview as someone unemployed. I've worked cleaning houses to make an extra [$100] a month to get out of debt.

We saw in chapter 3 how American job seekers playing the chemistry game can also feel forced to take downwardly mobile jobs. But their path down is different. Financial stress and family pressure are at work in both sites, but in the Israeli case, these forces are not counterbalanced, as they are in the United States, by a discourse encouraging job seekers to pursue their passions and dreams. In Israel work is predominantly seen in instrumental terms as an exchange of skills for money, not a reflection one's inner desires. In the specs game, then, the pressure to compromise down is thus not accompanied by a sense that one is betraying one's inner self.[14]

Beyond practical financial concerns, Israeli job seekers also hesitate to take downwardly mobile jobs for fear of undermining their social status. This fear of losing social status was evident in the internal discussions at an Israeli support organization called EzraSupport aimed at older unemployed workers. Cofounder Ehud, a sixty-four-year-old former manager of an industrial firm, explained that he formed this group when several years ago the "problem of unemployment among those older than fifty became clear as half of all unemployed are currently over the age of fifty."[15] Another cofounder, Rakefet, had been a manager of an organization focused on helping absorb new Russian immigrants into the Israeli economy. She noted the irony of how "now I am in a worse position than the Russians I used to help. It is punishment." She continued:

> We didn't expect this. We thought our jobs were safe until age sixty-five. We thought maybe jobs are not secure for the next generation. We never thought they would throw us out. Our generation didn't expect to have to look for work at this age.

The organization promises "solutions" for its members, but as Ehud explained—these "can't be that you'll again get a job with tenure. Those jobs are gone." EzraSupport's first efforts were to act as a kind of not-for-profit staffing agency, providing qualified workers to companies. Ehud claimed that "in the past five months, we referred 260 people to jobs." However, as other members were quick to point out, these referrals were for jobs involving significant drops in pay and status. According to an internal survey of the organization, only half of the members who received such referrals were even interested in them, and, of those, only 5 percent of the members actually took such jobs. Clearly, the vast majority of the members were not ready to take a significant cut in pay and status.

In light of this, Ehud decided to supplement the staffing agency idea with an effort focused on members taking "business initiative and creating income for themselves." Toward this end, EzraSupport members divided themselves into several cooperatives or "teams," each headed by a "team leader." The purpose of these teams is to start a profitable business that can help financially sustain the members. This, Ehud explained, was an attempt to "empower ourselves by taking initiative and making things happen." It was in the struggles to realize this attempt that tensions in the group became visible over the issue of downward mobility, with some members questioning others' willingness to work at anything but a cushy desk job.

Rakefet was the leader of the "educational team." She and her teammates had devised a workshop on how to start a small business, which they had been marketing to older unemployed Israelis. Unfortunately, despite the low fees, few had signed up. At an EzraSupport meeting, Rakefet reported that the team's bid for a government contract to run entrepreneurial workshops for "unemployed men" had been unsuccessful. This led to the following discussion:

ARI: Who are we to bid for such a contract? What can we show for ourselves? We are burning in illusions.

RAKEFET: Ari, I don't understand what your problem is.

ARI: I've been at these meetings for a year, and they are not encouraging me. Empires are being built here. Big huge projects. But we don't even have anyone [at EzraSupport] to answer and make phone calls [for the staffing agency]. There should be someone at all times at the desk to answer calls if a potential employer calls.

At this point the group erupted into cacophonous yelling on the issue of volunteering to answer the phone at EzraSupport:

MEMBER: We've been talking about this for three years. Answering phones can only happen if we pay people, not volunteer.

ARI: No one around here wants to work. I got the bus company to offer people jobs here, and only a few people took it. Older people don't want this kind of work.... Bibi [Netanyahu, the then finance minister] is right on this point. There are jobs around for the minimum wage, and no one here wants to take them....

The argument revealed conflicting views on downward mobility. Ari came down squarely, in word and deed, on the take-any-job side of the debate. He had taken a part-time minimum-wage job punching tickets at Tel Aviv's central bus station, although only a few years earlier he had been making a high salary, by Israeli standards, running a construction company where he managed over two thousand workers. He explained that accepting the job at the bus station was simply an adjustment to a new reality, one which many of his colleagues were unwilling to make:

They worked in big industries and in the public sector, and now they come to a new labor market where the employer doesn't want to give a long-term commitment. The big government companies that have been privatized want cheap labor. Older workers live in a world that has passed. Long-term jobs do not exist. If you were previously a manager and now you want a job, your best chances are to get a simple job, which involves a big status drop. People in EzraSupport, and I am one of the founders, want to turn it into a business. . . . They were previously managers, and now they look for a job where they can sit like before. So we can find volunteers to be the "managers" of this or that business group, but no one volunteers to answer the phones. The group gives titles to everyone, but there is nothing there. In the end, this illusion will do more harm than good. Their expectations are too high.

Ari claimed that "empowerment," which was the group's stated goal, is better achieved by "going to work like me. Punching tickets. Now I am talking to my boss about doing other projects like recruiting people." He explained that starting at the bottom is more likely to lead to a good job, and he was bitterly upset that he had managed to get jobs at the bus company for other members of EzraSupport but almost no one would take them because of the status drop. "Ehud's strategy is starting your own business," Ari told me. "Ehud has nothing to eat, but he's waiting."

Ehud later offered this response to Ari's point:

There are jobs, but not respectable ones. You can be a manual worker. Hard physical work exists. But someone like me can't do physical work. I would collapse. People here never did blue-collar work, and that's the work that exists. People are willing to compromise on the money but not on the essence of the work.

Whether or not job seekers should accept downward mobility is an enormous source of tension. In the American case, the tension is revealed in the telling of "success stories" and centers on whether the job seeker is actually doing work that he or she "wants" to do, that is aligned with his or her inner desires or is at least a step in that direction. A loser in the chemistry game is one who ends up in a job that does not correspond to who he or she really is—a subjective criterion. In Israel, one is a loser according to objective criteria of pay and position.

Under the stress of downward mobility, job seekers seek escape routes. The pseudo-job of participating in a cooperative team at EzraSupport is one form of potential escape to a space where the job seeker is protected from the punishing labor market and the mounting social pressures while maintaining a legitimate social identity. This is similar to taking a volunteer leadership position at AmeriSupport. In both Israel and the United States, such a protected place can found in support organizations through immersion in job equivalents. However, what counts as a job equivalent in each site is different and reflects the underlying differences between the two games. In the American case, since work is meant to be an enactment of your passion, you can be considered to be working if you are engaged in a personally meaningful activity—even if you are not being paid. As we saw in chapter 3, working as a volunteer for AmeriSupport could provide some legitimate professional cover. In the specs game, however, unpaid activities are not considered work and have no bearing on one's professional identity. For an unpaid activity to count as a kind of work, and thus provide cover from social stigma, it must be plausibly *intended* to make money. The attempt by EzraSupport to form profitable cooperative enterprises fits well with this instrumental understanding of work.[16]

Another form of escape, or at least escape fantasy, common among Israeli job seekers, is emigration. Driven partly by the painful sense of betrayal, at least a third of my interviewees brought up emigration as a hypothetical solution to their problems. They imagined that well-paying jobs were plentiful in places such as the United States and Europe. Most of them, however, viewed this option as impractical because of family ties, language, and legal barriers. Nonetheless, the nature of this escape fantasy revealed their understanding that their job-finding problem was an external problem rooted in particular social structures, which could therefore be escaped by physically leaving that social context. Such escape routes are not possible if the problem is perceived to lie within oneself. Indeed, I met only one American job seeker who mentioned emigrating; she had lost her health insurance and joked about moving to Canada for its health care system.

*   *   *

Stepping back, we see that on almost every dimension of the unemployment experience, American and Israeli job seekers diverge. Despite the fact that job seekers in both sites are looking for white-collar jobs, often at firms operating in the same global economic niche, the day-to-day search processes, the interpretations of the outcomes, and even the compromises are all markedly different. As I have argued, these differences come from playing two distinct job-search games.

This chapter discussed the unemployment experience of job seekers playing the specs game, which is characterized by self-objectification and low player prominence. This game ultimately generates system-blame: a subjective response to job-search difficulties as rooted in external determinants. Factors external to the game—including job seekers' expectations regarding the role of the state that were formed in the pre-neoliberal corporatist political-economic context—focus some of this blame specifically on the state, which is seen as betraying the job seeker.

The next chapter will explore yet a third game, the diligence game, found in the American blue-collar context. The findings will suggest that the structure of a given job-search game trumps both culture and class in shaping the unemployment experience.

CHAPTER SIX

A Cross-Class Comparison

The Blue-Collar Diligence Game

R eggie's first words to me were, "My mind is about to explode. Not having a job, it can drive you to go use drugs, can drive people to hit their wife, drive people crazy. I've seen it. I have seen a lot." Two months earlier, he had lost his job working in a warehouse. Like the American and Israeli white-collar workers discussed in prior chapters, Reggie had repeatedly hit frustrating roadblocks in his search for a new job. Yet his experience of unemployment, and that of most blue-collar American workers I interviewed, followed a different pattern. It was the product of a different job-search game.

The prior chapters described the workings of the chemistry game in the American context and the specs game in the Israeli context. Although these chapters described the specific labor-market institutions that underlie each of these games, a question may remain about the role of broader national cultures in ultimately shaping unemployment experiences. For example, it may be suggested that it is the American culture of individualism that explains the focus on chemistry and the personalized self-blame. The cross-class comparison described in this chapter will show a group of American job seekers—those seeking blue-collar jobs—who are *not* playing the chemistry game and who have a very different experience of unemployment. This comparison provides further evidence that it is the job-search games and the specific institutions that underlie them, and not a widely shared national culture, that drives the unemployment experience.

The American blue-collar job search does not focus on interpersonal connection, as in the chemistry game, or on the job seeker's list of objective skills, as in the specs game. Instead, it focuses primarily on whether the job seeker is an eager, compliant, and hard worker, a filter I summarize with the word "diligence."

True, as in the chemistry game, the focus is on an intangible attribute, but it is a very different attribute than the interpersonal fit sought in the chemistry game, as we will see below. In the diligence game, chemistry may in fact be a liability. The diligence game and the labor-market institutions dominant in the American blue-collar context ultimately generate a search experience that in important ways resembles the experience of playing the specs game. In a surprising finding, the job-search experience of blue-collar American job seekers is *closer* to that of white-collar Israelis than to that of their own white-collar compatriots. This suggests that to understand job-search and unemployment experiences, more important than culture or class is the specific job-search game one must engage in when looking for work and the concrete labor-market institutions that structure it.

The data presented in this chapter were gathered through in-depth interviews with job seekers who made use of a state-funded One-Stop job-search support center in the San Francisco Bay area (which I will refer to as "WorkSource"). This center is one of many similar One-Stop centers across the state of California and the United States and is part of the larger support structure that also encompasses AmeriSupport. WorkSource is geared toward the general population of job seekers—that is, those who do not self-identify as professionals who would join AmeriSupport—and the overwhelming majority of the people it serves are blue-collar workers. Their typical past jobs include assembly-line, maintenance, mechanical, and warehouse work. In addition to interviewing job seekers, I participated in job-search workshops at WorkSource and interviewed counselors and staff who provide these workshops and other support services.

The Structure of the Diligence Game

The chemistry, specs, and diligence games can be compared by the different approaches that employers take to conceptualize and evaluate a set of intangible characteristics often bundled together as soft skills. In the chemistry game, these are the inner qualities that make the job candidate a good fit. Hiring managers typically rely on their gut instinct and give much weight to whether or not they feel a connection with the job seeker at the interview. In the specs game, soft skills are understood as needed to carry out certain tasks, such as the leadership skills needed to manage a group of employees. Such skills are thought to be objectively assessable through elaborate pre-employment tests. In the diligence game, soft skills are foremost seen as a set of attitudes; with the relevant question being whether the job seeker is motivated to work hard and do whatever is asked of him or her, cheerfully obediently, and diligently.

Creating chemistry and exhibiting diligence are often conflated because both depend on the job seeker's self-presentation. Yet the necessary modes of self-presentation are distinct and are driven by different imperatives: connection versus compliant subordination. In the white-collar context, the goal is to achieve a sense of comfort and familiarity among social equals. In the blue-collar context, the goal is to exhibit a willingness to subordinate among social unequals.

Exhibiting subordination and creating chemistry require opposite signals. In trying to account for why employers in the low-wage market often prefer to hire less-educated immigrants over more highly educated native-born workers, Waldinger and Lichter (2003) explain that in the low-wage market, employers are *not* looking to hire people like themselves. Given the low wages and poor working conditions of the jobs they are offering, employers believe anyone who is "like them" will resist such conditions and thus not be a good, hardworking, diligent employee. The central question on the prospective employer's mind is whether a given worker will comply and work with diligence despite low pay and generally poor working conditions.

In this context, social similarity—the typical basis for chemistry as discussed in chapter 2—becomes a reason to expect that, just like oneself, the job candidate is not, in Waldinger and Lichter's words, "suitable for subordination." In other words, the social similarity that is so critical in the white-collar context becomes a liability in the working-class context. While Waldinger and Lichter focus on the very bottom of the labor market, their analysis of social similarity as a *negative* in this segment of the market reveals much about the fundamental cross-class difference in American job searching. The chemistry filter is relevant when hiring those with whom the manager will work in a collaborative fashion. The diligence filter is relevant when hiring blue-collar workers who will typically be subjected to command-and-control forms of management.

Moss and Tilly (2001) distinguish between two types of soft skills. One type focuses on "interaction" and refers to employer assessments of job seekers' friendliness and ability to fit in or project appropriate affect.

These are the factors that are in different ways assessed by the use of the chemistry and spec filters. The second type of soft skills in Moss and Tilly's (2001) typology focuses on motivation and refers to employer assessment of factors such as enthusiasm, a positive work attitude, commitment, and dependability. This second type of soft skills is the focus of the blue-collar diligence filter. In their comprehensive study of employers' hiring practices, Moss and Tilly (2001) report that when employers are asked to rate the *most* important qualities they look for in hiring entry-level blue-collar workers (specifically in this study auto-parts manufacturing workers), motivation-type soft skills were their top concern. Motivation not only ranked ahead of hard skills but notably was deemed far more important than interaction soft skills, which are critical in the white-collar and retail contexts. One factory owner explained that in hiring in the blue-collar context:

> We look for someone who basically has their personal life together. You have to have somebody you can rely on, who will get to work every day, call in when they're not going to show up, not come in drunk or having stayed up all night and not been to bed so that they could hurt themselves here, or stuff like that. As I say, their personal lives have to be stable to the point where they can maintain a constant effort to make it to work. (Moss and Tilly 2001, 60)

Similarly, after reviewing the existing research, Cappelli (2012, 42) concludes that in evaluating high school graduates and dropouts, employers' list of "deficiencies" is "topped not by a cluster of missing technical or academic abilities but by a lack of work attitudes and self-management skills such as punctuality, time management, motivation and a strong work ethic." A world of difference separates this filter from the sense of interpersonal chemistry sought in the white-collar context.

The institutionalization of the diligence filter creates distinct challenges and frustrations for blue-collar job seekers. In an economic context where blue-collar jobs are dwindling and there are large numbers of applicants for every position, an initial filtering of all candidates by their commitment to hard work and motivation is expensive. For this reason, employers are moving away from the traditional blue-collar filtering method of interviewing job seekers who "walk in" to establishments and apply on the premises, and are instead increasingly relying on online applications for the initial filtering. As this chapter will show, this shift is creating distinct difficulties and frustrations for job seekers who understand the importance of diligence to the ultimate hiring decision but feel systematically blocked from interactions in which they can display it. Job seekers often resist the advice to apply online partly due to barriers in using computer technologies and partly due to their understanding that applying online may diminish their abilities to distinguish themselves to employers in the ways that are ultimately most important to getting hired.

The Blue-Collar Job-Search Advice Discourse

Taken as a whole, WorkSource's advice discourse presents blue-collar job searching as a relatively straightforward process. Unlike AmeriSupport's weekly meetings with guest speakers, small-group strategy meetings, and continuous workshops, at the One-Stop where I conducted this research, as well as at similar support organizations around California, the extent of the support was far more limited in scope, with various workshops offered as one-time events with a set curriculum repeated each week.[1]

The advice discourse on finding blue-collar work begins with basic skills. In WorkSource workshops and in meetings with counselors, time was spent figuring out job seekers' relevant transferable skills. The presumption was that job seekers have more skills than they realize because they tend to think too narrowly about the relevance of their past experience. As Jenn, a WorkSource counselor, explained at an orientation:

> Believe it or not, the skills that you do have can be transferable. What are the similarities between a bartender and a police officer? Strange question? Both work with the public, use communication skills, and need to know how to deal with drunks. [*Laughter.*] We want to break the blinders. The skills you have are marketable to new jobs. You just need to look at it in new way.

In the blue-collar context, the term "skills" often refers to general capacities, such as being able to read competently, use a computer, communicate with others, and do basic math. These threshold skills are needed for many entry-level jobs that involve working in teams or with equipment.

While the advice discourse begins with skills, the consistent message to blue-collar job seekers is that basic skills are not enough and are not even the most important element in the hiring decision. As Jenn put it: "Employers are looking for more than just employees with qualifications. That's the baseline. They are looking for a *work ethic*." Marylin likewise told job seekers: "Employers say: Get rid of the mentality of 'my car' or 'my kids' as excuses for not showing up at work." Mia, yet another counselor, also echoed this message: "What employers really want is *devotion*. They want to identify people who will have a positive influence."

As in the chemistry game, intangible qualities matter most. What is different is that conveying diligence does not require customizing one's message. In the chemistry game, an interpersonal connection requires researching the hiring manager and the particular organization and projecting the appropriate inner qualities that will add up to a good fit. But in the diligence game, the quality of being a hard worker, although intangible, is generic and applies to one employer as well as to another. For this reason, it is possible to take more of a numbers-game approach like that of Israeli white-collar workers playing the specs game. As Mia, the counselor, put it: "The more employers you contact, the more likely you are to get a job." In both the specs and the diligence games, the targeted employer is perceived as looking for generic qualities, whether it be a particular skill or a particular attitude.

The blue-collar job seekers at WorkSource generally agreed with their counselors on the central importance of displaying diligence. They often, however, did not go along with the suggested tactics—particularly when it came to résumés and cover letters, as will be described below. While this section describes the dominant advice discourse coming from the counselors and workshop leaders, the next section will analyze the gaps between this advice and the job seekers' actual search practices.

Job seekers were advised to keep their résumés clean and clear. As Jenn put it: "It needs to be short, concise, easy-to-read bullets. The rule is KISS: 'Keep It Simple and Short.'" The counselors also advised job seekers to view their résumé as a "piece of advertisement." As Rob, a counselor, explained: "The thing is to catch the eye of the interviewer, make it snazzy." He elaborated:

A résumé is a gift to the employer. Do you want to just have a brown paper bag, or something snazzy? Which would you rather get? Snazzy up your résumé. It's a representation of you. You control what's on there.

When "snazzy" was unpacked, it boiled down to a résumé that is clean and clear. It is not sloppy and does not contain spelling mistakes that would convey carelessness. A snazzy résumé conveys conscientiousness, care for how one presents oneself, seriousness of purpose, and respect for the employer.

Advice on cover letters emphasized brevity but with a perfunctory sentence or two describing job seekers' interest in the work. In one workshop, for example, a former aviation mechanic shared his one-sentence draft cover letter: "I'm looking to get back to doing electrical work because I have realized there is no future in aviation." The counselor chuckled at the naive honesty and explained: "No. Can't say that. You need to state it in the positive. You *like* electrical work. Don't talk about 'no future' in aviation, even if that's the real reason." The same line of advice was seen in regards to interviewing. For example, Frank, who was looking for a job sorting mail, was advised to make a point of the "fact" that he *enjoyed* mail. Thus, in contrast to the specs game, where liking the job is irrelevant, and to the chemistry game, where liking the job can only be conveyed convincingly through revealing and heartfelt personal stories, the diligence game requires signaling an externally cheerful and positive attitude toward a particular line of work. In other words, some emotional labor is advisable, but of the "surface acting" as opposed to the "deep acting" variety (Hochschild 1983).

An often-repeated piece of advice for interviewing was to sound "appropriate." Clarice, a job seeker, offered an example to her peers during a workshop of how *not* to talk during an interview:

> Sometimes I sit there and I know, wow, I just blew it. They asked me about my hobbies. I said I studied world religions. They asked me which one I found fascinating. I said Islam. [*The room breaks into laughter.*]

A fellow job seeker chimed in: "Islam? That is not *the* buzzword. Maybe crossword puzzles?" The cause of the laughter, which took me a second to understand, was that Clarice had said something that the group perceived as obviously inappropriate. Interest in Islam was understood by the group to have negative connotations. The "appropriateness" strategy diverges from the chemistry game's focus on creating a personal connection, but it resembles the specs game's focus on presenting a suitable exterior.

Playing the Diligence Game

In the specs and chemistry games, the job seekers' practices are in general agreement with the advice discourse. In the American blue-collar case, there is a gap. As a threshold matter, blue-collar job seekers are generally skeptical of the need for advice from purported experts when they have had a lifetime of experience looking for jobs. Secondly, they are resistant to the substance of the counselors' advice, particularly with respect to "papers" such as résumés and cover letters. As this section will describe, the strategies that blue-collar job seekers actually pursue are typically not discussed in the workshops.

The job seekers I interviewed for this chapter were all registered members of WorkSource, and I approached them while they were in Work-Source's common area using the computers, newspapers, and phones for job searching. Yet despite being there, about half of them did not go to *any* of the workshops, which were free and right down the hall. When I asked where they got advice on job searching, the most common response was that they talked with friends and relied on past experience. Willie explained: "I learned by going from job to job. That's just the way it is. When you go to interviews over the years, you just learn how to conduct yourself, not read books about it." Jerry would talk with his friends: "We sit around and share ideas. No workshops. No books." In fact, one of the reasons job seekers come to WorkSource is to talk with fellow job seekers. Jerry explained: "This center here . . . the whole thing is trying to get leads, tips, what's in demand, who needs who. I involve myself in conversations here. Give input, ask others how they've been doing, putting our heads together."

When blue-collar job seekers do attend a workshop, the atmosphere is different from the corporate-like ambience at AmeriSupport. Work-Source workshops are more like a high school classroom, with the job seekers bantering and joking with each other. Their humor underscored their distant and uncomfortable attitude toward so-called expert advice.

For example, blue-collar job seekers understand the appearance of their résumés to be largely unimportant. For them, a résumé is just a straightforward list, as in the Israeli specs game. Bill took this approach: "Writing a résumé is not hard. . . . My story is I am a warehouse man, and I am good at what I do. And it speaks for itself."

In contrast to job seekers playing the chemistry game, endlessly trying to tailor their advertisement-like résumés to the constantly shifting target audience, players in the blue-collar diligence game (like those in the specs game) see no reason to alter a competently done résumé unless there is a change in their job history or credentials. As James put it:

> My résumé is pretty good, and there is no need to change it. It's a legit résumé. The only time I need to change it is if I get another job, then I have to add it. Otherwise it's good. No need to change.

When I asked Reggie if he might attend a free WorkSource workshop on writing résumés, he responded: "I know how to write a résumé. I can put fake businesses on there easily. I don't think there is much I can learn about this stuff." The advice to provide a cover letter explaining that you like the particular work was typically ignored. In fact, blue-collar job seekers generally do not use a cover letter at all.

Blue-collar job seekers defy the advice of job counselors for a number of reasons. As discussed above, based on their past experiences, many believe that résumés and cover letters are not important to the hiring process. Moreover, difficulties with access to and use of computers pose significant barriers to creating and editing these documents. The obstacles to access and use of computers are also a barrier to finding job postings, which are increasingly prevalent online, and to filling out online job applications. While white-collar job seekers are typically experienced computer users, many blue-collar job seekers feel ill equipped to use computers and navigate the Internet, and become frustrated when they try. A growing body of research documents a substantial digital inequality in access and use of computers along the lines of class, education, and race. I refer to digital *inequality* as opposed to the more commonly used metaphor of the digital *divide*, because under the binary distinction highlighted by the latter concept, the blue-collar job seekers in my study may well be categorized as workers who have crossed the "divide," given their access and use of computers, but such categorization would miss the significant barriers these workers face in making full use of digital technologies.[2] As DiMaggio and Bonikowski (2008) note in their review of this literature, capacities that are taken for granted by experienced users, such as the use of drop-down menus, can pose great challenges for neophytes. In the job-search context, conducting online searches for job postings can indeed be a daunting task for novice computer users. It requires learning how to navigate multiple websites and effectively use keywords to identify relevant postings. Responding to postings online is even more complicated, requiring one to open and fill out an online application, upload one's résumé and cover letter, and perform other tasks that are far from self-explanatory to an inexperienced computer user. Since most of the blue-collar workers I interviewed did not own computers, they used the old and slow computers at WorkSource. Because these computers were shared, job seekers had to learn to use security passwords and USB drives to upload résumés. During my participant-observations at WorkSource, job seekers frequently asked me for help with using the computers, and even I, a relatively experienced computer user, occasionally had trouble because of the various security and privacy systems of WorkSource's computers.

Frustration in using computers led some job seekers to conclude that it was time to enhance their computer skills by taking classes. Not only were job postings increasingly going online, but the California unemployment system put pressure on job seekers to become computer-literate by making the receipt of unemployment benefits conditional on posting and updating the status of your résumé on the state's job website.

As Harold explained:

> I rarely look online because I am not computer-literate. But I am getting involved in tech. I am going to have to improve my tech skills 'cause it's getting to be real competitive now. It's a must-know thing.

But Harold was in the minority. Most of his fellow job seekers avoided the Internet as much as possible and stuck with other means of searching for work. This was not only because of their difficulties with computers, but also because they perceived that most of the jobs listed online were office work, not the kinds of jobs they were looking for. As James put it: "I think these sites are a big gimmick. Some of them are not real jobs. The jobs they list are for people already with a degree, not for someone like me."

Most importantly, blue-collar job seekers share the perception that whatever competitive advantage they might have over other job seekers would be nullified by the anonymous process of applying for work online or by "paper." They experience the Internet as undermining their successful past strategies of getting a job, specifically the strategy of talking directly to the hiring manager and displaying their diligence. For this reason, they turn to search strategies that allow for personal contact with potential employers.

As an alternative to navigating online applications, blue-collar job seekers look for job postings that come with a phone number. Such postings can be found on a bulletin board at WorkSource and in smaller local community-based newspapers. Job seekers typically call the potential employer to confirm that they are accepting applications and then physically go to the employer to apply. If no relevant postings are found, some job seekers use the Yellow Pages. Ben explained this approach: "I look under 'warehouses,' and I call and see if they are accepting applications and then go down there and fill in the application." When responding to cold calls, employers frequently say that they are not hiring but that the the job seeker should come and fill out a job application anyway. Job seekers interpret this in different ways. Most, like Ben, think that employers "say that [they are not hiring] even if they are hiring just to see if you are coming." Showing a willingness to come to the place of business even if they are not currently hiring is one way to exhibit the kind of tenacity and diligence that the job seekers attempt to convey.

Once they reach the place of business, in addition to filling out applications, job seekers often try to speak to the hiring manager, though they are not always successful. As Frank explained: "I ask to speak to anyone giving interviews. I've not had a chance to talk to any manager yet." As I will later describe, difficulties in meeting hiring managers becomes increasingly frustrating and ultimately generates a sense of dehumanization that strongly resembles the *choser onim* of Israeli job seekers.

Another strategy for maximizing personal contact with the hiring manager is simply "walking in." Jerry explained:

> *I like* the old-fashioned way. If I see a place where they do the work that I do, I stop and walk in and ask if they are hiring or not. When you walk into an establishment, you see right away what it's about. You give your application to a person, and you present yourself. To me, a résumé is a part of you, but for someone to *really* see you, you have to be right there.

The core of the strategy is for the job seeker to be seen by the hiring manager as eager to work. As Jeff put it: "I want employers to understand that I am one of the most reliable workers they will find on the planet." In addition to showing up in person, diligence is also displayed by coming in early in the day. Willie explained:

> It looks bad if you are looking late in the day. You want to look for work in the morning, or else they think you're just laying around. If I do go late, then I go in there and throw in something like it's hot, I've been doing this all day, and this is the last place I will go into today.

Jeff agreed: "After lunch, nobody wants to see you. Do it from nine to noon."

Even though hiring managers are rarely available, Jeff explained, "I talk to the secretary. The secretary has influence, so I try to leave a good impression with her." George likewise said: "I go to places and I talk to the receptionist, make an impression. Not this impersonal stuff. Then you keep calling, and they know who you are. I tell them, 'I am going to keep calling you.'" Bill made sure not to "slouch" when he talked to employers "because that does not show enthusiasm." This level of persistence was not always easy. Jeff reported that after being told there were no positions available, "the toughest thing is putting a smile on my face, shaking the hand of the person, and saying, 'Thank you, anyway.' I really feel like saying, 'Motherfucker.'"

While Jeff's experience shows that maintaining a smile in the face of rejection is not easy, it is important to point out that blue-collar workers' interaction with hiring managers or other staff involves surface acting (Hochschild 1983). Unlike the deep acting at the core of the chemistry game, requiring the production of an internal emotion needed to establish a sense of connection, the emotional labor of the diligence game is more similar to the self-objectification of the specs game. In both the diligence and specs games, job seekers need only to produce a certain external display, professionalism in the specs game and good cheer under all circumstances in the diligence game.

In addition to directly talking to employers, blue-collar job seekers also perceive networking—or using word of mouth, as it is often called—to be an effective approach. Bill reported seeing in his former workplaces how employers "hire from within families. It's the mother, father, grandchildren, in-laws. . . . They all carpool." Likewise, Clarice recalled: "When I worked in production, entire families were working there. It was all families." Even so, word of mouth is seldom deliberately used as a job-search strategy. Personal networks are mainly used to find out who is hiring, but not for referrals. Jeff reported that when he tries to "use word of mouth, my friends say, 'Go apply,' or people bring me the flyer." This kind of word of mouth about job openings is typically from family and friends. Here again, the American blue-collar pattern is more similar to that of Israeli white-collar workers than to that of American white-collar workers. The networks of American blue-collar job seekers, like those of Israeli white-collar job seekers, are limited to long-standing relationships among family and friends. As in Israel, no blue-collar interviewee attempted to "network" in the sense of seeking out new contacts for the purpose of getting job leads or referrals.

Behind this similar pattern in networking lies an important difference. In the Israeli case, the reason for not engaging in broader networking was skepticism that a stranger would have any reason to help. In the American blue-collar case, the reason was social withdrawal and the awkwardness of asking anyone for help. Willie explained: "It would be hard for me to be-friend somebody and start a networking thing like that. I am a loner doing my own thing."[3]

Most blue-collar job seekers named a handful of family members and friends to whom they had turned for tips and leads, as compared to the more than twenty people typical in the Israeli case. One reason for this gap is the social withdrawal that accompanies blue-collar unemployment. This social withdrawal, which will be discussed below, is ultimately rooted in the social stigma attached to blue-collar unemployment in the United States. This stigma, in turn, deals a direct blow to one of the cornerstones of the blue-collar job seeker's legitimate identity—his or her diligence.

The Experience of Labor-Market Obstacles

In discussing labor-market difficulties, the most common theme brought up by blue-collar job seekers was the growing impersonalization and "pa-perization" of the hiring process. The increasing reliance on résumés, on-line applications, and formal rigid criteria was perceived as undermining attempts to communicate their diligence, which relied on personal inter-action. Most job seekers reported that this impersonalization of the job search was a sharp break with the past. Jerry said:

> They are asking to e-mail or fax the résumé, rather than interview. The inter-view is now on paper. These days, it's what's on paper and not so much the per-sonal. It used to be different. It used to be more based on face-to-face inter-views and not so much on résumés. Just speak to me.

Reggie echoed this experience: "Five years ago, I would not even need to put in a résumé. I got all those other jobs without a résumé. Before, I could just walk in."

The "paperization" of the process is frustrating for blue-collar job seek-ers, who generally believe that their strengths do not come through on paper. Résumés tend to highlight formal credentials, which is not where most blue-collar workers feel they can distinguish themselves. Dave explained:

> Since the electronic age, you've got to have exceptional and verifiable qualifi-cations for someone to look at your résumé. Even the skills that I have, there

are thousands of other people with the same qualifications. So what makes me distinguishable from the next guy? ... I walk into stores and ask to talk to the hiring manager, but it's much more rare than it used to be.... I used to just go talk to the person hiring there. Talk to the owner.

The impersonalization of the hiring process often presents unbending obstacles to the job seekers' strategies for presenting themselves as diligent and hardworking. Bearing a strong resemblance to the experience of the Israeli job seekers we met in chapter 5, George was frustrated by the invisibility that the rigid application process creates:

The hardest thing about job searching is access to the people who are offering these jobs. You can e-mail, fax, go fill out applications, but *that's just paper.* I have a personality that wants to work, but I have to see the guy. I need to look a person in the face and say, "Hey, I might want to work with you."

Résumés and formal processes highlight formal qualifications, and in most cases formal credentials or education requirements are perceived as artificial obstacles, not reflecting the necessary skills to perform the job. As James put it: "It used to be you didn't need a high school degree to work at McDonald's. Now they've put a clamp on that. Without a diploma, you ain't shit. You are a worthless person in the world.... There are criteria for every job. To be a dog-walker, [you] need a license."

Beyond formal qualifications and credentials, blue-collar job seekers also face a number of other rigid filters. For example, most job applications require a criminal background check, drug tests (which often involve having to urinate in front of the tester), credit checks, and in some cases pre-employment tests focusing on basic reading and math skills.[4] These rigid filters that do not see through to the job seeker's actual skills mirror the Israeli white-collar experience with staffing agencies.

As in the Israeli specs game, questions about salary expectations are raised as a threshold issue and can become an obstacle. While in the chemistry game, the salary issue is typically raised in the later stages of the hiring process and is a signal of strong interest from the employer, in the blue-collar diligence game, salary is raised as a threshold issue as part of the job application. Answering the question about expected salary poses a strategic dilemma. Job seekers are unsure how to answer the salary question in a way that does not foreclose the job opportunity but yet does not lock them into a low salary. For example, Jerry had not had any interviews in the past month, despite filling out countless applications. He was not sure why but feared it might be related to his salary expectations: "Only thing they are telling me is, 'We are not hiring at the moment,' or I am asking for too much money. But to live in California, I need at least eleven dollars [an hour]. I have learned now to leave it blank . . . not put the dollar amount, so that I don't get overlooked."

Losing the Diligence Game

This chapter opened with Reggie saying that his mind was about to explode. Jerry used the same metaphor to describe his unemployment experience: "It is a very stressful, very emotional period, feeling frustration, anger, anxiety. I see the logic of people exploding." As we have seen throughout this book, particular job-search games generate particular experiences and corresponding subjective responses. In the context of the diligence game, the subjective response to not finding work—and to the financial hardship that comes with unemployment—is frustration, anxiety, and humiliation. Jerry elaborated on his experience with labor-market rejections:

> They [employers] tell me, "If you had come in an hour earlier" or "You have insufficient skills." I tell myself they are feeding me a bunch of crock. I'd rather have a person be straight with me. Not waste my time. . . . Hardest part of it all is just taking the rejection. Just being rejected. These people don't look at me as being important. Hey, I have to make a living, too.

The humiliation described by blue-collar job seekers is different from the self-blame of American white-collar job seekers. In the chemistry game, the pain of rejection comes from revealing the self in an attempt to connect with the hiring manager and then being told you do not fit. In the diligence game, the social difference between job seeker and hiring manager, and the lack of interpersonal fit, is taken for granted. Moreover, because blue-collar job seekers' attempts to meet hiring managers are typically thwarted by impersonal and impenetrable filters, it is not the job seekers' presentations of self but these rigid filters that are the most salient determinants of the hiring outcome. In other words, the diligence game is characterized by low player prominence. It is not the job seeker's strategic actions that are perceived to ultimately determine the outcome but a system of hiring that increasingly relies on online applications, rigid credential requirements, and background checks. It is also a system that renders the job seeker's diligence invisible. As in the specs game, low player prominence produces system-blame not self-blame.

As the Israeli case showed, the absence of self-blame does not mean that the unemployment experience is not emotionally painful. The pain of rejection and of continued unemployment in the American blue-collar context stems from the interpretation that one's work contribution is not needed. As Jerry put it in the quote above, "These people don't look at me as being important." For many blue-collar workers, this is a direct blow to their sense of self. In Bill's words: "A job, no matter the pay, gives you a sense of self-respect. No matter how much you don't like it. The only thing I know to do is how to work. I could be wasting time, but I prefer having a job to anything." Bill had previously worked at Wal-Mart, which he described as the "worst working experience of my life" due to mistreatment by a capricious manager. Nevertheless, he recalled: "I could not stand Wal-Mart but I gave a hundred and ten percent." While Wal-Mart was a terrible job, it did allow Bill to maintain his worker identity and enact his ethic of being a hard worker.

The pain of blue-collar unemployment often also arises from the fact that the job seeker's family and friends may interpret his or her labor-market rejections through the lens of the diligence game; that is, as an indication of his or her lack of diligence and willingness to work. In the white-collar context, job seekers' friends and family are generally supportive. If tensions arise, it is typically because friends and family believe that the job seeker is holding out unrealistically for a high-level job. But in the blue-collar context, tensions with family and friends are more frequent, often arising when the job seeker feels (or knows) that others are doubting his or her diligence in looking for work. Denise reported an extreme case: "My husband kicked me out of the house. He doesn't think I am looking for work hard enough. He thinks jobs just fall from the sky. I told him I never been no lazy woman."

Social tensions with family and friends also arise as job seekers sense that their relative social status has been diminished to the point that their identity is now defined by their unemployment. This new identity—and the tensions that come with it—lead many blue-collar job seekers to withdraw from their social relationships. George explained how being unemployed had affected his social life:

I don't go around people like my uncle and children because of feeling less than [*pause*], 'cause of what I don't have. Friends are funny. I'd rather not par-

take of things unless I can reciprocate. People talk about social things, but I am
not able to do that. One of the guys I went to high school with, a friend, starts
being afraid you'll ask to borrow money.

Jerome described a similar experience: "I can sense it with my friends.
'He's lost his job.' They look at you different. 'He's down on his luck.' So
there is a slight change there. First thing out of their mouth is: 'I don't
have any money.'"

The financial deprivations of unemployment also affect one's ability
to form new relationships, which further contributes to social isolation.
James explained how lack of money makes it impossible to keep up a
regular social life: "No milk, no honey. No finance, no romance. Women
want to know what you're doing. When you can't even take them to the
dollar store to get a soda, [and instead say] go to the water fountain, it's
tough. I have to laugh to keep from crying."

This social withdrawal has important consequence for the job search.
To the extent that job seekers isolate themselves to avoid humiliation,
they limit the degree to which they can use existing networks for help.
Friends who are avoided cannot be enlisted to help. The one exception to
this dynamic was networking at WorkSource itself. The social risk of networking was significantly lower there because everyone was in the same
boat. For many job seekers, WorkSource was their only source of word-of-
mouth information and social support.

In addition to withdrawing from social relations, many job seekers
attempt to avoid humiliation by keeping their struggle to themselves.
Kim said:

> I don't like letting people in my life see that I feel kicked around. I keep up
> a good front. "I'll be all right." And if I tell people, people talk. They will say
> they understand but then tell other people, "She's got no prospects!" So I'm on
> my own.

This withdrawal can even apply to one's husband or wife. Willie explained
his bottle-it-up strategy:

> No one knows when I am having a bad day. I won't say anything. My wife will
> give me a hug and a kiss. I will not even tell my wife. I never let anyone know
> because I don't want anyone to feel sorry for me. If they know you're feeling
> bad, they feel sorry for you, and you may not want to talk about it. Talk may
> bring a whole bunch of emotions, and you may not want that.

Willie's self-containment is intended to protect not only his family, but also himself. Many job seekers reported engaging in a constant struggle with their own negative thoughts. Kim actively tried not to think about her difficulties: "It helps because I can fake myself out and forget about these problems."

In this emotional work on the self, the stakes are seen as very high. It is often perceived that losing the struggle to stay positive and letting oneself get down means one may not be able to climb back up. Ben put it this way:

> I can sit at home and fall into the void, [thinking] how can I let this happen? . . . You've got to climb out of the pit. When you're in the pit, you wonder if it's going to get better, second-guess yourself, lots of negative thoughts. That's what you don't want. If you have them, it will drop you like that. If you get depressed, boy, wow, that's a sad case. I've seen people fall into depression, and it's not pretty.

The struggle to stay positive is thus motivated on three fronts. Succeeding in the job search, sustaining social relations, and maintaining internal well-being—all seem to require remaining positive. Whether presenting yourself to a prospective employer, to a friend, or even to *yourself*, the consistent effort is to put on a positive attitude. While the positive-attitude imperative for the job search cuts across class lines in the American context, it is, however, only in the blue-collar context that maintaining a positive attitude becomes essential for maintaining close social relationships.

The social context of the diligence game has another effect. The anxiety about finances that accompanies unemployment is generally more intense in the blue-collar context. Blue-collar job seekers are generally closer to the financial abyss, with little in the way of savings or other cushions; even the expenses of the job search itself can become a significant burden. For example, showing up in person at an employer's place of business, though seen as preferable to applying online, is also more expensive. Jerry explained: "There is not enough funding just to go around job searching. At this point right now I am bankrupt. I have no ends. My back is up against the wall." George described his situation: "The choice is eating or paying [electricity]. To go to [WorkSource] is a seven-dollar round trip. This affects other parts of my life, like I run out of toilet paper." Such financial anxiety means, as George put it, "I don't sleep at night, tossing and turning. Then I'm not fully rested, but I got to get up. . . . The frustration and depression don't leave you."[5]

In addition to the anxiety brought about by actual financial deprivation, there can also be severe anxiety that you will need to ask your family or friends for money or that they are already afraid you are going to ask them for money. While some job seekers are fortunate enough to be able to get by with a combination of unemployment benefits, a working spouse's income, and help from parents, most are deeply afraid of imposing a financial burden on others, including their families. For example, Denise, whose husband kicked her out for allegedly being "lazy," went to live in a housing project with her adult daughter, grandson, and cousin, and was anxious because she could not contribute to the household expenses. She had received unemployment compensation after losing her job at a cereal factory. However, early in her job search, she had found a temporary job through an agency. After missing a day of work, she had been fired from this temporary job and, for that reason, no longer qualified for unemployment insurance. The resulting financial stress extended from how to pay the bills next month to how to cover her eventual funeral expenses so that she would not be a burden to her daughter. Denise related:

> I need benefits. I need insurance. I am forty-six, and when I pass, I want it to be taken care of with insurance from a funeral home as a packet [so that] my daughter will not have to worry about it.

Denise's case reflects a broader dilemma. While temporary work can generate badly needed cash, it also jeopardizes one's ability to receive unemployment benefits. As Karl put it: "Temp work messes with my unemployment." The temp agency offers "a day here or four hours there. I told them I need forty hours a week. I have teenage children." Jerry, a former forklift operator, avoided this dilemma by working in the informal economy: "I try to take one or two days a week to do catch-out, like stand on the street. Trucks will come through that require some workers. It's a fifty-fifty chance. You need to sell yourself to them. Full day of work is eighty dollars. Catch-out is my bread and butter these days." Another option is selling drugs. George explained: "I could easily be selling drugs and making quick money." But, he continued, "I know the downside. The jail part does not scare me. It's the respect of my children."

Like Denise, George was not receiving unemployment benefits. He had had a dispute with his former manager, who claimed that George was fired "for cause." To avoid being a burden to his extended family, George had opted to live in a homeless shelter. He explained:

I didn't want to move in with my cousins or sisters and not pay any bills. I went into a shelter, so I can start being independent now. They give you ninety days. They give extensions if you're making progress and have a good attitude. They know who's kicking all day long. I leave at six a.m. and I'm in bed by seven p.m.

Jerry, who also lived in a homeless shelter, said that his ability to stay there was, in his words, "all based on your performance. They see me as a go-getter." Thus, whereas Denise was deemed "lazy" by her husband, George and Jerry were evaluated as diligent by their shelters. All three were judged worthy, or not worthy, of a place to live according to the same ubiquitous "hard worker" standard.

The diligence game sharpens a dilemma that is present for all job seekers: How long do you hold out for a good job and when do you settle for a lesser job? Job seekers acknowledge that there may be some very low-wage jobs available, but they also recognize that these jobs do not pay enough to make ends meet. Michael put it this way: "Everyone is hiring but no one is paying enough." Kim agreed:

These days, "job" stands for "just over broke." There seems to be lots of work with low salary. I need more money to make ends meet. Seems like if you're not a professional, there are just scraps out there.

Low-wage jobs are not seen as a viable way to make a living. At the same time, the availability of such jobs creates a tension in the context of the diligence game because it suggests that perhaps the job seeker is unemployed because he or she is not willing to work hard. One way out of this dilemma is to seek retraining for better-paying jobs. But here again, job seekers at WorkSource face another form of the diligence filter.

Retraining: The Diligence Game Inside WorkSource

WorkSource offers some retraining funds, but to receive them, one must play the diligence game *inside* WorkSource.

Unlike AmeriSupport, which receives almost no state funding and relies on unpaid self-help speakers to provide content in exchange for an opportunity to market their services, One-Stop centers like WorkSource are funded by the state and the federal government.[6]

WorkSource is officially open to all job seekers. Anyone can become a member for free and have access to a common room with computers, phones, and newspapers to use for job searching. There are also weekly workshops, open to all job seekers. Yet, WorkSource's primary focus is to serve a select subset of the general population through counseling and retraining. Patricia, the director of WorkSource, explained: "We administer federal [retraining] funds to serve a number of people. We need to spend these funds to continue to get it." Sustaining this funding depends upon the "performance results" of the retraining, measured by the number of job seekers who obtain and retain employment upon finishing their retraining. This performance criterion generates a particular selection process. As Patricia plainly put it: "What we do is all tied up with the performance measures."

The performance-measure structure drives WorkSource to focus on identifying those job seekers who, as Patricia put it, give the staff a "sense that they will succeed." This "sense" is generated by assessing how job seekers jump through a series of hoops. The first hoop is invisible to the job seekers. Job seekers are not told about the availability of retraining funds when they first register at WorkSource or when they receive their mandatory orientation tour. They are told, however, that there are guidance counselors who are available for drop-in consultations to discuss their situation. It is then up to the job seeker to take the initiative to seek out one of the counselors. Unbeknownst to the job seekers who take this step, they have jumped through the first diligence hoop.

At the initial meeting with the counselor, a second invisible filter is applied to exclude job seekers who were "fired, or quit, or are chronically unemployed." Rob, one of the counselors, said that the first two groups do not qualify as unemployed and the circumstances surrounding their job loss are "red flags" about reliability. The latter group is simply presumed to be "difficult to place." From the perspective of WorkSource, as Jenn, another counselor, related: "The ideal job seeker is one who was recently laid off" because he or she is "used to a working schedule."

Job seekers who have made it through these two invisible hoops are then asked if they are interested in retraining. Those who express an interest are given a set of tasks, such as researching their targeted retraining field, by doing which they "prove" their commitment and seriousness. Jenn explained:

> If they do all the homework and they have the motivation and they want to succeed, we then do two more follow-ups. . . . It's all about them. If they call, schedule appointments, want to invest time and energy, do the stuff I tell them,

then they motivate me. I say, "By this date you should have five things done."
It's a long drawn-out process. They have to be thorough. . . . My red flags are
missed appointments or if they don't do their homework. I give everyone a
chance. They just need to prove it to me.

The core filter at this stage of the selection process is persistence.

For Jenn, using this standard feels appropriate: "I am helping the
people who really want to be helped." However, it is also clear that the filtering mechanism at WorkSource is likely to reproduce the inequalities of
the wider job-search world. I asked the Patricia about the creaming effect:

PATRICIA: Yes. The counselors help those who have a good likelihood of getting a
job, who are employable.
AUTHOR: Doesn't this mean that those who need help most don't get it?
PATRICIA: Yes. It's a flaw in the legislation. It bothers me, but the incentive for our
counselors is the end result. If you enroll someone who can get a job, we get
refunded. It's performance-measure based. We want hard exits, which means
you got retrained and then you got a job, and not soft exits, which mean you
stopped going to the retraining. This is bad, but the legislation dictates that.

At the end of my formal fieldwork at WorkSource, I proposed starting
a discussion group for job seekers as an opportunity to openly share experiences and frustrations among peers. This seemed important because
the imperative to keep up a positive attitude meant that job seekers typically had no one in their personal social network with whom to talk about
how hard it all was. Occasionally this role was played by compassionate
counselors at WorkSource, but that was not one of their duties. Willie, who
regularly met with Jenn, told me that the most useful support provided at
WorkSource was the "one-on-one conversation. Not about jobs, but just
to communicate, to know that someone knows what I am going through."
My proposal, however, was met with concern from the WorkSource administration that "talking" may replace diligent job searching. Patricia put
it this way:

We want to motivate job seekers to be serious job seekers. We want to encourage working. Meetings can sometimes replace employment as a source of contact. We want to make sure this doesn't happen.

My discussion-group proposal also seemed to have been initially opposed due to concern that I would reveal too much information and upset

the center's carefully constructed filtering system for receiving retraining funds. I was told that since I was not a trained employee, I may not accurately reflect WorkSource's policies on retraining. The group was approved once I agreed not to discuss retraining but only to refer job seekers to see the counselors. While the proposed group was approved partly because it justified making use of a grant for helping displaced workers, it was not put on the WorkSource listing of offerings on the bulletin board. When one attendee asked why the group was not posted on the bulletin, he was told: "That's because we don't want this to be your home. We want you to get a job."

Whether blue-collar job seekers are interacting with potential employers, social connections, or institutions such as homeless shelters and WorkSource, the consistent filter used to determine whether they will receive work, social support, shelter, or retraining is diligence.

*   *   *

If one only considered the differences in the American white-collar and blue-collar unemployment experiences, one might hypothesize that *class* plays an important role in shaping responses to unemployment. Similarly, if one only considered the differences in the American and Israeli white-collar unemployment experiences, one might hypothesize that *culture* plays an important role in shaping responses to unemployment. Yet the findings in this chapter show that the two groups whose unemployment experiences are most similar—Israeli white-collar workers and American blue-collar workers—have neither class nor culture in common.

The surprising parallels in their experiences suggest the importance of looking beyond class and culture to examine the labor-market institutions that structure job-search experiences. Specifically, as we have seen in this chapter, it is the structural similarities between the specs and diligence games—their low player prominence and the nature of their requisite emotional labor—that help us make sense of the similarities in subjective responses.

CHAPTER SEVEN

Conclusion

Job-Search Games and Unemployment Experiences

Unemployment experiences are neither universal nor simple reflections of particular cultural or economic conditions. My cross-national and cross-class comparative analysis revealed how different labor-market institutions give rise to different job-search games and how playing these games generates very different unemployment experiences.

In this concluding chapter, I present a brief side-by-side comparison of the key elements of the chemistry and specs games to illuminate some of the mechanisms underlying the cross-national variations in unemployment experiences. I then revisit the cross-class comparison and consider its implications for the role of institutions and culture. Finally, I discuss the implications of this book for our understanding of unemployment and our understanding of the relationship between social structures, individual experiences, and the possibility of social change.

Chemistry vs. Specs

This book's conceptualization of the chemistry game links American white-collar job-search practices to the experience of highly personalized self-blame. This previously untheorized link becomes evident through the comparison of the chemistry game to the specs game, which shows how two groups of white-collar job seekers, looking for similar kinds of jobs under similar economic conditions, end up having very different unemployment experiences.

At first glance, white-collar job searching in Israel and the United States seems similar. In both places, employers post openings on various Internet websites and job seekers respond. Yet beneath the surface, the concrete job-search practices and strategies—how American and Israeli job seekers construct résumés and cover letters, use networks, and present themselves at interviews—are strikingly different. They are playing different games.

White-collar Israeli and American workers have different understandings of what it takes to find a job. Israelis describe finding a job as a process of identifying an employer that happens to need one's precise package of skills, experiences, and education—one's specs. Americans describe finding a job as a process of proving that one is a good fit. Skills are perquisites to be in the running, but, ultimately, what matters most are intangible inner qualities that come through in one's self-presentation.

These distinct understandings emerge not from national or class-based characteristics, but from institutional differences. Although employers in both sites sift potential candidates using a mixture of objective specs and subjective chemistry filters, the different ways in which hiring is mediated by labor-market institutions make the specs filter more *salient* to Israeli white-collar job seekers and the chemistry filter more *salient* to American white-collar job seekers.

The specs discourse resonates with Israeli job seekers because of the practices of staffing agencies and testing institutes, the front lines of the Israeli labor market with which Israeli job seekers have direct and frequent contact. The chemistry discourse resonates with white-collar American workers in part because the chemistry-based filtering practices used by American hiring managers are the job seeker's only direct personal experience with the hiring process. But more importantly, the salience of the chemistry filter is greatly magnified by the American career-success self-help industry, which focuses on interpersonal fit as *the* key for getting hired and provides advice on improving one's self-presentation skills in a wide array of books, workshops, and coaching practices.

In each site, dominant labor-market institutions and corresponding discourses generate job-search games with distinct strategic logics. Israeli job seekers playing the specs game focus on identifying every job opening in the market and maximizing the sheer volume of applications. Given the structure of this game, Israeli job seekers see the success of any given application as being largely outside their immediate control. The only aspect of the search that does seem to be within their strategic control is the number of potential employers that are approached.

In contrast to the specs game's focus on the *external job market*, the chemistry game focuses strategic attention on the *self*. The job seeker must look inward in order to find, develop, and articulate the inner qualities that will convey fit with a given employer. These articulations take written form in résumés and cover letters and verbal form in rehearsed sound bites (elevator speeches) to be used while networking and interviewing. The different strategic logics of the two games are evident when we compare, side by side, the most common and concrete practices of job searching, such as writing résumés and cover letters, networking, and interviewing.

Israeli résumés are conceived of as a straightforward list of skills and credentials, while the American résumé is an advertisement, the construction of which involves strategic customization for each targeted employer in order to convey fit. In the chemistry game, the aesthetic quality of the résumé is given great weight, and a core activity at AmeriSupport is critiquing résumés, with a heavy emphasis on aesthetics and style. IsraSupport members, in contrast, typically do not look at each other's résumés. While American bookstores have shelves of books on how to write a résumé, Israeli bookstores have none. In the chemistry game, how a résumé looks matters. In the specs game, it does not.

In the chemistry game, cover letters, even more than résumés, provide an opportunity for job seekers to reveal the self behind the credentials and to persuade the potential employer of a good fit. In the specs game, on the other hand, cover letters are usually a two-sentence formality.

Honing an elevator speech and networking to develop *new* contacts is a central strategy in the chemistry game because personal references are perceived as more efficient conveyors of one's fit than even one's carefully crafted and customized résumés or cover letters. However, this strategy is not viable in the specs game. Given that game's formal and rigid screening institutions, to use personal referrals is to ask the employer to deviate from routine hiring practices—a deviation that even Israeli job seekers themselves typically view as corrupt or as "beating the system." In this context, personal connections and referrals are still important but work only as a personal favor to a family member or longtime friend.

Finally, the differences between the specs and chemistry games are evident in job interview strategies. In preparing for an interview, American white-collar job seekers conduct focused research and develop ways to articulate their passion for—and fit with—that particular company. They are advised that, during the interview itself, they should look around the interviewer's office for hints of children or hobbies that can suggest areas

TABLE 1: **Summary of Job-Search Games***

Game	Specs	Chemistry
Strategic Focus	Market	Self
Résumés	List	Advertisement
Cover Letters	Two-sentence formality	Self-revealing
Networking	Corrupt	Efficient
Interviews	Oral exam	First date

*This table previously appeared in Sharone (2013).

of potential personal connection. Israeli interviews, on the other hand, require job seekers to project the image of a consummate professional and to suppress personal or non-work-related dimensions of the self. Revealing personal details would call one's professionalism into question. Whereas American job seekers most often compare interviews to first dates, the common metaphor in Israel is an oral exam.[1]

Table 1 summarizes some of the important differences between the two job-searching games. In short, whether in writing or in person, American job seekers attempt to externalize the self in order to connect and to project fit, while Israeli job seekers attempt to efface the self and project a competent professional with the right specs. Playing these different games gives rise to very different unemployment experiences.

Unemployment Experiences and Game Structures

The initial responses of newly unemployed job seekers in Israel and the United States are strikingly similar. They typically understand their job loss as having been outside their control, attributing it to factors such as corporate restructuring. Once they begin searching, however, differences emerge. In the first few months, American white-collar job seekers devote significantly more time to the search than their Israeli counterparts do and are more likely to report being excited about it. However, if they have not found a job after three months or so, their job-search intensity plummets. They typically report feeling personally rejected and often attribute their continued joblessness to what they begin to see as a flawed self. Unsuccessful Israeli job seekers, on the other hand, come to feel a sense of invisibility and increasingly blame their continued joblessness on a flawed system. Despite their anger at the system, however, they continue their search with only slightly diminished intensity.

To explain such diametrically opposite subjective responses—and their important implications for job-search intensity—requires comparing and analyzing the underlying structures of the games. Two critical differences need to be highlighted. First, the games have different levels of player prominence. The chemistry game is characterized by high player prominence because what is perceived to be the central determinant in the hiring decision—effective self-presentation and the projection of appropriate inner qualities to establish fit—is also perceived to be within the job seeker's strategic control. The specs game is characterized by low player prominence because few short-term strategies are available for piercing through the rigid specs filter. In most cases, the specs are fixed elements that broadly determine what kinds of jobs one can apply for. Thus, it is the filtering practices of the dominant labor-market institutions—*not* the job seeker's strategic moves—that are perceived to be the central determinants of the outcome.

The second important difference is that the chemistry and specs games demand different kinds of emotional labor, which map on to Hochschild's (1983) distinction between surface acting—requiring only an external display of emotions—and deep acting, which requires the internal production of the requisite emotion. The specs game requires surface acting: a job seeker must submerge the subjective self and externally present himself or herself as nothing more and nothing less than a professional with the necessary specifications. This *self-objectification* demands that job seekers reduce themselves in writing to a set of marketable elements and, in person, suppress their individuality and nonprofessional attributes in an effort to display an understanding of the strictly professional nature of the hiring process. The chemistry game, on the other hand, demands the deep acting of *self-subjectification*: producing and projecting the emotional tonalities of a subject with the requisite internal attributes. While Israeli job seekers compartmentalize the self and attempt to project a personality-free professional exterior, American job seekers externalize the self in an attempt to connect. While the emotional labor of self-subjectification is perhaps most easily observed in the job-search context, it is not limited to it. Whereas Hochschild's (1983) theoretical breakthrough was in identifying and naming the emotional labor required of workers in certain interactive service work, this book points to a form of emotional labor that pervades the American white-collar world of work.

The games' differences with respect to player prominence and emotional labor generate distinct search experiences that unfold over time. In the initial stages of play, the chemistry game provides players with a boost of excitement that corresponds to intense levels of engagement in the job search. This is attributable to the game's high level of player prominence, which puts job seekers in control of their career fates. It is *their* strategic moves—how they write their résumés and cover letters and how widely and wisely they network—that will determine the outcome. The intensity of the absorption at this stage is evident in support-group meetings in which American job seekers engage in heated brainstorming sessions about ideal cover letters or elevator speeches. The intensity of engagement is also boosted by the emotional labor of self-subjectification. In the initial phase of the search, this emotional work generates vulnerability but is also experienced as self-exploration and even creative self-expression.

The initial stage of the specs game, on the other hand, is far less engaging. The game's low player prominence means that Israeli job seekers perceive themselves to have far less strategic control from the outset. The search experience is rote and requires, more than anything else, the stamina to keep scouring the market for new postings. Moreover, the emotional labor of self-objectification requires dispassionate attention to the market and its demands. Rather than the excitement of self-discovery and self-expression, the specs game's self-objectification only generates detachment.

The two games not only start differently but also unfold differently over time. In the chemistry game, after three or more months of unsuccessful job searching, the high player prominence has a boomerang effect, resulting in self-blame. The same player prominence that made the job seeker the enthusiastic master of his or her own fate now brands him or her as the one who has failed to find work.

But player prominence alone is not enough to explain the highly specific nature of American self-blame. As the preceding chapters showed, American job seekers are typically not blaming themselves for lacking the right job skills or for otherwise losing out in a meritocracy, but rather for failing to present themselves well enough or for having only a flawed or defective self to present. This more insidious form of self-blame can be traced to the game's emotional labor. Self-subjectification requires job seekers to bring to the fore and externalize inner elements of the self. It is this highly subjectified self that American labor-market institutions place at the center of the job-search game, and it is this highly subjectified self to which repeated failures are attributed. High player prominence leaves American job seekers with no one but themselves to blame for losing, while self-subjectification gives this blame a particularly personal edge. The deeply personalized quality of American self-blame is thus the mirror image of the structure of the American chemistry game.

The specs game generates a very different dynamic of subjective responses over time. Israeli job seekers who continue to look for work for three or more months begin to feel angry at a system that they perceive as only seeing them as a collection of buzzwords. The specs game's low player prominence means that losing in this game does not reflect much on the job seeker's strategies; she or he is decentered, and their strategic moves are not perceived as determinative of the negative outcome. As in the chemistry game, the focus of the blame is projected toward whatever elements are perceived to be decisive, which in this case are the labor-market institutions that increasingly seem to arbitrarily exclude certain job seekers and their skills.

As in the American case, understanding the precise nature of the Israeli subjective response to the system requires looking beyond low player prominence and turning to the effects of the emotional labor of self-objectification. This emotional labor demands that job seekers suppress all aspects of the self and reduce themselves to a set of specs. It is this reduction of the self that leads Israeli job seekers to feel that they have become invisible. Turning themselves into a set of buzzwords to be filtered by highly rigid institutions generates the common feeling of *choser onim* and the sense that "no one is checking *me* out for real."

At the heart of the lived experience of playing the specs game is a growing sense of being betrayed by a system that discursively claims to be meritocratic but that in practice appears increasingly arbitrary and unfair because it blindly excludes job seekers from the labor market. Low player prominence and self-objectification combine to render each successive failed attempt at finding work further proof of the arbitrariness of the rigid filtering mechanisms, and of a system that does not see the full potential—not to mention the humanity—of the person behind the specs.

Job-Search Discouragement

One of the most troubling consequences of unemployment is job-search discouragement. In the United States, millions of workers routinely report that they would like to work—often desperately so—but have ceased searching. This book's comparative analysis of the dynamics of the chemistry and specs games helps explain patterns of job-search intensity and discouragement. As previously described, the nature of the chemistry game leads over time to a much more precipitous drop in job-searching activity than the specs game. High player prominence and self-subjectification mean that once self-blame has begun, each further unsuccessful attempt to find work is yet another experience of highly personalized failure. Continuing to search only intensifies the sense of personal failure and rejection; it becomes very hard to carry on. In contrast, the low player prominence and self-objectification of the specs game generate a dynamic in which continued job searching intensifies the apparent contradiction between the hiring system's claims of fairness and its blind and arbitrary methods, while leaving the job seeker's sense of self untouched. Whereas in the chemistry game each unsuccessful attempt rubs salt in the wound, in the specs game unsuccessful attempts leave job seekers more angry but nonetheless feeling they have nothing to lose by continuing their search.

These different trajectories can be explicated by analogy to two familiar games: chess, a game of strategy with high player prominence, and the lottery, a game of luck with low player prominence. Israeli job seekers' experience is akin to playing the lottery, where losing is understood to reflect the low odds built into the game. American job seekers' experience, however, is more like playing chess, where losing is understood to reflect one's own abilities. If you play chess and keep losing, you are unlikely to enter a chess tournament. This decision would reflect not only your perception that you would be unlikely to win, but also your perception that losing would reflect poorly on *you*. In contrast, as the booming lottery industry suggests, many players will keep playing a low player-prominence game despite repeated losses, hoping that their time has come for a lucky break but feeling none the worse about *themselves* in any case.

These imperfect analogies aim to convey an essential but generally overlooked element underlying the dynamic of job-searching intensity: The continued intensity of job searching over time depends on the understandings and interpretations that job seekers develop about the determinants of prior failed attempts. The game framework captures this dynamic because it focuses on the unfolding experience in which the job seeker's subjective understanding of the outcome at any stage of the search affects his or her level of activity in the next stage.

These findings have practical implications for combating discouragement. The currently dominant theory of job-search discouragement is that unsuccessful job searching diminishes a job seeker's sense of self-efficacy.

This leads some to argue that the appropriate antidote to discouragement is "empowerment training" to challenge job seekers' beliefs about their limited power.[2] My findings suggest that, in fact, too much perceived empowerment may backfire. A self-help message that finding work is wholly within one's control and that it largely depends on one's job-searching skills (themselves consisting largely of self-presentation) may provide an initial boost but sets the stage for later self-blame and, in fact, for the curtailment of effort and engagement. My findings point to the need for support programs that not only focus on a job seeker's individual power, but also make clear the structural nature of the obstacles he or she faces. As the Israeli case suggests, job seekers' recognition of forces and constraints beyond their control helps them maintain the intensity of job searching over time because it provides a way to understand labor-market difficulties without debilitating self-blame.[3]

The Role of Culture and the Blue-Collar Diligence Game

What is the role of culture in shaping American workers' subjective responses to unemployment? As discussed in chapter 1, the American cultural tool kit (Swidler 1986) provides both individualistic and structural accounts of career hardships. Explaining why white-collar workers turn to individualistic narratives when discussing their difficulties in finding work must therefore reach beyond culture. This book shows that the American white-collar unemployment experience—and particularly self-blame—is generated by playing the chemistry game. But one might ask whether the chemistry game and the institutions that underlie it are themselves reflective of the American culture of individualism, in which case the culture of individualism would indeed explain self-blame, although indirectly.

Responding to that question calls for an examination of the relationship between cultures and institutions. Throughout this book, I have highlighted findings that suggest that broad cultural differences are *insufficient* to explain the dominance of the labor-market institutions that structure the games in each site. Surely, each country's dominant labor-market institutions are partly constituted by discourses drawn from the wider culture. American hiring institutions draw on discourses of individual uniqueness and interpersonal fit, while Israeli institutions draw on discourses of objectivity and modernization. The availability of these discourses in the wider culture is indeed a prerequisite for the viability of these particular institutions. Yet while institutions draw on cultures, they are not the inevitable products of those cultures. The American culture of individualism is, in fact, consistent with a whole array of possible hiring institutions to filter candidates—including those that focus on specs, as evidenced by American staffing agencies' use of specs discourses and practices that mirror those of their Israeli counterparts (as discussed at the end of chapter 2). Strikingly, both the specs and chemistry "logics"[4] play important roles in *both* societies in social spheres outside the hiring context. The specs discourse is used in both Israel and the United States in the context of buying certain products, such as an automobile, whereas the chemistry discourse is used in both the United States and Israel in the context of romantic dating. Labor-market institutions' use of specs in Israel and chemistry in the United States are not cultural inevitabilities, but rather selections driven, at least in part, by political-economic forces and legal considerations.[5]

My cross-class comparison of American job seekers provides particularly important evidence that unemployment experiences are more linked to specific job-search games generated by specific institutions than to widely shared national cultures. As discussed in chapter 6, of the three groups of job seekers examined in this book, the two groups that share *neither culture nor class* report the most parallel unemployment experiences. The similarities between American blue-collar and Israeli white-collar job seekers' experiences particularly highlight the importance of job-search game structures—that is, the degree of player prominence and the depth of the emotional labor—in shaping subjective responses.

American blue-collar job seekers play a distinct game that focuses on displaying their diligence and ethic of hard work. While the diligence filter ostensibly resembles the chemistry filter in its attention to intangible characteristics of the job seeker, the actual structure of the diligence game, with its rigid hiring practices, more closely resembles that of the specs game. And it is this structural similarity in the games that, in turn, generates the similarity in unemployment experiences.

In the United States, the dominant institutions that mediate between job seekers and employers look very different across class lines. While hiring managers in the white-collar context look for interpersonal chemistry, which often stems from social similarity, hiring managers in the blue-collar context look for signs of compliant subordination and willingness to engage in hard work, attitudes that may in fact be undermined by social similarity.[6] American blue-collar hiring processes are also far more rigid because they typically involve criminal background checks, drug tests, credit checks, threshold questions about salary expectations, and, in some cases, pre-employment tests. Moreover, in the blue-collar context, the dominant sources of job-search advice are peers and personal experience rather than the self-help industry, which plays only a marginal role. These institutional differences generate blue-collar job-search strategies that are less focused on tailored résumés and cover letters or well-rehearsed elevator speeches for networking and more focused on what many blue-collar job seekers consider the most effective modes of job searching: showing up at the employers' place of business and attempting to meet the hiring manager to convey one's readiness to work hard.

The diligence game is characterized by low player prominence. It involves repetitive attempts by job seekers to meet hiring managers that are most often rebuffed by an impenetrable bureaucratic hiring process. As in the specs game, given these impersonal and immovable filters, job seekers' strategic moves are not perceived as central to determining the hiring outcome. The diligence and specs games are also similar in terms of emotional labor; both require surface acting rather than the deep acting necessary in the chemistry game.[7] As the prior chapters reveal, deep acting leaves job seekers far more vulnerable to personalizing their labor-market difficulties than surface acting does.

Parallel game structures result in similar unemployment experiences. In explaining labor-market difficulties, blue-collar job seekers often discuss how the "paperization" of the process does not allow employers to see their hard-work ethic, much as white-collar Israeli job seekers discuss how the staffing agencies' rigid checklists make them feel "invisible." American blue-collar job seekers often express themselves in words that could just as easily have come from Israeli white-collar job seekers. For example, consider the similarity between an Israeli job seeker's frustration that "they [employers] don't look you in the eye to see who you are" and an American blue-collar worker's assertion: "I have a personality that wants to work, but I have to see the guy. I need to look a person in the face." The diligence game and the specs game, while played in different cultural and class contexts, share an underlying structure that generates a subjective experience of invisibility and arbitrariness.

*   *   *

Stepping back, a vast line of studies correlates unemployment with a decline in individual well-being. Bourdieu (2000, 222) discusses how exclusion from the social game of paid work deprives individuals of the "countless tokens of a socially known and recognized *function*," and leaves them feeling "purposeless and meaningless." Yet the nature of this difficult experience is not universal. This book reveals profound variations. In some cases, we see job seekers feeling personally rejected and internally flawed, while in others we see job seekers feeling invisible and arbitrarily excluded by a flawed system. While such feelings and thoughts may at first appear deeply individual and personal, the findings described in this book show that they fall into clear patterns and correspond to the structures of the games that shape the experience of job searching.

Beyond unemployment, the theory of social games[8]—as extended and developed in this book with the theorization of player prominence and the incorporation of emotional labor—may shed light on how other variations in social structures generate distinct individual-level experiences. It may be easier to observe the engendering of self-blame and discouragement in the context of long-term unemployment than in other contexts, but the theoretical framework developed in this book can be applied in a wide range of social contexts—such as workplaces, schools, or even personal relationships—to analyze how particular structural characteristics of institutional contexts explain systematic variations in the experiences of and responses to various life outcomes.

Social Games and Social Change

The chemistry and spec games not only produce different individual outcomes, but also generate different levels of collective action aimed at transforming the institutional underpinnings of unemployment. In Israel I observed numerous instances of collective action initiated and led by unemployed white-collar workers. When gathered together in support groups, Israeli job seekers consistently expressed a sense of being collectively wronged by external forces, which was often followed by a discussion of what could or could not be done about it. In the specs game, the longer the job seekers searched, the more they perceived and openly discussed the problem as rooted in the hiring system. System-blame does not guarantee collective action—many Israeli job seekers expressed skepticism about the value of any effort to change the system—but there were some who insisted on the need for collective action. I observed one group organize a public teach-in on neoliberalism and its effects on employment conditions, inviting speakers from a local NGO and a local university. Another group organized a letter-writing campaign to politicians, demanding improved unemployment benefits and more job creation.[9]

A revealing moment occurred in the summer of 2011, when an Israeli woman, working as a video editor and unable to secure more than low-paying temporary jobs, was evicted from her Tel Aviv apartment. Unable to find an affordable apartment, she pitched a tent on the grass divider in one of Tel Aviv's major boulevards. She also put out a call on a social media website for others to join her in protesting escalating housing prices and, more broadly, the state's embrace of neoliberal policies and the evisceration of the welfare state. Within days thousands had joined her protest, and within a month Israel witnessed the largest protest in its history, with over 300,000 people chanting, "The people demand social justice." While this particular protest did not originate with the unemployed, many unemployed Israeli workers immediately joined in. Members of IsraSupport reported reaching out to the protest organizers as a group and, together with others, organizing a demonstration that specifically addressed the issue of staffing agencies. One unemployed job seeker explained: "We must bring to the agenda the issue of the staffing agencies as part of the larger struggle of social justice."

By contrast, among my sample of American white-collar job seekers, I found only rare attempts to discuss the possibility of collective action and no actual instance of it. During my year at AmeriSupport, in the context of a group for whom the shared nature of labor-market difficulties was manifest, every attempt by a member to engage others in discussing their shared plight as a public issue was shot down as self-sabotage and reflecting a "bad attitude."[10]

My findings and analytical framework suggest an approach to answering the question of *why* collective action among unemployed white-collar job seekers in the United States is rare. Contrary to the claims of some theories (e.g., Schlozman and Verba 1979), this absence of collective action is not simply the result of job seekers being so steeped in individualistic ideologies that they cannot conceive of structural causes—or collective solutions—to their predicament. In fact, as previously shown, white-collar workers typically recognize their job loss as structurally determined (by practices such as offshoring), and in the wider American society, there is no shortage of discussion of unemployment as a public and political issue—in fact, unemployment was *the* dominant issue in the 2012 presidential elections. Rather, as this book shows, it is the day-to-day experience of playing the chemistry game, with its particular structure arising from its particular institutions, that gives white-collar unemployment its individualizing and apolitical focus. The game initially boosts the job seeker to the status of a captain, charting his or her own career path, but eventually generates a subjective understanding of a flawed inner self. Whether in the boost or bust phase, the game pushes structural constraints and public solutions to the background, rendering the direct lived experience of unemployment as a private rather than a public matter.

In the fall of 2011, in the midst of the ongoing labor-market crisis sparked by the Great Recession, protests arose around the United States under the banner of Occupy Wall Street. These protests focused significant attention on the issue of economic inequality, as suggested by the commonly used slogan, "We are the 99%." But despite historically high levels of unemployment, there was little visible participation by unemployed workers in these protests on the issue of unemployment.[11] I interviewed the few self-identified unemployment activists at the Occupy Wall Street protests in New York City—where the first and largest protests took place—about their efforts to mobilize fellow unemployed workers. One of the main obstacles described by these activists was self-blame, unemployed workers' "obvious sense of shame and thinking it's their fault." One openly unemployed activist offered this explanation of the difficulty of mobilizing other unemployed workers: "People feel shame. They don't want family members to see them. They don't tell their friends that they are unemployed, especially if they are unemployed for a long time."[12]

These cross-national differences in collective action are surface manifestations of a deeper underlying divergence in the extent to which unemployment is perceived as a public or private issue. My analysis and comparison of the specs and chemistry games suggest the conditions under which games have the effect of masking their underlying structures, as well as the opposite effect of rendering these underlying structures more visible and contestable. In the specs game, low player prominence and self-objectification tend to focus the players' attention outward to its structural foundations. As the preceding chapters show, playing the specs game generates feelings of anger and betrayal because the longer the game is played, the more intensely job seekers perceive a contradiction between the public claims of meritocracy and their private experiences of arbitrary exclusion. This generates an impetus for collective action oriented toward changing the structures of the specs game.

My analysis of how a game's internal contradictions can lead to dissent and resistance is similar to Burawoy's (2012) discussion of how games in "despotic regimes" may sow the seeds of their own destruction, which differs from Bourdieu's (1988) conceptualization of social games where resistance and collective action may arise from a change in social conditions that create a mismatch between a field and the habitus, but not from a social game's own dynamics, as further discussed in appendix B.

The chemistry game has the opposite effect. Rather than generating an impetus for collective action, its high player prominence and self-subjectification produce an inward focus and lead individuals to pin the blame for unemployment on their apparently flawed selves. While the chemistry game's individualizing focus renders collective action unlikely, the framework of social games developed in this book does allow one to be hopeful about the possibility of change. It is important to emphasize that the chemistry game is a product of institutions that are themselves mutable. Unlike theories that root the absence of collective action in an obdurate American individualism impermeable to experience (Schlozman and Verba 1979), my findings and theoretical framework suggest that the absence of collective action and the reproduction of existing social structures are the products of historically contingent institutional configurations. As the analysis in chapter 2 shows, the labor-market institutions underlying the chemistry game are not cultural inevitabilities, but the result of changeable political-economic conditions.

*   *   *

It may be surprising that a book on unemployment—the lack of work—would turn for an explanatory framework to theories of social games and emotional labor, which have deep roots in the sociology of work. This book in fact treats job searching as a form of work. Just as sociologists interested in understanding people's work experiences would typically examine what workers do each day (their labor process), a similar examination of what job seekers have to do each day to find a job (their job-search process) is necessary to comprehend unemployment experiences. Perhaps one reason why this approach has not been used before is that it runs counter to the dominant stereotype of unemployment as a void. The very word *un*employment signifies an absence. In societies in which people are identified, understood, and valued largely according to the paid work they do, the absence of employment implies disorientation, idleness, and passivity. Conceptualizing job searching as a form of work flips this image of unemployment on its head by emphasizing that, in fact, as this book shows, selling one's labor in the job market typically requires considerable unpaid labor.

Looking for work may be the hardest work of all. The job-search experience is one of being told: *No. No. No. No. No.* In a society such as ours, in which one's social existence requires a job, the work of job searching puts this very social existence on the line day in and day out. Depending on the institutionalized mechanisms of inclusion and exclusion, an unemployed white-collar job seeker may come to feel, as in Israel, invisible, dehumanized, and betrayed, or, as in America, personally exposed, flawed, and rejected.

Yet nothing about these unemployment experiences is inevitable. The institutions underlying them are changeable. It is up to us to change them.

APPENDIX A

Methodology

My initial in-depth interviews were conducted with 57 American white-collar job seekers in the San Francisco Bay Area in 2005, and 48 Israeli white-collar job seekers in the Tel Aviv area in 2006. I conducted the interviews in the United States in English and the interviews in Israel in Hebrew. Having spent half of my childhood in Israel and the other half in the United States, I am bilingual and was able to probe the nuances of interviewees' responses in both languages. I subsequently supplemented my data by interviewing two more groups of job seekers:

(i) I interviewed 30 blue-collar unemployed workers in the San Francisco Bay area, as discussed in chapter 6, to explore cross-class differences; and

(ii) I interviewed 27 white-collar job seekers in the Boston area in 2009–11. These interviews allowed me to explore the extent of any regional variations in the white-collar unemployment experience in the United States. In addition, since these interviews were conducted four to six years after my original interviews in the San Francisco Bay area, I used these interviews to examine the effects of technological changes that occurred during this period, such as the growth of social media and online networking, as well as any specific effects of the labor-market crisis that came in the wake of the Great Recession.

In addition to job seekers, I also obtained supplementary data by interviewing American and Israeli recruiters in human resources departments and staffing agencies, job-search coaches, and counselors.

To facilitate comparability, I limited my interviews to unemployed job seekers in the middle years of their working lives, between the ages of thirty and sixty. The age parameters aimed to reduce the likelihood that the job-search intensity or duration would be tangled with indecision about career paths, which is more typical of younger workers, or with considerations of possible retirement, which is more common for older workers.

I also limited my sample to job seekers looking for work in the private sector, and maintained comparable proportions of managers, technical workers, and other white-collar workers.

The goal of my purposive recruiting strategy was not a random sample but variation along significant independent variables to allow comparisons across subcategories (Lamont and White 2009; Small 2009; Trost 1986). Specifically, in recruiting white-collar job seekers, I sought a range of respondents along the dimensions of location (e.g., San Francisco and Tel Aviv), white-collar occupation, gender, marital status, age, and length of unemployment. The ultimate number of interviews was determined by saturation, the point at which further interviews provided little new and surprising information (Small 2009). This purposive recruiting approach has been recognized as appropriate when seeking to understand variations in particular processes and dynamics, with the aim of developing or "extending" theories (Becker 1998; Burawoy 1998; Trost 1986) and for "unraveling the mechanisms underlying causal processes, especially those that occur over time" (Lamont and White 2009, 10; Small 2009; Mitchell 1983). In this case, the recruiting strategy is well-suited for developing a theoretical framework that unravels the mechanisms producing variations in subjective response to unemployment and for generating causal inferences (Mitchell 1983; Small 2009).

Table A.1 summarizes the basic demographic characteristics of the San Francisco and Tel Aviv area interviewees, and compares these to the general population of unemployed job seekers in each site.

All interviews were transcribed and coded. The job-seeker interview data were initially coded with broad concepts covering different search strategies such as "customizing résumés" or experiences such as "personal rejection." Codes that corresponded to large amounts of interview data were also broken down to into several subcodes. For example, interviews that stressed the importance of résumé appearance and formatting were labeled "résumé aesthetics." A similar coding strategy was applied to field notes from support groups meetings of job seekers and presentations of speakers to job seekers.

I recruited interview subjects by a variety of means, including randomly approaching people at government unemployment offices and job fairs (40 percent), approaching job seekers at support groups (50 percent), and snowballing (10 percent).

TABLE A.1: **Sample Demograhics**

Site	San Francisco–area sample	General unemployed population (SF area)		Tel Aviv–area sample*	General unemployed population (Israel)
Number of interviewees	57			48	
Percentage male	55%	53%		58%	44.9%
Age (median)	48	36.4		43	37.2
Percentage married	37%	32%		56%	48.6%
Over one year unemployed	38%	35%		36%	40%
Race/Ethnicity					
White	74%	42%	European descent	48%	18%
African American	12%	13%	Middle Eastern descent	28%	43.8%
Hispanic	5%	20%			
Asian American and other	9%	25%	Other	24%	37.6%
Occupations					
Technical	35%			39%	
Managerial	28%			24%	
Professional	13%			10%	
Other white collar	24%			27%	

*My Israeli sample only includes Jewish Israelis (roughly 80 percent of the Israeli population). After conducting several pilot interviews with Arab Israeli job seekers, I concluded that the deep economic, social, and cultural schism meant that researching unemployment experiences among Arab Israelis would constitute an entirely different project.

As discussed in chapter 1, a significant advantage of recruiting job seekers at support groups was that it allowed me to observe my interviewees in action and interaction. The potential drawback of recruiting at support groups is that my respondents, in both sites, overrepresent job seekers who attend such groups, introducing a potential bias. However, since my interviews included *both* members and non-members of support groups, my analysis of the data can confirm that with respect to the general patterns of job-search practices and subjective responses (e.g., self-blame), there was no significant difference in the responses of job seekers who were members of support groups and those who were not. Moreover, the self-selection mechanism for participating in these groups is similar in both sites. Comparing my data for job seekers who belong to such groups and those who do not belong suggests that the groups attract job seekers who typically differ from the general population in two ways: First, at the point of joining, they are less likely to have promising job leads through their preexisting networks and are therefore feeling more anxious about their prospects. Second, from among job seekers who are facing difficulties, those who join support groups appear more motivated than non-members to seek advice about their job-search strategies and gain an edge by networking with fellow job seekers. Thus, both the most well-connected and the most discouraged job seekers that I interviewed did not attend these groups. The selection bias for job seekers who put more effort into job searching and who have a harder time finding work is helpful for the purposes of this study. The greater intensity of both the search effort and the labor-market difficulties brings into sharper focus processes that may be harder to discern in other job seekers.

I specifically chose to conduct participant-observations at AmeriSupport, as described in chapter 2, in part because participation in this group is free, which means that the membership is not biased toward job seekers who can afford paying for such a group. Moreover, based on my own visits to five other support groups around the United States and my review of studies of other support organizations, I concluded that AmeriSupport is similar to other public and private support organizations throughout the United States (Lane 2011; Garrett-Peters 2009; Ehrenreich 2005; Smith 2001; Newman 1999). While to my knowledge no data exists about the total number of white-collar workers who make use of such organizations, a 2009 small-case survey of newly unemployed workers reveals that 36 percent of job seekers go to One-Stop centers, where groups such as AmeriSupport meet and where other discrete job-search support services—such as workshops on writing résumés and interviewing—are provided (Zukin, Van Horn, and Stone 2011). Moreover, Lane (2011) finds that a quarter of American churches provide their members with some kind of job-search program. My selection of IsraSupport, as discussed in chapter 4, was based on its similarities to AmeriSupport. Both organizations focus on supporting unemployed white-collar professionals through regular meetings, where job seekers interact with both peers and career coaches to discuss job-search strategies.

Finally, in addition to my interviews and participant-observations, I also drew data from less conventional sources. After one year of participant-observations at AmeriSupport, I facilitated a weekly informal gathering called "Let's Talk about It" that focused on discussing emotional difficulties arising from the job search and unemployment. I also asked eight job seekers at AmeriSupport to keep a journal of their daily experiences and to share their journals with me. The open sharing that took place in these informal gatherings and in the journals greatly enriched my data.

APPENDIX B

Notes on Social Games

The theory of social games as developed, independently, by Michael Burawoy (1979) and Pierre Bourdieu (1976, 1997), attempts to bridge the agent-structure divide in a way that both comprehends the agent as a conscious decision maker and strategic actor, and, at the same time, recognizes (i) the constraints, limits, and obstacles posed by social structures external to the individual agent, and (ii) the constitutive power of social structures to shape the practices, strategies, and subjectivities of agents. Thus, for both theorists, the game metaphor accounts for our lived experience of strategizing and making decisions that have real consequences, while also explaining the patterned nature of actions and experiences in a given social context.

To explicate this conception of social games, it is useful to begin by contrasting it with other theories that also conceptualize social action as a kind of game, starting with the well-known theoretical tradition of game theory most often associated with economics. Game theory originated with John von Neumann and Oskar Morgenstern's 1944 publication of *Theory of Games and Economic Behaviour.* This theory defines games as "any interaction between agents that is governed by a set of rules specifying the possible moves for each participant and a set of outcomes for each possible combination of moves" (Hargreaves and Varoufakis 1995). It attempts to formally model the decision-making processes of players involved in various kinds of social situations. In economics, game theory has been deployed to develop understandings of how agents attempt to maximize utility in complex situations involving interactions with other utility-maximizing agents. Depending on factors such as whether the games are simultaneous or sequential, zero-sum or non-zero-sum, different possible sets of strategies are analyzed for the optimal approach. The essential assumption of game theory is that human actions can be understood, at least roughly, as mirroring instrumentally rational behavior and are therefore amenable to mathematical modeling. Behind this assumption lie two further related and often unstated assumptions. First, players' strategies are constrained by the rules and structure of the game but are not constituted by it—that is, there is no conception of social structures exerting any positive or constitutive power in shaping players' goals and strategies. Second, players have independent knowledge about the likely outcomes of moves to enable strategic decisions based on instrumentally rational calculations.

Social games theory is critical of game theory's conception of the instrumentally rational player. Bourdieu argues that game theory is a "scholastic representation" that projects on to players a "conscious project aiming at ends" and engagement in deliberate calculations that can only seem plausible in the imaginations of scholars far removed from practical experiences of daily life (1997, 207; 1998b, 2005). Bourdieu claims that games are in fact embodied experiences where players are not engaged in conscious calculation or strategizing but typically make moves based on deeply ingrained dispositions, which he calls *habitus*, or a *feel* for the game. Habitus is Bourdieu's conceptualization of the positive power of social structure to shape the very rationality of the player. For example, in analyzing marriage patterns among French peasants, Bourdieu (1976) finds that the regularities in practices are not based on obedience to any rule but are the result of strategies aimed to reproduce the family lineage and safeguard its patrimony. Bourdieu describes families deploying a whole array of "parries" and "moves" similar to those used in fencing and chess. The strategies, however, are not consciously considered but derive in a subconscious way from "strongly interiorized principles." As Bourdieu (1976, 141) puts it: "These strategies are the product of habitus, meaning the practical mastery of a small number of implicit principles that have spawned an infinite number of practices and follow their own pattern."

Burawoy (1979) implicitly shares with Bourdieu the same critique of game theory as ignoring the positive and constitutive power of social structures over the agent. Both Bourdieu and Burawoy see social games as shaping the subjectivities of agents, the logic underlying their strategies, and their interpretations of outcomes. They disagree, however, on the durability and stability of this positive constitution. Bourdieu's habitus posits that structures forge a deep, durable, and stable pattern of thoughts and practices that are carried by agents across social games. Burawoy theorizes a more fluid constitutive process resulting in sets of practices that are continuously reconfigured by the dynamics of the current game (Burawoy 2012).

It is this core difference regarding the habitus that leads to their different understandings of the relationship between games and social change alluded to in chapter 7. Whereas Burawoy's (2012, 1979) more fluid conception of agents' subjectivities opens the possibility of games with internal dynamics that ultimately generate resistance from players to their very rules, Bourdieu's conception of the habitus makes this kind of resistance much less likely. For Bourdieu (1988), resistance may arise from external conditions producing a mismatch between a field and the habitus, but absent such a mismatch a habitus adjusted to its external conditions is deeply embodied and difficult to change without arduous and improbable counter-training (Bourdieu 2000, 172). Bourdieu (1976, 1990a, 1997) suggests that the play of games typically leads to reproduction of their underlying structures because the experience of playing "adjusts" players' habitus—including their subjective hopes and expectations—to the objective probabilities of the game. This adjustment, Bourdieu claims, ultimately "ensures unconditional submission" to the established order that is implied in the *doxic* relation to the world" (2000, 231). In other words, agents submit to external structures because the extent of their hopes and expectations are produced by such structures. This process, Bourdieu claims, "puts the most intolerable conditions from the point of view of a habitus constituted in other conditions, beyond questioning and challenge" by those whose habitus is thereby constituted (2000, 231). Bourdieu's (1997) framework imagines that over time habitus and structure become so fused that deprivations inflicted on agents are made invisible by the deeply internalized and taken-for-granted understandings and expectations of the structure. Yet reflecting on the job-search games and dynamics described in this book suggests that social games do not always produce a relationship between agent and structure that moves toward fusion and adjustment of subjectivity to structure, but may instead produce a relationship of increasing tension. As described in chapter 5, playing the specs game generates anger because it intensifies the perceived contradiction between expectations of meritocracy and the experience of arbitrary exclusion. The chemistry game, as described in chapter 3, does not generate resistance; however, this is not the result of the adjustment of the habitus to "objective probabilities," but rather is due to the dynamic of a growing inward focus and self-blame. Instead of experiencing a growing sense of fusion between agent and structure, like the proverbial fish in water, American job seekers engaged in the chemistry game increasingly feel like defective fish unable to swim.

The theory of social games can also be fruitfully analyzed in relation to Johan Huizinga's (1950) anthropological theory in *Homo Ludens*. While game theory focuses on rational strategic calculations, an entirely different dimension of games is highlighted by Huizinga, who argues that the act of playing is essential to the human species. He rejects both the Smithian idea of *Homo Economicus* and the Marxist idea of *Homo Faber*, and instead proposes *Homo Ludens*: "Man the Player." Playing games for Huizinga is not about solving mathematical equations to find optimal strategies, but about the pull of "tension and solution," and mirthful fun. Huizinga focuses on the lure of games. He claims that we must delve beyond rationality or even functionality to understand why "the gambler loses himself in his passion" (1950, 4–11). The power of the game is based on tension arising from uncertainty or "chanciness" and a striving for resolution. Competition with others can increase this tension to fervent levels, as a "testing of the player's prowess: his courage, tenacity, resources." With its suspense and drama, "play casts a spell over us; it is 'enchanting' and 'captivating,'" such that the "consciousness of its being 'merely' a game can be thrust into the background." One of the enchanting elements of games is that they create an order. "Into an imperfect world and into the confusion of life it brings a temporary, a limited perfection." As Huizinga explains:

> All play has its rules. They determine what "holds" in the temporary world circumscribed by play. The rules of the game are absolutely binding and allow no doubt.... Indeed as soon as the rules are transgressed the whole play-world collapses. The game is over. The umpire's whistle breaks the spell and sets "real" life going again.... [The one who breaks the rules] [r]eveals the relativity and fragility of the play-world in which he had temporarily shut himself with others. He robs play of its *illusion*.... Therefore he must be cast out, for he threatens the existence of the play community. (1950, 11)

Huizinga's portrayal of human play is powerfully resonant because it corresponds to a familiar experience of absorption. For Huizinga, games are defined as being removed and "different from 'ordinary' life" because, he claims, true play must be free and voluntary activity. The condition of voluntariness conjures childhood memories of carefree play, but renders most social action as beyond the limits of Huizinga's theory. In sum, whereas economic game theorists examine the games of everyday life as if players were abstract mathematicians in a social vacuum, Huizinga explores the very human and social qualities of games but insists on distinguishing games from the everyday.

This luring and captivating quality of games is also at the heart of the theory of social games (Burawoy 1979; Bourdieu 1976, 1997). Yet there is an important difference between the theory of social games and Huizinga's theory. Social games share with game theory the presumption that games are a pervasive part of everyday life. Everyday life play may not be characterized by "mirthful fun," but due to the "chanciness" of social life, it nonetheless constantly and deeply engages us in strategizing. Unlike Huizinga's theory, the theory of social games recognizes that social activity admits of no easy or pure designation of "voluntary" versus "involuntary" action, and instead claims that for games to arise what is essential is that agents enjoy some minimal level of strategic "discretion." For example, the machinists that Burawoy (1979) describes are hardly free from economic coercion in their need to work for a living, but discretion over the precise manner, tempo, and rhythm of work provides enough space to open up the possibilities of strategizing and, thus, of absorbing play.

In sum, there are three common threads to the theory of social games. First, a conception of games' positive or constitutive power of the agent to account for agents' lived experience of engaging in strategic action while at the same time explaining the patterned nature of actions in a given structural context. Second, theories of social games are also characterized by a premise, shared with Huizinga (1950), that humans are drawn to games by the pull of "tension" that arises from uncertainty or "chanciness." Theorists of social games have emphasized the need for some level of uncertainty to generate the essential play experience of absorption. The outcome must be indeterminate ex-ante, but not random or unattainable. A game will not "absorb" players if "uncertainty is too great and outcomes are entirely beyond the control of players," or if "uncertainty is too slight" and outcomes are "completely controlled by players" (Burawoy 1979, 87). Or as Bourdieu puts it, for players to be invested in the game, the probabilities of fulfillment of the players' expectations must be "neither nil . . . nor total," but somewhere in between "absolute necessity and absolute impossibility" (Bourdieu 1997, 213). The third and final common thread of social games theory is the idea that ordinary life is infused with games. Games may arise in virtually any area of social life where social structures generate uncertainty over obtaining a desired outcome and where agents have some discretion to engage in strategic actions in an attempt to achieve this outcome.

Notes

Chapter One

1. It is important to note that this book focuses job seekers' *perceptions* of what it takes to get hired and the institutions behind these perceptions. As I will emphasize throughout the book, the chemistry game of white-collar American job seekers as well as the other job-search games focus job seekers' attention to particularly salient elements of the hiring process, rather than to all the elements considered by potential employers.

2. I note that this quote, and certain other quotes of job seekers that appear throughout this book, appeared previously in earlier articles (Sharone 2007, 2013) that draw on my interview data and in which some initial versions of the ideas developed in this book were first presented.

3. Bakke 1933; Newman 1999; Schlozman and Verba 1979; Sharone 2007; Uchitelle 2006.

4. Kalleberg 2009, 2011; Osterman 1999.

5. Osterman 1999; Cappelli 2008.

6. See Kalleberg 2009; Cappelli 2008; Farber 2008; Fantasia and Voss 2004; Mishel, Bernstein, and Allegretto 2007.

7. Reich's analysis is greatly indebted to Piore and Sabel (1984).

8. Mishel, Bernstein, and Allegretto 2007; Rifkin 2004.

9. Economic effects are typically seen as *mediated* by institutions. For example, according to Kalleberg (2009), the postwar era ended due to macroeconomic and technological changes that led to heightened global competition, but in each country, these changes were mediated by distinct institutions such as government regulations and labor unions. This mediating effect is seen in the European-American comparison, which does not prove that economic factors do not matter but does suggest that economy is not destiny and that institutions, such as labor laws and welfare policies, can and do counteract the economic forces generating inequality and insecurity (Fantasia and Voss 2004; Mishel, Bernstein, and Allegretto 2007).

10. See Farber 2005; Gardner 1995; Jacobs and Newman 2006; Rodriguez and Zavodny 2003. While there is no disagreement that white-collar job security has decreased in recent decades, there is some debate in the literature regarding the overall levels of job security. On the one hand, an analysis of Current Population Survey data from 1973 to 2006 by Princeton economist Henry Farber (2007) suggests an overall decline in job security. Farber finds that the fraction of male workers age thirty-five to sixty-four with a mean tenure of at least ten years with the same employer has substantially fallen while the number of workers with a tenure of less than one year has increased. Women have even shorter average tenures than men, but their average tenure has been increasing. Farber argues that the pattern in women's tenure "reflects the common factors reducing tenure for all workers offset for females by their dramatically increased commitment to the labor force over the past half century" (2007, 20). Another recent study, however, finds that the *overall* median tenure for males has not changed in recent decades (Stevens 2005). In trying to make sense of these conflicting data, Valletta (2007) argues that overall population measures do not reflect changes in job stability because they ignore the significant aging of the American workforce. Because older workers tend to have longer tenures, such measures mask the fact that for workers between the ages of thirty-five and fifty-four, work tenure has decreased.

11. Farber 2011; Shierholz and Mishel 2009.

12. Center on Budget and Policy Priorities 2004; Stettner and Wenger 2003.

13. Mishel, Bernstein, and Allegretto 2007; Stettner and Allegreto 2005.

14. Bureau of Labor Statistics, Household Data Annual Averages, table 32, 2009. As a result of declining white-collar job stability, levels of family income instability for those with a college degree are now comparable to levels for those without a high school diploma. Even before the Great Recession, half of all American families, regardless of class, experienced a drop in real income over any given two-year period, and the size of that drop has substantially increased over the past thirty years. And it is white-collar and college-educated workers who experience the greatest earnings drop upon losing a job. See Hacker 2006; Farber 2005; Newman 1999; Valletta 2007.

15. Challenger, Gray, and Christmas 2009.

16. For example, see Strully 2009; Sullivan and Wachter 2009; Cottle 2001; Broman, Hamilton, and Hoffman 2001; Dooley, Fielding, and Levi 1996; Thomas, Benzeval, and Stansfeld 2005.

17. Zukin, Van Horn, and Stone 2011.

18. Mishel, Bernstein, and Allegretto 2007.

19. Gangl 2004; Hipp 2011.

20. Kalleberg 2011; Osterman 1999; Farber 2008; Autler 2002; Ram 2008; Samuel and Harpaz 2004.

21. Gangl 2004; Gal 2005; Hipp 2011.

22. Plocker 2005. For detailed descriptions of Israel's high-tech economy, see

Rosenberg and Vainunska 2007; Carmel and de Fontenay 2004; and Ram 2008. Israel's high-tech sector has led to the growth of other post-industrial sectors such as financial services. The general structure of employment in Israel is now nearly as "post-industrial" as it is in California, with white-collar workers constituting 52 percent of all workers in Israel, compared to 59 percent of all workers in California (Fligstein and Sharone 2000; Ram 2008). Given these uniquely high levels of high-tech concentration, my sample in both countries overrepresents job seekers in the technology sector. This limitation is somewhat mitigated to the extent that one considers the technology sector to be a harbinger of trends in others economic sectors.

23. Mishel, Bernstein, and Allegretto 2007; Stettner and Allegreto 2005; Samuel and Harpaz 2004.

24. As a participant-observer, I wore two hats. The job seekers knew I was a graduate student doing research, but at same time I was invited to take full part in all activities as someone who in the future (i.e., upon finishing graduate school) would be looking for a job. I participated in group brainstorming sessions about job-searching strategies and acted as a volunteer peer-to-peer coach for members seeking feedback about their own search processes.

25. This theory is most closely associated with Marie Jahoda (1982). Her "latent deprivation" model argues that unemployment deprives job seekers not only of the manifest benefits of work—wages—but also, and more importantly, of such "latent" benefits as the imposition of a daily time structure, enforcement of regular activity, and regular contact with people outside the nuclear family. These latent benefits help explain "why employment is psychologically supportive even when [work] conditions are bad"; as Jahoda claims, "Even unpleasant ties to reality are preferable to their absence" (189). Pierre Bourdieu uses this theoretical model to explain the conditions of the unemployed both in Algeria in the 1960s and in Europe in the 1990s. In both cases, he conceptualizes unemployment as the "destructing of existence, which is deprived among other things of its temporal structures, and the ensuing deterioration of the whole relationship to the world, time and space" (1998a, 82). Bourdieu posits that lack of structure generates passivity and resignation. William Julius Wilson follows Jahoda and Bourdieu in explaining the effects of unemployment in the American inner city ghetto: "Work is not simply a way to make a living and support one's family. It also constitutes a framework for daily behavior and patterns of interaction because it imposes discipline and regularities.... Regular employment provides the anchor for the spatial and temporal aspects of daily life" (1996, 73). Numerous other studies have explicitly or implicitly followed Jahoda's latent-deprivation framework for analyzing the hardships associated with unemployment. Examples include Creed and Macintyre (2001), Evans and Haworth (1991), and Karsten, Geithner, and Moser (2007).

26. This line of research emphasizes diminishing "self-efficacy" (Wilson 1996; Bandura 1982) or declining "internal locus of control" (Levenson 1974), focusing

on whether individuals perceive events in their life to be contingent on their own actions, which is the mark of high self-efficacy, or as contingent upon chance or powerful others, which suggests low self-efficacy. Wilson defines "self-efficacy" as the "belief in one's own ability to take steps necessary to achieve the goals required in a given situation" (1996, 75). In this model, the experience of unemployment wears down job seekers' self-efficacy because failure to find work challenges their sense of "power and command over the environment" (Waters and Moore 2002, 602). Declining self-efficacy, Wilson claims, affects the "amount of effort expended in a given venture, and the degree of perseverance when encountering difficulties" and "can give rise to feelings of futility and despondency" (1996, 75). In this theory, it is not the absence of formal employment structures but the experience associated with unemployment and job searching—particularly the "continued exposure to uncontrollable outcomes" (Kaufman 1982, 113)—that is at the core of the unemployment experience. Self-efficacy theory has led researchers of unemployment, in both psychology and sociology, to focus on indices of diminished self-efficacy (Gianakos 2002; Ross and Mirowsky 1992; Waters and Moore 2002).

27. Swidler 1986.

28. See Kluegel and Smith 1986; Bellah et al. 1985; Wolfe 1999. Newman's (1999) cultural argument follows in the theoretical tradition of Geertz (1973), who understood cultures to be deeply coherent webs of significance. Empirically, Newman provides a description of a coherent and integrated managerial culture similar to the descriptions offered by American culture scholars from Alexis de Tocqueville (2000) to Seymour Martin Lipset (1997). Yet, as the studies cited above reflect, recent sociological accounts of American culture point to a cultural system that is complex and contradictory.

29. See Sharone 2013; Smith 2001; Cottle 2001; Newman 1999.

30. Newman claims that structural explanations, such as corporate restructuring, "dissolve, especially under the influence of the business press, which reminds the unemployed manager that 'you are out of a job, not because of impersonal forces, but because of your personal failings'" (1999, 69).

31. Swidler 1986.

32. Newman 1999.

33. While Smith's (2001) chapter on white-collar unemployment points the way to an institutional analysis of the unemployment experience, my book goes beyond her single-site study in several important ways. My cross-national and cross-class comparisons of job searching bring to light some of the distinct but taken-for-granted dimensions of American job searching that I conceptualize as the "chemistry game." Moreover, the comparative examination of job-searching practices and experiences suggests a novel theory of the *links* connecting labor-market institutions, the day-to-day practices of job searching, and subjective responses to unemployment.

34. See also Bourdieu 1998b, 121; 2001, 35.

35. Bourdieu and Passeron 1977, 204–5.

36. Ibid., 210; emphasis added.

37. Bourdieu 2004, 6. Bourdieu similarly discusses the experience of workers' encountering "anonymous sanctions of the labor market" (Bourdieu and Passeron 1977, 28; see also Bourdieu 1984, 386).

38. Bourdieu 2001, 37; 1990a.

39. Bourdieu 1990b. For example, in the context of explaining gender inequality, the experience of the "social order" leads girls to "internalize in the form of schemes of perceptions and appreciation not readily accessible to consciousness, the principles of the dominant vision" (Bourdieu 2001, 95).

40. Bourdieu 2001, 42, 95.

41. Bourdieu and Wacquant 1992, 168. According to Bourdieu, the naturalness and taken-for-grantedness of structures is at its strongest when the internalization occurs early in life. Bourdieu makes the analogy to learning games or a language. The earlier in life you learn the game, the greater the "unawareness of the unthought presuppositions that the game produces and endlessly reproduces, thereby reproducing the conditions of its own perpetuation" (1990a, 67).

42. Bourdieu 2000, 173. See also Bourdieu 1990a, 53.

43. Bourdieu and Passeron 1977, 206; Bourdieu 1990a; 2001, 2. Bourdieu refers to this invisibility as "doxa," which is defined as the "relationship of immediate adherence that is established in practice between a habitus and a field to which it is attuned, the preverbal taking for granted of the world" (Bourdieu 1990a, 68).

44. Bourdieu 1988.

45. In his later works, Bourdieu (1998a) writes about this transformation and the rise of job insecurity, acknowledging that "there will be no return to those social universes in which the quasi-perfect coincidences between objective tendencies and subjective expectations made the experience of the world a continuous interlocking of confirmed expectations" (2000, 234). While Bourdieu empirically observes the rapidly changing world of work under neoliberalism, which requires constant reinvention of the self, his theoretical writing on careers continues to assume conditions of a stable external environment gradually internalized by agents. For example, Bourdieu describes how "the process of transformation through which one becomes a miner, a farmer, a priest, a musician, a teacher, or an employer, is long, continuous and imperceptible. . . . It starts in childhood sometimes even before birth" (2000, 165).

46. Smith 2001.

47. Ehrenreich 2005; Smith 2001.

48. Sherman 2007, 112.

49. Buroway 1979; Bourdieu 1997.

50. Buroway 1979, 82.

51. Different games can be thought of as falling along different points on the continuum of player prominence. For example, consider chess and poker—two familiar games in which there is uncertainty over the outcomes and players exer-

cise strategic discretion. Chess is a game with high player prominence because the sum total of the players' moves is understood as wholly determinative of the outcome; nothing but the players' own moves matter. Poker has a more moderate level of player prominence because its structure renders the luck of the draw an important determinant of the outcome. In both games, players exercise discretion in each round of play, but the exercise of discretion is more determinative of the outcome in chess than in poker. In social life, unlike chess and poker, the relationship between the exercise of discretion and outcomes is not always clear. For example, Sherman (2007) describes hotel workers with different views on the degree to which getting a tip depends on one's strategy to elicit the tip or on the guest's own tipping practices. The degree of player prominence in the job-search game ultimately turns on how players *perceive* the relationship between actions and outcomes.

Chapter Two

1. Bergsma 2007; Ehrenreich 2005; McGee 2005; Starker 1988.

2. The concept of "self-help" as a distinct set of practices and discourses for improving the *self* has only recently crystallized (McGee 2005). As recently as the 1970s, the term "self-help" often referred to mutual aid and cooperative efforts for improving *conditions*. For example, the Boston Women's Health Collective was considered a "self-help" effort by women to collectively provide an alternative to male-dominated medical expertise.

3. Huffcutt and Youngcourt 2007; Moss and Tilly 2001.

4. Huo, Huang, and Napier2002.

5. Finlay and Coverdill 2002.

6. Foschi and Valenzuela 2007.

7. Garnett, Guppy, and Veenstra 2008, 160.

8. Miller and Rosenbaum 1997, 509.

9. Jackall 1988.

10. Rivera 2012.

11. Burton 2001.

12. Finlay and Coverdill 2002.

13. Smith 2001.

14. This class-based segregation in job-searching support is not unique to Ameri-Support but is found in similar state institutions throughout California (Smith 2001).

15. AmeriSupport members identified themselves as 72 percent white, 15 percent African American, 10 percent Asian American, and 3 percent other categories. AmeriSupport members' ages broke down as follows: 3 percent were 20–30, 13 percent were 31–40, 40 percent were 41–50, 35 percent were 51–60, and 9 percent were 61 and over.

16. Advice is offered on countless other aspects of impression management, such as how to dress for interviews. There are two schools of thought on what to wear. One is that job seekers should go sit in the prospective employer's parking lot and see how employees dress and then dress in a similar way. The other is that the job seeker should always wear a suit regardless of what the employees are wearing.

17. Some job seekers raise concerns about including their picture, most commonly regarding age discrimination that may be facilitated by their inclusion of a picture on their social networking profile. Guest speakers typically acknowledge that discrimination may exist but typically respond with the question: "In the spirit of networking, isn't it more inviting to connect with people with pictures than without?"

18. Although this is one point on which self-help practitioners appear to rely on the findings of sociologists regarding the importance of personal networks (e.g., Granovetter 1974; Fernandez, Castilla, and Moore 2000), there is an important difference. The academic research suggests that using one's network may help in hiring while the self-help discourse goes further and advocates the importance of actively creating *new* connections for the purpose of obtaining referrals. The efficacy of this practice is not supported by existing studies.

19. Sandra Smith's (2012) research, focusing on the behavior of referrers, reveals that people may indeed make referrals to employers based on very limited "thin slice" instantaneous assessment.

20. The use of formulas for job-searching tasks is ubiquitous and reflects the rationalization process. One speaker even presented a formula for writing a networking e-mail: "Use the recipient's name in the body of the e-mail in the sentence you most want them to read, and follow up with another e-mail once a week and voice mail twice a week. Following this formula, you have a forty percent chance of getting in the door."

21. Hochschild 1983.

22. As Ibarra (2002, 43) observes, "The foundation for most career advice" is "based on the notion of an 'inner core' or a 'true self.'"

23. To understand the focus of self-help speakers on following one's passions, it is also important to note that in many cases these ideas were developed with a different audience in mind, not the unemployed, who usually face an urgent need to find a job for financial reasons, but currently employed workers, who are much more likely to be able to focus on the meaningfulness of their work.

24. The rise of the self-help industry is documented by McGee (2005), who finds that between 1972 and 2000, the number of self-help books, as a percentage of all books in print in the United States, more than doubled. Sales of self-help books rose by 96 percent in the five years between 1991 and 1996, and by 2005 one-third to one-half of all Americans had bought a self-help book. Beyond books and audiovisual products, the ideas and practices of self-help are institutionalized in self-help support groups, workshops, and personal coaching practices (McGee 2005). Vallas

and Cummins (2012) also show the rapid rise in recent decades of career-oriented self-help books focusing on "branding" oneself for labor market success.

25. Other social commentators have understood the rise of self-help as reflecting a growing form of American narcissism (Lasch 1979) or as an attempt to reconcile the "Bohemian" counterculture of the 1960s with the resurgent bourgeoisie culture of the 1980s (Brooks 2000).

Chapter Three

1. This finding is consistent with Lane 2011.

2. The structuring of job searching into a daytime job contradicts what would be expected under Jahoda's (1982) theory of "latent deprivation" (as discussed in chap. 1, n. 9) focusing on the disorientation of workers deprived of externally imposed work schedules.

3. For example, Hochschild 1983; Leidner 1993.

4. See Smith 2001; Ehrenreich 2005; Lane 2011.

5. Bourdieu 1998b, 2000.

6. Jackall 1988.

7. Lane similarly describes one job seeker's belief that a "perfect" résumé, "were it to exist, could have landed him a job months earlier" (2011, 76).

8. Lane (2011) similarly finds an intense focus on networking among high-tech workers.

9. This form of technology-focused self-blame was rare among white-collar workers before the rise of online social networking technologies. Using job boards such as Monster.com or sending e-mails does not pose a perceived technological obstacle for most white-collar job seekers in the same way as using social media tools.

10. Shierholz 2009.

11. This effect of absorption is also supported by findings in social psychology concerning the "attention bias," whereby people tend to attribute fault to whatever factors they attended to prior to the outcome (e.g., Nisbett and Ross 1980).

12. Newman 1999. In chapter 1, I discussed other difficulties with arguments focusing on the American culture of individualism as an explanation for American self-blame, notably the availability and use by unemployed workers of non-individualistic narratives about career outcomes.

13. For example, Zukin, Van Horn, and Stone 2011.

14. Sharone 2007.

15. My finding that women are more likely to turn to non-worker roles is consistent with survey data showing that women more likely than men to withdraw from the labor force following job loss (Farber 2011). The existing literature on gender differences in job searching (e.g., Campbell 1985; Marx and Leicht 1992)

does not focus on whether differences appear over time after an initial convergence, as my findings suggest.

Chapter Four

1. Autler 2002; Ram 2008; Samuel and Harpaz 2004.

2. Dagan-Buzaglo 2007. The provision of welfare benefits by a labor federation as opposed to the state is unusual (Esping-Andersen 1990). Israel's unique institutional trajectory, where many of the roles of the welfare state were performed by the Histadrut, was partly due to the historical legacy of the Histadrut fulfilling state functions prior to the establishment of the State of Israel in 1948. This arrangement continued after the founding of the state, in part because the Labor Party desired to maintain workers' dependence on the Histadrut (Shalev 1992).

3. Shalev 1992.

4. At its height, the Histadrut was the country's second-largest employer (after the state), employing 28 percent of the workforce (Samuel and Harpaz 2004). This unusual circumstance was the product of the Histadrut's original mission to help absorb Jewish immigrants to pre-Israel Palestine through programs of job creation. To achieve this goal, the Histadrut started its own companies, many of which became dominant in the Israeli market.

5. Harpaz 1990; Freeman 1994. Collective agreements were not extended to all workers. Ten to twenty percent of the workforce—predominantly consisting of Sephardic Israelis (Jews of Middle Eastern origins) living in peripheral towns and of Arab workers, mostly working in construction and agriculture—were not included in collective agreements or their extensions, and constituted a source of flexible and cheap labor.

6. Shalev 1992.

7. Ibid.

8. Gal 2005.

9. Shalev 1992.

10. Ram 2008.

11. Ibid.; Rosenberg and Vainuska 2007.

12. Kristal and Cohen 2007; Dagan-Buzaglo 2007.

13. Israeli wage inequality has dramatically risen in recent decades, making the gap between the top and bottom deciles in Israel as wide as it is in the United States. The Gini index rose in Israel from .36 in 1964 to .42 in 1994 (Ram 2008). Moreover, Israel's minimum wage is now among the lowest in the OECD, alongside that of the United States, and the poverty rate is skyrocketing. Even Israel's communal kibbutzim, once a global model for egalitarian principles, are increasingly privatizing and employing wage earners who are not kibbutz members (Samuel and Harpaz 2004; Ram 2008).

14. Shalev 1992.

15. Ram 2008.

16. Samuel and Harpaz 2004.

17. The high-tech sector in Israel took off in the 1990s and grew at the astonishing pace of 13 percent a year from 1990 to 2002 (Ram 2008). Israeli high-tech
exports, as a proportion of total exports, grew from 30 to 48 percent in the decade
from 1996 to 2006 (Rosenberg and Vainunska 2007). The growth of the high-tech
sector is partly the result of the entry into the Israeli market of American high-tech
giants such as IBM, Intel, and Motorola. IBM's and Intel's largest research and development laboratories outside of the United States are in Israel, and forty-three
of the fifty largest American high-tech corporations have set up research and development centers there (Ram 2008). Alongside these American companies are a
rapidly growing number of Israeli high-tech companies. For more data on the rise
of the high-tech sector in Israel, see Senor and Singer (2009).

18. Azaryahu 2000.

19. The adoption of the "American model" of employment relations was met
with very little cultural or intellectual resistance. According to Azaryahu (2000),
while European intellectuals resist American culture on the grounds of vulgarity, the Israeli cultural elite had, by the 1970s, become less concerned with avoiding American vulgarity than with not being "swallowed up" by the twin threats of
(i) the "third world," as represented by the culture of Sephardic Jews and Israeli
Arabs and (ii) the ultra-religious Israeli Jews seeking to establish greater religious
control over everyday life.

20. Klein and Polisar 1997.

21. Ibid., 23.

22. Ibid., 54–56. To help implement the "American model," the Bank of Israel
brought prestigious Americans to Israel. In the 1990s, it appointed as its governor
Jacob Frenkel, the former chair of the department of International Economics at
the University of Chicago. Frenkel was followed by Stanley Fischer, the former
vice chairman of Citigroup.

23. Samuel and Harpaz 2004; Ram 2008.

24. Ram 2008; Nadiv 2005.

25. In Israel more than three-quarters of staffing agencies engage in both temporary hiring and permanent placement services (Nadiv 2005). These functions
are often combined with the hiring of temporary workers who are also being considered by the employer for a permanent position. Temporary workers constitute
more than 5 percent of Israeli workers, the highest proportion in the advanced
capitalist world (Ram 2008). Because the proportion in most other advanced capitalist countries, including the United States (Kalleberg 2000), is around 1.5 to
2.5 percent, Israeli social critics often joke that in their zeal to Americanize, they
have become "more American than the Americans."

26. Data reported by the Israeli Central Bureau of Statistics' "Labor Force Survey" (2007) indicates that 50 percent of unemployed Israeli job seekers look for

work through staffing agencies. The survey does not break down these responses by occupations or levels of education. My findings suggest that for white-collar private-sector jobs, the use of staffing agencies by large- and medium-size employers is nearly universal.

27. Ram 2008; Dagan-Buzaglo 2007.

28. Nadiv 2005; Dagan-Buzaglo 2007.

29. Ram 2008.

30. Dagan-Buzaglo 2007. This function of circumventing protective legislation is most clearly seen in staffing agencies whose sole purpose is to act as the legal employer. Such agencies are used by employers who have already found the worker they want to hire (and thus do not need recruiting services) but do not want to be the legal employer. As Vasil, the manager of one such agency, told me, the employers come to his agency and say, "Hire this guy for me and you deal with all the employment stuff," because they do not want to be limited in their flexibility to lay off workers.

31. Ibid.

32. Davidov 2006, 8–9; Ram 2008. This logic leads the state to utilize subcontractors who pay poverty wages, claiming that it is obligated by anti-corruption laws to accept the "lowest bid" (Ram 2008). As Dagan-Buzaglo explains, "Government tenders do not distinguish between products and people, reflecting the commodification of labor—turning labor into a product and ignoring the person who does the work" (2007, 33).

33. Fizer 2003. According to Stryker (2008) and Cappelli (2008), in the 1950s pre-employment tests were also widely used in white-collar hiring the United States. The rarity of pre-employment tests in the United States as compared to Israel is the result of American legal challenges focusing on the discriminatory "disparate impact" of pre-employment tests on applicants from minority groups.

34. See www.pilat.co.il.

35. Israeli employers are not alone in using pre-employment tests. A cross-national survey of hiring managers found that tests are not an important factor in hiring in the United States but are among the most important criteria in other countries, including China, South Korea, and Indonesia (Huo, Huang, and Napier 2002).

36. For private employers, tests are relatively expensive, typically costing more than $200 (US) per candidate. As a result, private companies use the staffing agencies to limit the number of candidates to be tested. The state, by contrast, runs its own testing agency and therefore can avoid having to interview before testing.

37. In one case, an employer asked applicants to send in handwritten résumés in order to use the handwriting analysis as an initial screen. Most typically, such handwriting samples are sent to the Anna Koren institute (www.annakoren.co.il), which claims to be "the largest graphological center in the world," with thousands of global clients. On its website, the institute cites research claiming that graphologists performed better than laypersons and that laypersons performed better than

psychologists. Performing "better" is not defined. This research also claims that 80 percent of Israeli and French firms use such tests before hiring (Edwards and Armitage 1992).

38. Amos eventually found a job as a manager in a large hotel, but his simultaneous pursuit of a job and self-employment is very common. This dual approach is encouraged by IsraSupport to a much greater degree than by AmeriSupport.

39. Improve Inc., another organization that provides workshops for job seekers who have completed state-sponsored retraining programs, also emphasizes the imperative of individual action and initiative. At one workshop, Miriam, the facilitator, showed a graph of changes in the Israeli labor market, with agricultural and manufacturing work both decreasing and service work increasing. She explained to a group of job seekers that while in the earlier eras of agriculture and manufacturing, "mechanical and physical power and working within a hierarchy were of great importance," today's world of service work requires "self-management." And self-management begins with disciplining yourself to take action to find work. Ironically, Miriam told me that her workshop was "heavily influenced" by the American self-help book *What Color Is Your Parachute?*—the same book by Richard Bolles that animates the chemistry game discourse of many of AmeriSupport's speakers. Yet from this same book, different elements are emphasized in the Israeli context: Finding and following your passions is ignored; taking initiative is emphasized.

40. It is important to note that this is not a reflection of a general lack of use of social media. Israelis, in fact, may use online social networks even *more* extensively than Americans. Based on a combination of average daily visitors and page views, LinkedIn is the ninth most popular site in Israel, while it ranks as the eleventh most popular site in the United States. http://www.appappeal.com/maps/linkedin/.

41. Swidler 1986.

42. Brooks wrote the following observations after a 2009 visit to Israel:

Israel is a country held together by argument.... Subordinates in companies feel free to correct their superiors.... Israelis don't observe the distinction between the public and private realms. They treat strangers as if they were their brothers-in-law and feel perfectly comfortable giving them advice on how to live. One Israeli acquaintance recounts the time he was depositing money into his savings account and everybody else behind him in line got into an argument about whether he should really be putting his money somewhere else. Another friend tells of the time he called directory assistance to get a phone number for a restaurant. The operator responded, "You don't want to eat there," and proceeded to give him the numbers of some other restaurants she thought were better.

43. In addition to directness, Israeli culture is also traditionally distinguished by solidarity. Whereas the United States is described as "individualistic," Israel is

seen as "familistic," with social relations and dense networks of friends being a very important feature of daily life. See Danet 1989; Fischer and Shavit 1995; and Katriel 1986a, 1987. Katriel (1986a) argues that despite a fundamental economic transformation, Israeli society maintains strong solidarity. She points to practices of solidarity building ("*gibush*") that are built into educational structures, such as the practice of keeping kids together in the same class from first through sixth grade. Whether Israeli culture can still be characterized by solidarity is contested by studies showing a growing individualism in Israeli society (e.g., Harpaz 1990, 1999). Nevertheless, to the extent it still exists, this culture of solidarity may support the readiness of strong connections to help with *protectzia*, but it bears no relationship to the practices of the dominant Israeli labor market institutions. In fact, these institutions may in part be perceived as necessary precisely to counteract solidarity among Israelis through practices that impersonalize and objectify the hiring process.

Chapter Five

1. The actual experience of being repeatedly filtered out by the staffing agencies for age and other proxies has generated various folk theories of how else the system is arbitrary or unfair. For example, Channan, a high-tech engineer who had been screened out over twenty times by staffing agencies, had come to believe, along with a sizable minority of other Israeli job seekers, that "companies often just interview without there being a job. They just want to *appear* to be recruiting to create the impression that the company is big and successful." Gil, another engineer, felt that "companies sometimes like to interview people *for the hell of it*, even if they are not really hiring, to have a reserve pool when they need workers."

2. See www.pilat.co.il.

3. Resentment toward the testing companies seems to be bottomless. Another sore point is that the institutes will only provide job seekers with the test results for a fee. As one job seeker put it, "You need to pay them to know what you were not good at. They are trying to make money from the unemployed. It's like stepping on a corpse. It is such exploitation."

4. As with the screening by the staffing agencies, one of the most upsetting elements of the tests is the sense that one's fate is being determined by unqualified and untrained personnel. As Tova put it, "A girl of twenty-five, a B.A. in psychology, is asking me about my relationship with my mother, my childhood. I feel it's humiliating how my fate is determined."

5. While my interview subjects claim the *tests* caused their *choser onim*, it may be argued that it is not the structure of the tests per se that generate this feeling but some other factor, such as Israeli culture. Perhaps Americans taking a similar kind of test would interpret the experience through a different cultural lens and

have a different subjective response. To untangle the cultural and institutional roots of the subjective reactions I encountered, it is useful to look at some studies of tests outside of Israel. The literature reflects a consistent subjective experience of pre-employment tests as unfair. This includes responses from American test takers, who, like Israelis, consider personality tests to be "unrelated to the job, invasive of individual privacy, and lacking face value or procedural justice." These studies show that when such tests are used, job seekers' reactions cut across cultural boundaries. The Israeli response does not appear to be unique to Israelis or to reflect Israeli culture (Gilliland 1993; Rosse, Miller, and Stecher 1994; Rynes and Connerley 1993; Smither et al. 1993). As Lane (2011, 93) finds, pre-employment tests are "despised" by American high-tech workers in the Dallas area who are required to take them as part of their job-application process.

6. While it is hard to enlarge one's group of close friends and family members, such groups are often quite large. For example, Ariella explained: "I do not turn to everyone, just the people that are close. . . . My close circle of friends is thirty to forty people." She was not unusual; many interviewees reported turning to at least twenty close friends and family members.

7. I note that from the perspective of the social psychology literature, this Israeli response of system-blame is less surprising than the American response of self-blame. Theories of attribution and self-serving biases in social psychology generally find that actors tend to explain failures by finding fault in the external environment as opposed to internal attributes (Kruger 1999; Miller and Ross 1975; Roese and Olson 2007).

8. While white-collar job seekers in both Israel and the United States faced challenging labor-market conditions, at the time of my first round of interviews in San Francisco and Tel Aviv, the San Francisco area did have a lower overall unemployment rate. It may be argued that Israeli responses are therefore simply reflecting a tougher labor market, while in San Francisco a lower unemployment rate suggests the availability of employment opportunities and thus may explain the greater self-blame among American job seekers. However, a closer look at unemployment rates for specific occupations shows that the cross-national differences in subjective responses persist even for workers in occupations with the same unemployment rates. During the time of this first round of interviews, the unemployment rates for managers in both sites were nearly identical. According to data obtained from the Integrated Public Use Microdata Series (IPUMS), the 2005 unemployment rate for managers in the San Francisco–Oakland area was 3.64 percent (Ruggles et al. 2010), while the 2006 unemployment rate for managers in Israel was 3.5 percent (Central Bureau of Statistics of Israel 2007). Because the diverging subjective responses held for managers, despite nearly identical labor-market conditions, we cannot attribute self-blame to the unemployment rate. Moreover, the insufficiency of unemployment rates to explain self-blame is suggested by my in-depth interviews with unemployed American job seekers in

2009–11 and by surveys from the same period in the United States, revealing self-blame even during periods of historically high unemployment (Zukin, Van Horn, and Stone 2011).

9. While in the United States (re)training funds have always focused on workers without a university education, in Israel it has historically been more common for workers of all educational backgrounds to be given funding for mid-career retraining, even as late as the 1990s. However, in recent years the budget for retraining has been decimated, and particularly for white-collar workers, where it was slashed from NIS 34 million in 2001 to NIS 1.8 million in 2007 (Dagan-Buzaglo 2007). Several of my interviewees had completed trainings in the past, but these did not always lead to jobs, which becomes another reason to blame the state. As one recent graduate of a retraining program put it: "In a normal country, the government would give you consultation on how to move forward. Here they just send you to a course in the latest buzzword, and people finish the course and can't get jobs afterward."

10. One striking similarity between the Israeli and American (un)employment agencies is the clear class division in the provision of services. The Israeli office has one space for those with university degrees and another for those without a degree, much like the American division between "professionals" and "others." The difference is that in Israel the boundaries are clear-cut. You either have a degree or not. In the United States, the line is more blurry and depends on the job seeker's own definition of himself or herself as a "professional" or not. These different boundary demarcations reflect the deeper differences I have discussed between the Israeli and American employment regimes: the importance of job seekers' self-definition in the American case and of objective credentials in the Israeli case.

11. This coercive element was made possible by specific legislation and only applies to job seekers under the age of thirty-five. While the American and Israeli regimes of unemployment benefits are generally similar in amounts and duration, in 1994, to minimize so-called "negative incentives," the Israeli Parliament passed a law that changed the condition for receiving unemployment benefits from requiring that job seekers accept any "appropriate work" to requiring them, after three months of searching, to take "any" job offered to them at any salary. The unemployment compensation system in California, by contrast, only requires that you look for work in your "field." This change in Israel's unemployment benefits regime was part and parcel of the increasingly restrictive eligibility rules for unemployment insurance over the past thirty years (Shalev 1992).

12. The most aggressive attempt to institutionalize this ideology, and the most widely discussed government reform at the time of my research, was the adoption of a welfare-to-work program. In Israel the program is informally but widely called the "Wisconsin Plan," referring to the fact that it was purportedly first used in Wisconsin and giving it the aura of something that comes from the United States and is therefore modern and efficient. On the first day of the implementation of Jeru-

salem's welfare-to-work program, I observed both heavy reliance on the American discourse of individual responsibility and extreme anger and bewilderment on the part of welfare-reliant citizens.

13. Drawing on follow-up interviews with a subset of my sample of Tel Aviv– and San Francisco–based job seekers who remained unemployed for over twenty weeks (twenty-seven American and twenty-two Israeli job seekers), the table below summarizes the number of hours spent on job searching per week and how that number changes over time:

Hours Searching Per Week	Weeks 2–5	Weeks 12–15	Weeks 20+	Change
Israel	22	16	14	–36%
U.S.	34	12	9	–73%

14. The instrumental view of work is increasingly expressed by Israeli workers, which Harpaz (2002) ties to rising insecurity. With perceived precariousness, he argues, work is increasingly viewed simply as something for which one gets paid. This is in contrast to the more traditional Israeli view of work as a source of social contribution, as an expression of creative power, or as intrinsically interesting (Harpaz 2002). The pre-neoliberal work ideal can be found in speeches of early Zionist leaders who idealized work for its own sake. Israel's first prime minister, David Ben-Gurion—the equivalent of George Washington as a mythical founding father—famously said: "We do not see work as a curse and as bitter necessity or only a means of living . . . but as a social duty, a human duty, discovering the creative power of human beings and their domination of nature" (Harpaz 1990). Yet from 1981 to 1993, the percentage of workers who reported valuing work as a way to contribute to society fell from 40 to 18 percent, those who found work intrinsically interesting fell from 26 to 19 percent, and those who defined work as something for which one gets paid rose from 68 to 83 percent (Harpaz 1999). These changes in Israel are consistent with the expectations of Abramson and Inglehart (1995), who argue that changes such as the rise of inflation and unemployment lead to an increase in the importance of earning money and material values.

15. In referring to unemployment, Ehud did not use the conventional Hebrew word *muvtal* because, he explained, its etymology comes from a root meaning "idle" and thus connotes laziness. Instead, he used the phrase *bilti meusak*, a literal translation of the English word "unemployed," which he considered more precise and less pejorative. Ironically, job seekers in the United States avoid the "unemployed" label for similar reasons and instead use labels such as "in transition."

16. As in the American case, job equivalents are characterized by a gender divide, which is even more stark in the Israeli case. In both sites there is a strong link between masculinity and work, and it is more commonly men who opt for a job equivalent that maintains their identity as workers. At EzraSupport business meetings, the ratio of men to women was two to one. When compared to

men, Israeli women more frequently take an approach similar to that of American women, investing their identities in familial or social roles, particularly as mothers, aunts, daughters, and friends.

Chapter Six

1. One likely reason for the more limited support structure is the fact that blue-collar workers' more limited budgets make them far less likely to become customers and clients of the self-help authors and coaches who are eager to speak to white-collar audiences.

2. A national survey in 2002 by the National Telecommunication and Information Administration (NITA) showed that while Internet use was increasing across all categories of users, adoption rates were higher for those with higher incomes and education levels, producing an ever-*widening* "digital divide" between those who have access and use digital technologies and those who do not (Hargittai 2008). The "digital divide" in basic access is troubling, but exclusive focus on the binary question of "access" versus "no access" or "use" versus "no use" has been criticized for missing key dimensions of digital inequality *among* Internet users (see DiMaggio et al. 2004; Robinson 2009; Hargittai 2008; Halford and Savage 2010). Scholars have urged researchers and policy makers to replace the "divide" metaphor with the broader concept of "digital inequality," which captures differences among the increasing number of individuals who have crossed the digital divide but with varying depth of access and range of abilities to make use of such access. As DiMaggio et al. (2004, 375) explain, since Internet access continues to grow— for example, with more people being able to get online at public libraries or One-Stop centers—the pressing questions now are what are people doing and what are they able to do when they go online? Recent research has shown significant variations among *users* of the Internet (Robinson 2009). This research shows that the quality of one's Internet connection and computer hardware, the need to drive or take a bus to places like the WorkSource, and the limitations on one's autonomy of use at such public facilities are all important determinants of the efficacy of using digital technologies. No less important are one's navigation skills and the extent of one's training to find and evaluate information from searches, and to have access to technical support when difficulties arise.

3. This finding is consistent with Sandra Smith's (2007) work describing the hesitation to network among working class African American job seekers. Also consistent with Smith (2007) was the degree to which working-class job seekers were concerned about the perceived character of their networking counterparts. As one job seeker shared with her peers at a One-Stop workshop: "I only [use a referral] if I am absolutely sure of their track record. Otherwise I go in there like I don't know you, 'cause you never know what friends do on their time."

4. Moss and Tilly 2001.

5. The relationship between unemployment and stress and between anxiety and sleep issues are well established. For example, see a recent study entitled "The Anguish of Unemployment" by the Heldrich Center at Rutgers University (2009). The report can be accessed at: http://www.heldrich.rutgers.edu/sites/default/files/content/Heldrich_Work_Trends_Anguish_Unemployment.pdf.

6. While federal funding for retraining is channeled through the roughly 2,750 One-Stop Career Centers around the United States, the level of available funding has substantially declined in recent decades (Gatta 2012).

Chapter Seven

1. I am often asked which of these profoundly different ways to filter job seekers is "better" for companies. First, it must be reiterated that while the specs and chemistry games make different filters *salient* to job seekers, employers in both countries make some use of both specs and chemistry factors in their hiring decisions. Second, while this is not the focus of this book, the data certainly show how both the chemistry filter (focusing on interpersonal fit) and the specs filter (rigidly focusing on external markers of qualifications) can miss talented job seekers and undermine fairness and efficiency. For example, a problem with more informal hiring mechanisms that rely on personal interviews and social networks is that they can bring to the fore subjective valuations that may have little to do with the job seeker's qualification to do the job. As other scholars have noted, these informal methods clearly create an opportunity for factors such as race and gender to play an important role, consciously or not, in the filtering of job seekers (Moss and Tilly 2001). Yet formal and rigid processes such as staffing agency screenings and tests are not a panacea. Such filters also systematically exclude candidates who may be missed through the rigidity of filters that depend on buzzwords and proxies to evaluate skills and qualifications. It is my hope that the stories of the job seekers described in this book spur reflection on how hiring processes can more fairly evaluate job seekers' abilities and potentialities.

2. Gianakos 2002; Waters and Moore 2002.

3. Helpfully, recent editions of Richard Bolles's highly influential job search advice book *What Color Is Your Parachute?* (2013, 3) move precisely in this direction, discussing how "a huge proportion of the situation [job seekers] are facing is out of [their] control," while at the same time as encouraging them to "throw all [their] energy" into whatever aspects of their situation is in their control.

4. Friedland and Alford 1991.

5. In other words, labor-market institutions in Israel and the United States are not reflective of enduring and coherent configurations of cultural schemas in the way that Biernacki (1995) argues that employment practices in England and Germany reflect deeply rooted conceptions of labor. The comparatively dominant role

of staffing agencies and testing institutes in Israel relative to the United States is not due to any inherent incompatibility of these institutions with the American culture of individualism. As discussed in chapter 4, staffing agencies in Israel have grown rapidly since the 1980s due to legal and political-economic pressures (Ram 2008). Likewise, the widespread use of pre-employment testing in Israel but not in the United States is not easily attributable to cultural differences between Israel and the United States. In the American white-collar context, testing was in fact widely used in the 1950s (Stryker 2008; Cappelli 2008). It only became rare due to legal challenges focusing on its discriminatory "disparate impact." As with testing, Cappelli (2012) suggests that some American employers also hesitate to use a "specs"-like listing of specific qualifying requirements for positions due to fear of violating anti-discrimination regulations. To the extent that scholars have identified a distinct Israeli culture, it is characterized by interpersonal informality and the abhorrence of rigid interactions (Katriel 1986b) and is therefore in deep tension with Israel's labor-market institutions. Finally, arguments pointing to the causal role of shared enduring schemas in shaping institutions are less effective at explaining rapid institutional changes such as the rise of staffing agencies in Israel or of the career-success self-help industry in the United States.

6. Waldinger and Lichter 2003.

7. Hochschild 1983.

8. Buroway 1979; Bourdieu 2000.

9. As described in chapter 5, in the Israeli context, the most intense anger motivating collective action is not directed at employers but at the state. This anger stems from the contrast between the state's historical role in helping unemployed workers and its present policies, which appear to support the dominant labor-market institutions and to be indifferent to the plight of unemployed workers. This focus of blame on the state is thus a product of a particular political-economic and historical context and not a necessary consequence of the specs game. The structure of the game leads to an external focus, but not to a specific external focus such as the state. Like the specs game, the diligence game also produces a subjective response of system-blame, but how—or whether—this system-blame is outwardly channeled depends on the social context in which the game is embedded. In the American blue-collar context, the subjective response of system-blame is mediated by a different social context that leads job seekers, as they often put it to me, to "bottle it up." As discussed in chapter 6, the social context of blue-collar job searching gives rise to the humiliating experience of being perceived by others as suspect in terms of one's work ethic. To minimize this social humiliation, blue-collar job seekers typically refrain from openly discussing their hardships and their feelings of frustration with the hiring system. Given that such frustrations are rarely voiced, there is no impetus for collective action in the American blue-collar context.

10. Sharone 2007.

11. A survey of Occupy Wall Street protesters in New York suggests that almost

a quarter were working less than full-time jobs, and almost a third had lost their jobs sometime in the past five years (Milkman, Luce, and Lewis 2013).

12. The other major obstacle discussed by Occupy Wall Street unemployment activists was that unemployed workers "don't want to be outed because unemployed workers are not getting hired." One unemployed worker, when recruited to attend a rally, responded: "If I'm there, a guy is going to drive by and remember my face forever, and he might be the guy who could give me a job tomorrow." Along the same lines, another activist observed: "People worry about messages they will send to employers, whether they will be blacklisted" due to participation in protest rallies.

References

Abramson, Paul, and Ronald Inglehart. 1995. *Values Change in Global Perspective.*
Ann Arbor: University of Michigan Press.

Autler, Gerald. 2002. "Global Networks in High Technology: The Silicon Valley–
Israel Connection." MA thesis, Department of City and Regional Planning,
University of California, Berkeley.

Azaryahu, Maoz. 2000. "McIsrael?: On the Americanization of Israel." *Israel Studies* 5(1): 41–64.

Bakke, Edward W. 1933. *The Unemployed Man: A Social Study.* London: Nibset
and Co.

Bandura, Albert. 1982. "Self-Efficacy Mechanism in Human Agency." *American
Psychologist* 37: 122–47.

Becker, Howard S. 1998. *Tricks of the Trade: How to Think about Your Research
While You're Doing It.* Chicago: University of Chicago Press.

Bellah, Robert, et al. 1985. *Habits of the Heart: Individualism and Commitment in
American Life.* Berkeley: University of California Press.

Bergsma, Ad. 2007. "Do Self-Help Books Help?" *Journal of Happiness Studies* 9:
341–60.

Biernacki, Richard. 1995. *The Fabrication of Labor: Germany and Britain, 1640–
1914.* Berkeley: University of California Press.

Bolles, Richard. 2004. *What Color Is Your Parachute?* Berkeley, CA: Ten Speed
Press.

Bourdieu, Pierre. 1976. "Marriage Strategies as Strategies of Social Reproduction."
In *Family and Society: Selections from the Annales, Economies, Sociétés, Civili-
sations*, edited by Robert Forster and Orest Ranum, trans. Elborg Forster and
Patricia M. Ranum, 117–44. Baltimore: Johns Hopkins University Press.

———. 1984. *Distinction: A Social Critique of the Judgment of Taste.* Cambridge,
MA: Harvard University Press

———. 1988. *Homo Academicus.* Stanford, CA: Stanford University Press.

———. 1990a. *The Logic of Practice.* Stanford, CA: Stanford University Press.

———. 1990b. *In Other Words: Essays toward a Reflexive Sociology.* Stanford, CA: Stanford University Press.

———. 1997. *Pascalian Meditations.* Stanford, CA: Stanford University Press.

———. 1998a. *Acts of Resistance: Against the Tyranny of the Market.* New York: New Press.

———. 1998b. *Practical Reason.* Stanford, CA: Stanford University Press.

———. 2000. *Pascalian Meditations.* Stanford, CA: Stanford University Press.

———. 2001. *Masculine Domination.* Stanford, CA: Stanford University Press.

———. 2004. "The Peasant and His Body." *Ethnography* 5(4): 579–99.

———. 2005. *The Social Structures of the Economy.* Malden, MA: Polity Press.

Bourdieu, Pierre, and Jean-Claude Passeron. 1977. *Reproduction in Education, Society and Culture.* London: Sage

Bourdieu, Pierre, and Loïc J. D. Wacquant. 1992. *An Invitation to Reflexive Sociology.* Chicago: University of Chicago Press.

Broman, Clifford, V. Lee Hamilton, and William S. Hoffman. 2001. *Stress and Distress among the Unemployed.* New York: Kluwer Academic.

Brooks, David. 2000. *Bobos in Paradise: The New Upper Class and How They Got There.* New York: Simon & Schuster.

———. 2009. "A Loud Promised Land." *New York Times,* April 17.

Burawoy, Michael. 1979. *Manufacturing Consent.* Chicago: University of Chicago Press.

———. 1998. "The Extended Case Method." *Sociological Theory* 16(1): 4–33.

———. 2012. "The Roots of Domination: Beyond Bourdieu and Gramsci." *Sociology* 46(2): 187–206.

Burton, M. Diane. 2001. "The Company They Keep: Founders' Models for Organizing New Firms." In *The Entrepreneurship Dynamic,* edited by C. B. Schoonhoven and E. Romanelli, 13–39. Stanford, CA: Stanford University Press.

Campbell, Karen. 1985. "Job Search and Job Mobility." *Research in the Sociology of Work.* Vol. 3. Greenwich, CT: Jai Press.

Cappelli, Peter. 2008. *Talent on Demand: Management Talent in an Age of Uncertainty.* Boston: Harvard Business Press.

———. 2012. *Why Good People Can't Get Jobs.* Philadelphia: Wharton Digital Press.

Carmel, Erran, and Catherine de Fontenay. 2004. "Israel's Silicon Wadi: The Forces Behind Cluster Formation in Building High-Tech Clusters." In *Silicon Valley and Beyond,* edited by Timothy Bresnahan and Alfonso Gambardella. New York: Cambridge University Press.

Carnegie, Dale. 1936. *How to Win Friends and Influence People.* New York: Simon & Schuster.

Center on Budget and Policy Priorities. 2004. "The Lukewarm 2004 Labor Market." http://www.cbpp.org/2-16-05ui.htm.

Central Bureau of Statistics of Israel. 2007. Labor Force Surveys. Table 5.3: "Unemployed Persons Who Worked During the Last 12 Months by Last Industry and Last Occupation." *Statistical Abstract of Israel.*

Challenger, Gray, & Christmas, Inc. 2009. "More on White-Collar Job Loss." Challenger@Work. October 6. http://challengeratworkblog.blogspot.com/2009/10/more-on-white-collar-job-loss.html.

Chinoy, Ely. 1955. *Automobile Workers and the American Dream.* Boston: Beacon Press.

Chopra, Deepak. 1994. *The Seven Spiritual Laws of Success.* San Rafael, CA: New World Library.

Cottle, Thomas. 2001. *Hardest Times: The Trauma of Long-Term Unemployment.* Amherst: University of Massachusetts Press.

Covey, Stephen. 1989. *The Seven Habits of Highly Effective People.* New York: Simon & Schuster.

Creed, Peter A., and Sean R. Macintyre. 2001. "The Relative Effects of Deprivation of the Latent and Manifest Benefits of Employment on the Well-Being of Unemployed People." *Journal of Occupational Health Psychology* 6(4): 324–31.

Dagan-Buzaglo, Noga. 2007. *The Right to Work in Israel: A Legal and Fiscal Perspective.* Tel Aviv: Adva Center.

Danet, Brenda. 1989. *Pulling Strings: Biculturalism in Israeli Bureaucracy.* New York: State University of New York Press.

Davidov, Guy. 2006. "Enforcement Problems in 'Informal' Labor Markets: A View from Israel." *Comparative Labor Law & Policy Journal* 27: 3–26.

DiMaggio, Paul, and Bart Bonikowski. 2008. "Making Money Surfing the Web?: Impact of Internet Use on the Earnings of U.S. Workers." *American Sociological Review* 73(8): 227–50.

DiMaggio, Paul, Eszter Hargittai, Coral Celeste, and Steven Shafer. 2004. "Digital Inequality: From Unequal Access to Differentiated Use." In *Social Inequality*, edited by K. Neckerman, 355–400. New York: Russell Sage Foundation.

Dooley, David, Jonathan Fielding, and Lennart Levi. 1996. "Health and Unemployment." *Annual Review of Public Health* 17: 449–65.

Edwards, A. G. P., and P. Armitage. 1992. "An Experiment to Test the Discriminating Ability of Graphologists." *Personality and Individual Differences* 13(1): 69–74.

Ehrenreich, Barbara. 2005. *Bait and Switch: The (Futile) Pursuit of the American Dream.* New York: Metropolitan Books.

Esping-Andersen, Gøsta. 1990. *The Three Worlds of Welfare Capitalism.* Princeton, NJ: Princeton University Press.

Evans, Stephen, and John Haworth. 1991. "Variations in Personal Activity, Access to Categories of Experience and Psychological Well-Being in Unemployed Young Adults." *Leisure Studies* 10: 249–64.

Fantasia, Rick, and Kim Voss. 2004. *Hard Work: Remaking the American Labor Movement.* Berkeley: University of California Press.

Farber, Henry S. 2005. "What Do We Know about Job Loss in the United States?:

Evidence from the Displaced Workers Survey, 1984–2004." Federal Reserve Bank Chicago. *Economic Perspectives* 29(2): 13–28.

———. 2007. "Is the Company Man an Anachronism?: Trends in Long Term Employment in the U.S. 1973–2006." Working Paper 518. Princeton University.

———. 2008. "'Short(er) Shrift': The Decline in Worker-Firm Attachment in the United States." In *Laid Off, Laid Low: Political and Economic Consequences of Employment Insecurity*, edited by K. S. Newman, 10–37. New York: Columbia University Press.

———. 2011. "Job Loss in the Great Recession: Historical Perspective from the Displaced Workers Survey, 1984–2010." Working Paper 564. Princeton University, Industrial Relations Section.

Fernandez, Roberto, Emilio Castilla, and Paul Moore. 2000. "Social Capital at Work: Networks and Employment at a Phone Center." *American Journal of Sociology* 105(5): 1288–356.

Finlay, William, and James Coverdill. 2002. *Headhunters: Matchmaking in the Labor Market.* Ithaca, NY: ILR Press.

Fischer, Claude, and Yossi Shavit. 1995. "National Differences in Network Density." *Social Networks* 17(2): 129–45.

Fizer, Carlos. 2003. *Preparing for Employment Tests.* Tel Aviv: Center for Occupational Advice and Science. (Hebrew).

Fligstein, Neil, and Ofer Sharone. 2000. "Work in the Postindustrial Economy of California." In *The State of California Labor.* Berkeley: University of California Press.

Foschi, Martha, and Jerilee Valenzuela. 2007. "Selecting Job Applicants: Effects from Gender, Self-Presentation and Decision Type." *Social Science Research* 37(2008): 1022–38.

Freeman, Richard. 1994. *Working under Different Rules.* New York: Russell Sage Foundation.

Friedland, Roger, and Robert R. Alford. 1991. "Bringing Society Back In: Symbols, Practices, and Institutional Contradictions." In *The New Institutionalism in Organizational Analysis*, edited by Walter W. Powell and Paul J. DiMaggio, 232–63. Chicago: University of Chicago Press.

Gal, John. 2005. "The Rise and Fall of Unemployment Insurance in Israel." *International Social Security Review* 58: 107–16.

Gangl, Markus. 2004. "Welfare States and the Scar Effects of Unemployment: A Comparative Analysis of the United States and West Germany." *American Journal of Sociology* 109(6): 1319–64.

Gardner, Jennifer. 1995. "Worker Displacement: A Decade of Change." *Monthly Labor Review* 118: 45–57.

Garnett, Bruce, Neil Guppy, and Gerry Veenstra. 2008. "Careers Open to Talent: Educational Credentials, Cultural Talent and Skilled Employment." *Sociological Forum* 23(1): 144–64.

Garrett-Peters, Raymond. 2009. "'If I Don't Have to Work Anymore, Who Am I?':
Job Loss and Collaborative Self-Concept Repair." *Journal of Contemporary
Ethnography* 38(5): 547–83.

Gatta, Mary. 2012. *All I Want Is a Job! The Experience of Jobless Workers Navigating the Public Workforce System.* Unpublished manuscript.

Geertz, Clifford. 1973. *The Interpretation of Cultures.* New York: Basic Books.

Gianakos, Irene. 2002. "Predictors of Coping with Work Stress: The Influence of
Sex, Gender Role, Social Desirability, and Locus of Control." *Sex Roles* 46:
149–58.

Gilliland, Stephen. 1993. "The Perceived Fairness of Selection Systems: An Organizational Justice Perspective." *Academy of Management Review* 18: 694–734.

Gramsci, Antonio. 1971. *Selections from the Prison Notebooks.* New York: International Publishers.

Granovetter, Mark. 1974. *Getting a Job: A Study of Contacts and Careers.* Cambridge, MA: Harvard University Press.

Hacker, Jacob S. 2006. *The Great Risk Shift: The Assault on American Jobs, Families, Health Care, and Retirement and How You Can Fight Back.* New York: Oxford University Press.

Halford, Susan, and Mike Savage. 2010. "Reconceptualizing Digital Social Inequality." *Information Communication and Society* 13(7): 937–55.

Hargittai, Eszter. 2008. "The Digital Reproduction of Inequality." In *Social Stratifi-
cation*, edited by David Grusky, 936–944. Boulder, CO: Westview Press.

Hargreaves, Shaun Heap, and Yanis Varoufakis. 1995. *Game Theory: A Critical In-
troduction.* London: Routledge.

Harpaz, Itzhak. 1990. *The Meaning of Work in Israel.* New York: Praeger.

———. 1999. "The Transformation of Work Values in Israel." *Monthly Labor Review* 122(5): 46–50.

———. 2002. "Expressing a Wish to Continue or Stop Working as Related to the
Meaning of Work." *European Journal of Work & Organizational Psychology*
11: 177–98.

Heldrich Center at Rutgers University. 2009. "The Anguish of Unemployment."
http://www.heldrich.rutgers.edu/sites/default/files/content/Heldrich_Work_
Trends_Anguish_Unemployment.pdf.

Hipp, Lena. 2011. "Contracts, Confidence, and Continuous Employment: The Relationship between Labor Market Policies and Perceived Job Security." PhD
diss., Cornell University.

Hochschild, Arlie. 1983. *The Managed Heart: Commercialization of Human Feeling.* Berkeley: University of California Press.

Huffcutt, Allen, and Satoris Sabrina Youngcourt. 2007. "Employment Interviews."
In *Applied Measurement: Industrial Psychology in Human Resources Management*, edited by Deborah L. Whetzel and George R. Wheaton, 181–99. Hills-
dale, NJ: Erlbaum.

Huizinga, Johan. 1950. *Homo Ludens: A Study of the Play-Element in Culture.* Boston: Beacon Press.

Huo, Paul, Heh Jason Huang, and Nancy Napier. 2002. "Divergence or Convergence: A Cross-National Comparison of Personnel Selection Practices." *Human Resource Management* 41(1): 31–44.

Ibarra, Herminia. 2002. "How to Stay Stuck in the Wrong Career." *Harvard Business Review* 80, no. 12 (December): 40–47.

Jackall, Robert. 1988. *Moral Mazes: The World of Corporate Managers.* New York: Oxford University Press.

Jacobs, Elisabeth, and Kathryn Newman. 2006. "Rising Angst?: Change and Stability in Perceptions of Economic Insecurity." In *Privatization of Risk.* Social Science Research Council. http://privatizationofrisk.ssrc.org/Jacobs_Newman/.

Jahoda, Marie. 1982. *Employment and Unemployment: A Social-Psychological Analysis.* Cambridge: Cambridge University Press.

Kalleberg, L. Arne. 2000. "Nonstandard Employment Relations: Part-Time, Temporary and Contract Work." *Annual Review of Sociology* 26: 341–65.

———. 2009. "Precarious Work, Insecure Workers: Employment Relations in Transition." 2008 ASA Presidential Address. *American Sociological Review* 74: 1–22.

———. 2011. *Good Jobs, Bad Jobs: The Rise of Polarized and Precarious Employment Systems in the United States, 1970s–2000s.* New York: Russell Sage Foundation.

Kanter, Rosabeth Moss. 1993 [1977]. *Men and Women of the Corporation.* New York: Basic Books.

Karsten, Ingmar P., Eva Geithner, and Klaus Moser. 2007. "A Test of Jahoda's Latent Deprivation Model with Persons Who Are Out of the Labor Force." Unpublished manuscript. University of Erlangen-Nuremberg.

Katriel, Tamar. 1986a. "Gibush: The Rhetoric of Cohesion in Israeli School Culture." *Comparative Education Review* 30(2): 216–31.

———. 1986b. *Talking Straight: 'Dugri' Speech in Israeli Sabra Culture.* New York: Cambridge University Press.

———. 1987. *Communal Webs: Communication and Culture in Contemporary Israel.* New York: State University of New York Press.

Kaufman, Harold G. 1982. *Professionals in Search of Work: Coping with the Stress of Job Loss and Underemployment.* New York: John Wiley & Sons.

Klein, Yitzhak, and Daniel Polisar. 1997. *Choosing Freedom: Economic Policy for Israel, 1997–2000.* Jerusalem: Shalem Center.

Kluegel, James R., and Eliot R. Smith. 1986. *Beliefs about Inequality: Americans' Views of What Is and What Ought to Be.* 2nd ed. Piscataway, NJ: Aldine Transaction.

Kristal, Tali, and Yinon Cohen. 2007. "Decentralization of Collective Wage Agreements and Rising Wage Inequality in Israel." *Industrial Relations* 46: 613–35.

Kruger, Justin. 1999. "Lake Wobegon Be Gone! The 'Below-Average Effect' and the Egocentric Nature of Comparative Ability Judgments." *Journal of Personality and Social Psychology* 77: 221–32.

Krugman, Paul. 2007. *The Conscience of a Liberal.* New York: Norton.

Lasch, Christopher. 1979. *The Culture of Narcissism: American Life in an Age of Diminishing Expectations.* New York: Warner.

Lamont, Michèle, and Patricia White. 2005. *Workshop on Interdisciplinary Standards for Systematic Qualitative Research.* National Science Foundation Workshop for Cultural Anthropology, Law and Social Sciences, Political Science, and Sociology Programs, May 19–20; Arlington, Virginia.

Lane, Carrie M. 2011. *A Company of One: Insecurity, Independence, and the New World of White-Collar Unemployment.* Ithaca, NY: Cornell University Press

Leidner, Robin. 1993. *Fast Food, Fast Talk: Service Work and Routinization of Everyday Life.* Berkeley: University of California Press.

Levenson, Hanna. 1974. "Activism and Powerful Others: Distinctions within the Concept of Internal-External Control." *Journal of Personality Assessment* 38: 377.

Lipset, Seymour Martin. 1997. *American Exceptionalism: A Double-Edged Sword.* New York: Norton.

Marx, J., and K. T. Leicht. 1992. "Formality of Recruitment to 229 Jobs: Variations by Race, Sex, and Job Characteristics." *Sociology and Social Research* 76: 190–96.

McGee, Micki. 2005. *Self-Help, Inc.: Makeover Culture in American Life.* New York: Oxford University Press.

Milkman, Ruth, Stephanie Luce, and Penny Lewis. 2013. "Changing the Subject: A Bottom-Up Account of Occupy Wall Street in New York City." Murphy Institute. http://sps.cuny.edu/filestore/1/5/7/1_a05051d2117901d/1571_92f562221b8041e.pdf.

Miller, Dale T., and Michael Ross. 1975. "Self-Serving Biases in the Attribution of Causality: Fact or Fiction?" *Psychological Bulletin* 82: 213–25.

Miller, Rafiullah, and James Rosenbaum. 1997. "Hiring in a Hobbesian world: Social Infrastructure and Employers' Use of Information." *Work and Occupations* 24(4): 498–523.

Mills, Wright C. 1953. *White Collar: The American Middle Classes.* New York: Oxford University Press.

Mishel, Lawrence, Jared Bernstein, and Sylvia Allegretto. 2007. *The State of Working America 2006/2007.* Ithaca, NY: Cornell University Press.

Mitchell, Clyde. 1983. "Case and Situation Analysis." *Sociological Review* 31(2): 187–211.

Moss, Philip, and Chris Tilly. 2001. *Stories Employers Tell: Race, Skill, and Hiring in America.* New York: Russell Sage Foundation.

Nadiv, Ronit. 2005. "Licensed Manpower Companies in Israel." Jerusalem: Report of The Israeli Parliament Research and Information Center.

Neumann, John Von, and Oskar Morgenstern. 1944. *Theory of Games and Economic Behaviour*. New York: Wiley Science Editions.

Newman, Katherine. 1999. *Falling from Grace: Downward Mobility in the Age of Affluence*. Berkeley: University of California Press.

Nisbett, Richard E., and Lee Ross. 1980. *Human Inference: Strategies and Shortcomings of Social Judgment*. Englewood Cliffs, NJ: Prentice-Hall.

Osterman, Paul. 1999. *Securing Prosperity: The American Labor Market, How It Has Changed and What We Can Do about It*. Princeton, NJ: Princeton University Press.

Piore, Michael J., and Charles F. Sabel. 1984. *The Second Industrial Divide*. New York: Basic Books.

Plocker, Sever. 2005. "Gates: Israel Part of Silicon Valley. Microsoft Chairman Praises Successful Local High-Tech Industry during Israel Visit." Ynet. http://www.ynetnews.com/articles/0,7340,L-3159576,00.html.

Ram, Uri. 2008. *The Globalization of Israel*. New York: Routledge.

Reich, Robert. 2007. *Supercapitalism: The Transformation of Business, Democracy, and Everyday Life*. New York: Knopf.

Rifkin, Jeremy. 2004. *The European Dream*. New York: Penguin.

Rivera, Lauren A. 2012. "Hiring as Cultural Matching: The Case of Elite Professional Service Firms." *American Sociological Review* 77(6): 999–1022.

Robinson, Laura. 2009. "Digital Inequalities among American Youth: Access, Attitudes, and Information Seeking," *Information, Communication, and Society* 12: 4.

Rodriguez, Daniel, and Madline Zavodny. 2003. "Changes in the Age and Educational Profile of Displaced Workers." *Industrial and Labor Relations Review* 56(3).

Roese, Neal J., and James M. Olson. 2007. "Better, Stronger, Faster: Self-Serving Judgment, Affect Regulation, and the Optimal Vigilance Hypothesis." *Perspectives on Psychological Science* 2: 124–41.

Rosenberg, Yael, and Karen Vainunska. 2007. "Israel: The New Silicon Valley." MA thesis. Tel Aviv University Faculty of Management.

Ross, Catherine E., and John Mirowsky. 1992. "Households, Employment, and the Sense of Control." *Social Psychology Quarterly* 55(3): 217–35.

Rosse, Joseph G., Janice L. Miller, and Mary D. Stecher. 1994. "A Field Study of Job Applicants' Reactions to Personality and Cognitive Ability Testing." *Journal of Applied Psychology* 79: 987–92.

Ruggles, Steven, J. Trent Alexander, Katie Genadek, Ronald Goeken, Matthew B. Schroeder, and Matthew Sobek. 2010. *Integrated Public Use Microdata Series: Version 5.0* [Machine-readable database]. Minneapolis: University of Minnesota.

Rynes, S., and M. L. Connerley. 1993. "Applicants' Reactions to Alternative Selection Procedures." *Journal of Business and Psychology* 7: 261–77.

Sallaz, Jeffrey. 2009. *The Labor of Luck: Casino Capitalism in the United States and South Africa.* Berkeley: University of California Press.

Samuel, Yitzhak, and Itzhak Harpaz. 2004. *Work and Organizations in Israel: Studies of Israeli Society.* Vol. 11. London: Transaction.

Schlozman, Kay Lehman, and Sidney Verba. 1979. *Injury to Insult: Unemployment, Class and Political Response.* Cambridge, MA: Harvard University Press.

Senor, Dan, and Saul Singer. 2009. *Start-Up Nation: The Story of Israel's Economic Miracle.* New York: Grand Central Publishing.

Sewell, William. 1999. "The Concept(s) of Culture." In *Beyond the Cultural Turn: New Directions in the Study of Society and Culture,* edited by Victoria E. Bonnell and Lynn Hunt. Berkeley: University of California Press.

Shalev, Michael. 1992. *Labour and the Political Economy in Israel.* New York: Oxford University Press.

Sharone, Ofer. 2004. "Engineering Overwork: Bell-Curve Management at a High-Tech Firm." In *Fighting for Time: Shifting Boundaries of Work and Social Life,* edited by C. F. Epstein and A. L. Kalleberg. New York: Russell Sage Foundation.

———. 2007. "Constructing Unemployed Job Seekers as Professional Workers: The Depoliticizing Work-Game of Job Searching." *Qualitative Sociology* 30(4): 403–16.

———. 2013. "Why Do Unemployed Americans Blame Themselves While Israelis Blame the System?" *Social Forces.* Advance access published May 2, doi:10.1093/sf/sot050.

Sherman, Rachel. 2007. *Class Acts: Service and Inequality in Luxury Hotels.* Berkeley: University of California Press.

Shierholz, Heidi. 2009. "More than Four Unemployed Workers for Every Job Opening." *Economic Policy Institute Issue Brief* (April 7). http://www.epi.org/publication/more_than_four_unemployed_workers_for_every_job_opening/.

Shierholz, Heidi, and Lawrence Mishel. 2009. "Highest Unemployment Rate since 1983." Economic Policy Institute. June 16. http://www.epi.org/publication/jobspict_2009_july_preview/.

Small, Mario Luis. 2009. "'How Many Cases Do I Need?': On Science and the Logic of Case Selection in Field-Based Research." *Ethnography* 10(1): 5–38.

Smith, Sandra. 2007. *Lone Pursuit: Distrust and Defensive Individualism among the Black Poor.* New York: Russell Sage Foundation.

———. 2012. "Why Weak Ties Help and Strong Ties Don't: Reconsidering Why Tie Strength Matters." Paper presented at Institute for Work and Employment Research workshop, MIT Sloan School of Management, October.

Smith, Vicki. 2001. *Crossing the Great Divide: Worker Risk and Opportunity in the New Economy.* Ithaca, NY: Cornell University Press.

Smither, James W., Richard R. Reilly, Roger E. Millsap, Kenneth Pearlman, and Ronald W. Stoffey. 1993. "Applicant Reaction to Selection Procedures." *Personnel Psychology* 46: 49–76.

Starker, Steven. 1988. *Oracle at the Supermarket*. Piscataway, NJ: Transaction Publishers.

Stevens, Ann Huff. 2005. "The More Things Change, the More They Stay the Same: Trends in Long-Term Employment in the United States, 1969–2002." NBER Working Paper 11878.

Stettner, Andrew, and Sylliva Allegreto. 2005. "The Rising Stakes of Job Loss." *Economic Policy Institute Issue Brief.* 162 (May 25). http://www.epi.org/publication/bp162/.

Strully, Kate. 2009. "Job Loss and Health in the U.S. Labor Market." *Demography* 46(2): 221–46.

Stryker, Robin. 2008. "Scientific Mediation of Civil Rights Law." In *Droit et Regulations d'Activités Économiques*, edited by Jerome Pelisse, Thierry Delpeuch, and Christian Bessy. Paris: La Découverte.

Sullivan, Daniel, and Till von Wachter. 2009. "Job Displacement and Mortality: An Analysis Using Administrative Data." *Quarterly Journal of Economics* 124: 1265–306.

Swidler, Ann. 1986. "Culture in Action: Symbols and Strategies." *American Sociological Review* 51: 273.

———. 2001. *Talk of Love: How Culture Matters*. Chicago: University of Chicago Press.

Thomas, Claudia, Michaela Benzeval, and Stephen Stansfeld. 2005. "Employment Transitions and Mental Health: An Analysis from the British Household Panel Survey." *Journal of Epidemiological Community Health* 59(3): 243–49.

Tocqueville, Alexis de. 2000. *Democracy in America*. Edited and translated by Harvey C. Mansfield and Delba Winthrop. Chicago: University of Chicago Press.

Trost, Jan E. 1986. "Statistically Nonrepresentative Stratified Sampling: A Sampling Technique for Qualitative Studies." *Qualitative Sociology* 9(1): 54–57.

Uchitelle, Louis. 2006. *The Disposable American: Layoffs and Their Consequences*. New York: Knopf.

Vallas, Steven, and Emily Cummins. 2012. "Learning to Labor Revisited: Marketing the Worker's Soul in an Age of Neoliberalism." Paper Presented at Organizational Studies Conference, Rhodes, Greece, May.

Valletta, Robert. 2007. "Anxious Workers." *Federal Reserve Bank of San Francisco Economic Letter*, no. 2007-13 (June 1). http://www.frbsf.org/publications/economics/letter/2007/el2007-13.html.

Waters, Lea E., and Kathleen Moore. 2002. "Self-Esteem, Appraisal and Coping: A Comparison of Unemployed and Re-Employed People." *Journal of Organizational Behavior* 23(5): 593–604.

Waldinger, Roger, and Michael Lichter. 2003. *How the Other Half Works*. Berkeley: University of California Press.

Wenger, Jeffrey, and Andrew Stettner. 2003. "The Broad Reach of Long-Term Unemployment." *Economic Policy Institute Issue Brief*: 194 (May 15). http://www.epi.org/publication/issuebriefs_ib194/.

Wilson, William Julius. 1996. *When Work Disappears.* New York: Knopf.

Wolfe, Alan. 1999. *One Nation, After All: What Americans Really Think about God, Country, Family, Racism, Welfare, Immigration, Homosexuality, Work, the Right, the Left and Each Other.* New York: Penguin Books.

Zukin, Cliff, Carl Van Horn, and Charley Stone. 2011. *Out of Work and Losing Hope: The Misery of Bleak Expectations of American Workers.* John J. Heldrich Center for Workforce Development, Rutgers University. http://www.heldrich .rutgers.edu/sites/default/files/content/Work_Trends_September_2011.pdf.

Index

Made in the USA
Lexington, KY
20 February 2014